American Exceptionalisms

I0866676

American Exceptionalisms

From Winthrop to Winfrey

Edited by

Sylvia Söderlind

and

James Taylor Carson

SUNY PRESS

Published by State University of New York Press, Albany

© 2011 State University of New York

All rights reserved

Printed in the United States of America

No part of this book may be used or reproduced in any manner whatsoever without written permission. No part of this book may be stored in a retrieval system or transmitted in any form or by any means including electronic, electrostatic, magnetic tape, mechanical, photocopying, recording, or otherwise without the prior permission in writing of the publisher.

For information, contact State University of New York Press, Albany, NY
www.sunypress.edu

Production by Kelli W. LeRoux
Marketing by Michael Campochiaro

Library of Congress Cataloging-in-Publication Data

American Exceptionalisms from Winthrop to Winfrey / edited by Sylvia Söderlind and James Taylor Carson.
p. cm.
Includes bibliographical references and index.
ISBN 978-1-4384-3575-6 (hardcover : alk. paper)
ISBN 978-1-4384-3574-9 (pbk. : alk. paper)
1. Exceptionalism—United States. 2. National characteristics, American. 3. United States—Civilization. I. Söderlind, Sylvia, 1948– II. Carson, James Taylor, 1968–

E169.1.A4719825 2011
973—dc22 2010026045

10 9 8 7 6 5 4 3 2 1

To Olov Fryckstedt
and
in memory of
Peter Walker

Contents

List of Illustrations ix

Introduction: The Shining of America 1
Sylvia Söderlind

1 Witch-hunting: American Exceptionalism and Global Terrorism 15
Deborah L. Madsen

2 Both East and West: Asia and the Origins of American Exceptionalism 31
James J. Allegro

3 "The cause of America is in great measure the cause of all mankind": American Universalism and Exceptionalism in the Early Republic 51
Emily García

4 Burlesquing America's Errand: Savage Satire in Irving's *History of New York* and Melville's *The Confidence-Man* 71
Matthew Brophy

5 Exclusion Acts: How Popular Westerns Brokered the Atlantic Diaspora 93
Christine Bold

6 America as "World-Salvation": Josiah Strong, W. E. B. Du Bois, and the Global Rhetoric of American Exceptionalism 125
Nathaniel Cadle

7 American Exceptionalism and Immigration Debates in the Modern United States 147
Carl J. Bon Tempo

8 Giving the People What They Want: The African American Exception as Racial Cliché in Percival Everett's *Erasure* 167
Anthony Stewart

9 "Just an American Boy": American Exceptionalism and Steve Earle versus Capital Punishment 191
Roxanne Harde

10 Oprah's Vigilante Sentimentalism 207
Sara Humphreys

11 The City under the Hill: Allegorical Tradition and H. P. Lovecraft's America 223
Matthew Strohack

Afterword: American Exceptionalism in American Intellectual Conversation, or How I Finally Submitted to Literary Criticism 243
Terri Baker

Notes on Contributors 255

Index 259

Illustrations

Figure 5.1	The Frontier Club	95
Figure 5.2	The Cheyenne Club, 1888 (Wyoming Stock Growers Association Records, American Heritage Center, University of Wyoming)	97
Figure 5.3	Ella "Cattle Kate" Watson (Wyoming State Archives, Department of State Parks and Cultural Resources)	99
Figure 5.4	The Johnson County War "The Invaders," May 4, 1892 (Wyoming Stock Growers Association Records, American Heritage Center, University of Wyoming)	100
Figure 5.5	Owen Wister, ca. 1895 (Owen Wister Papers, American Heritage Center, University of Wyoming)	101
Figure 5.6	Joseph Keppler, "Looking Backward," *Puck* January 11, 1893	105
Figure 5.7	Immigration Restriction League pamphlet, 1903 (Library of Congress, Rare Book and Special Collections Division)	106
Figure 5.8	Frederic Remington, "The Last Cavalier," *Harper's New Monthly Magazine* September 1895	109

Figure 5.9 Harper Brothers, between 1855 and 1865 (Library of Congress, Prints and Photographs Division, Brady-Handy Collection, LC-DIG-cwpbh-02806) 113

Figure 5.10 Advertising flyer for *The Virginian*, 1902 (Box 79, Owen Wister Papers, Manuscript Division, Library of Congress, Washington, D.C.) 118

Figure 7.1 Sign in the window of Joey Vento's Philadelphia restaurant that ignited a furious debate over immigration and assimilation (Kyle Gradinger) 160

Introduction

The Shining of America

Sylvia Söderlind

In the first televised debate between presidential candidates John McCain and Barack Obama, on September 26, 2008, the Democratic nominee expressed his wish to restore "that sense of America being that shining beacon on a hill." His use of the demonstrative *that* indicated his confidence that the audience—at least the voting audience—would know to what particular sense and, most crucially, to what particular beacon he referred. That the allusion would be familiar to the white, educated, and, especially, Christian voter is indisputable. More questionable is whether it would be recognized by the disenfranchised as a positive sign of the change envisioned by the Democratic Party. The Puritans' hill is not Martin Luther King Jr.'s Mountaintop; Beacon Hill may be a distinctly American location, but it is no Mount Pisgah. In using this timeworn image Obama showed his command of Yankee oratory, even if he seemed to confuse the beacon and the city. However opportune his incorporation of the adjective "shining" to modify "beacon," it is important to note that it was Ronald Reagan who first borrowed "shining" from the sea of "America the Beautiful" in his farewell address to amplify, rather redundantly, that original beacon. Using a rhetoric associated with righteousness and moral responsibility Obama took the high moral ground away from his opponent's recourse to mere personal experience and pragmatic policymaking (at least in this particular instance).[1]

What is significant in Obama's use of that most common of all presidential allusions is that it appeared in response to a specific question about America's safety: "What do you think the likelihood is that there would be another 9/11-type attack on the continental United States?" Whether calculated or not, Obama's response pointed directly to the dependence of the idea of America's role as example to the world on the existence of an enemy. It was less a direct answer than an attempt to address the restoration of American credibility in the world in a way that indirectly blamed the Bush regime for jeopardizing the country's standing in the world. Yet Obama's use of the allusion provided what politicians would refer to as a "big tent"—with all its revival meeting resonances—to which the only entrance requirement is a desire to be American and to belong. As an encapsulation of the providential role of the United States in the world, the allusion to the founding text of American exceptionalism reinforced that the core of the country is neither a nation nor a state, but an idea that somehow possesses the force to guarantee the safety of the country's citizens.

The founding text in question is, of course, John Winthrop's famous sermon delivered on board the *Arbella* as the Puritans set out on their perilous but emancipatory "errand into the wilderness" in 1630. Although the notion of "exceptionalism" is a later coinage, the idea of America as charged with a mission to be an example to the world permeates narrative reconstructions of the nation's political and cultural history. And as the new millennium shapes itself on an increasingly globalized stage, on which the United States continues to play a crucial, if not always appreciated, role, the rhetoric of exceptionalism is experiencing a return to its most extreme variant, the typological thinking of the Puritan divines who divided the world into good and evil and read the events of their day as enactments of scriptural fate. Even as it came under fire over the following centuries, the rhetoric continued to pervade a number of discourses, such as when Obama voiced its redemptive promise in a moment when he needed, above all, to appear presidential.

In a disciplinary context, the exceptionalist myth is generally seen as having launched American Studies in the 1930s and produced its first cohort of interdisciplinary Americanists in the aftermath of World War II, "the first [generation] to take exceptionalism as an American given" (Noble 2002, 26). Although it has since waxed, aided and abetted by the cold war, and waned, in the wake of the presumed "end of history" heralded by the fall of the Berlin Wall, serious challenges to it still come up against established institutional as well as popular obstacles such as the Tea Party movement. As Seymour Lipset shows in *American Exceptionalism: A Double-Edged Sword* (1996) the term has undergone a significant transformation from Alexis de Tocqueville's early-nineteenth-century understanding of exception as simply denoting a difference—however complex—from a known norm or rule, to a value judgment implying "better than" or "superior to" that norm. The exceptionalism vaunted by the United States is not equivalent to the perceived uniqueness to which most nations subscribe, nor is it important simply because the country's actions are "more consequential" (Shafer, vi) on the global scale. Rather, the ethos of exceptionalism provides the nation with justifications for making exceptions to norms, rules, and laws established, and adhered to, by other nations in ways that are often baffling to outsiders.

The distinction between rule and exception has taken on new urgency as we witness a state of exception becoming the rule in a country that has always prided itself on its principled adherence to the rule of law. It is as if we are witnessing the logical conclusion of an inherently paradoxical tension between rule and exception, where, because of its emblematic role in a national allegory, the latter is destined to triumph whenever the tension is heightened into crisis. It is not surprising, of course, that American foreign policy continues to have consequences for the world, but the economic crisis of the fall of 2008 that has had worldwide repercussions arguably began with a change in domestic policy—regarding sub-prime mortgages—which pertained to the political promotion of the "American dream" of equal opportunity, a central tenet of the exceptionalist ethos. The continued emphasis on exceptionalism today, when the name of the game is difference, is also a bone of contention in the debates between the neoconservatives and their ideologues, such as Samuel P. Huntington, or even liberal Americanists of the "old school" like Leo Marx, and the "New Americanists" represented by the likes of Donald Pease, John Carlos Rowe, Amy Kaplan, and George Lipsitz.

The present book began as a conference held in Kingston, Ontario, Canada, whose participants were mainly literary and cultural critics and historians. The emphasis on the humanities is reflected not only in the subject matter of the essays included but also in the methodologies used. The emphasis is squarely—and this was indeed the intention of the conference—on the persistence of exceptionalist *rhetoric* as symptomatic of the survival of its ideology in a variety of cultural and historical documents. Although the conference theme was prompted by the resurgence of this long-criticized rhetoric in the context of the "War on Terror," the latter is only tangentially addressed here, even as it inevitably haunts any contemporary discussion of the role of exceptionalism in the construction of a national identity. What we have tried to do is bring together a historically and politically varied repertoire that illuminates the pervasiveness of the ethos of exceptionalism through history and through fields of human—cultural, social, and political—endeavor. The generative force of this powerful rhetoric is reflected in the variety of contexts in which it appears, which also accounts for the plural in our title. As our collection shows, however, as long as the rhetoric itself is not seriously questioned, all of these apparently disparate phenomena do, in the end, contribute to the continuance and foreclose any profound scrutiny of what is an inherently nationalist and racialist ethos.

Most reconstructions of the genealogy of American exceptionalism situate its birth in the Puritan sermon, a religious expression of sincere dedication to a Christian mission, with scant thought given to the concept of nation to which it would become so fatefully wedded. What emerges in this endeavor is a coherent narrative stretching from the "city on a hill" in the seventeenth century, through the Declaration of Independence in the eighteenth, Manifest Destiny in the nineteenth, *Pax Americana* in the twentieth, and the War on Terror in the budding twenty-first century.

It is not surprising, of course, that American exceptionalism, with its inevitable grounding in an assumption of the centrality of "nation"—absent from its foundational moment on board the *Arbella*—has become subject to debate in an age of globalization. How can any claim to exceptional national status be reconciled with a postnational world, in which cultures and identities are no longer coextensive with political boundaries and where transnational or diasporic affiliations are stronger than national ones? One answer is found in David Noble's *Death of a Nation: American Culture and the End of Exceptionalism* (2002), whose title illustrates the interdependence of nation and ethos. Noble shows the—salutary—end of exceptionalism to be inevitably linked to the challenges posed by feminists and antiracists, but he also shows that, even as the ideological construction became increasingly accepted as a social fact, it was nevertheless questioned in Americanist circles as early as the

1940s. He thus shows the "Great Divide" that his contemporary Leo Marx identifies with the sixties as less a generational than a political one. This view is hardly comforting at a time when the discourses of neoconservatism and neoliberalism often sound peculiarly similar, with differences remaining on a level of policy rather than in any questioning of the assumptions underlying America's national self-fashioning.

Recent events show the rumor of the death of exceptionalism to be highly exaggerated, however. The resurgence of religion in political rhetoric is equally shared by almost all poles on the political spectrum. As the debate between Leo Marx and George Lipsitz and Amy Kaplan shows,[2] it is exactly the status of the "nation" and the affect it elicits that lie at the heart of the disagreements. What Leo Marx, with tongue in cheek, labels the "ur-theory" of American Studies was a matter of double allegiance: to political opposition against capitalism and a deeply felt "belief" in the ideals of America. As Marx indicates in recounting an anecdote about a meeting between British Cultural Studies pioneer Richard Hoggart and an unidentified American Fulbright scholar in 1957, the role played by "belief" in the founding of the discipline is what has led outside observers to identify the United States as "a nation with the soul of a church" (Chesterton 2009, 10) and its ideology as "the American Creed" (Myrdal 2009, 573). Among American Americanists it is perhaps Richard Hofstadter who expressed it most succinctly: "It has been our fate as a nation not to have ideologies, but to be one" (qtd. in Lipset 1996, 4).

If the beliefs, however differently defined, in America were what held together an otherwise varied group of scholars in the early days of American Studies, it is the realization, implied in Noble's title, that "America" is only one of many aspects of identification of a number of what Huntington calls "subnational identities" within the United States that hold the New Americanists together. A loosely defined group of scholars whose critique of exceptionalism is closely allied with the social movements originating in the sixties, particularly those related to questions of race, gender, ethnicity and—though not nearly enough, according to Walter Benn Michaels—class, the New Americanists are scathing in their refutation of the recent Bush government's recourse to an imperialism of brute force under the aegis of an exceptionalist rhetoric that sees "dissent as a minor form of treason" (Pease 2006, 73). William Spanos's analysis of the willful forgetting of the Vietnam War reminds us that this fundamentally paranoid move was not unique to the George W. Bush regime. The war, Spanos argues, was the logical consequence of exceptionalist thinking, and the American defeat proved the untenability of the premise underlying its national ethos: the brutal extermination of those perceived to stand in the way of its providential task. American interventions in Vietnam, and now Iraq, repeat the same "errand into the wilderness" that Perry Miller first identified as the origin of the national narrative, and which Sacvan Bercovitch convincingly reinterpreted so as to explain the paradoxical conflation of lament and optimism at the heart of the American jeremiad.

It is that paradox that still makes of every mission whose accomplishment turns out to be illusory an occasion for a call to the nation to come together ever more determined to brave whatever obstacles are put in the way of its democratizing mission. The wilderness into which light has to be thrown at all costs is now the Old World, more specifically the Middle East, the cradle of both Western and Eastern civilization, and liberal democracy—and market capitalism—the new gospel to be spread, the new product to be exported whether the recipient wants it or not. It is the stubbornness of the discourse of exceptionalism that makes it so difficult to turn the ground of the debate from the moral high one to the more pragmatic and political, yet profoundly ethical one, concerning the definition and limits of democracy and the role of nations that is subject to lively debate among scholars of globalization.

If the critique of exceptionalism has taken a more vociferous turn since September 11, 2001, the revival of interest in the notion precedes the events of that day. It is sobering to read Daniel Bell's premature lament for its death, "The End of Exceptionalism" (1975) a generation later. Where Spanos in retrospect sees the Vietnam War as hoisting exceptionalism on its own petard, as it were, Bell in 1975 saw the war as a corollary of the "end of ideology," the subject of his controversial 1965 book to which his essay clearly alludes. The fact that Bell attributes the demise of exceptionalism to the death of political partisanship seems prophetic in the aftermath of a presidential election that has shattered so many received views of partisanship. But it is also ironic insofar as the reactions to the outcome of the election are frequently couched in the very rhetoric of exceptionalism. But it is the end of the cold war that inspires a renewed critique of exceptionalism, an ideology premised on the existence of an identifiable antagonist external to the nation. The reexamination began with Byron Shafer's collection *Is America Different? A New Look at American Exceptionalism* (1991)[3] and Michael

Kammen's "The Problem of American Exceptionalism" (1993), followed by Lipset's magisterial *American Exceptionalism: A Double-Edged Sword* (1996). Deborah Madsen, whose essay leads our collection, published her analysis of the cultural uses of the myth, focusing on the influence of religion and biblical exegesis on American literary and cultural discourse, *American Exceptionalism,* in 1998. The consensus among all of these seems to be that the exceptionalist narrative is likely to survive, as it has through history, even as its actors change.

Noble's *Death of a Nation* inaugurates the questioning inspired by the events of 9/11 and their aftermath which led to a heightened interest in the moral and legal ramifications of exceptionalism illustrated in Michael Ignatieff's collection *American Exceptionalism and Human Rights* (2005). Non-Americans who may never have heard the word *exceptionalism* are almost certain to know something about extraordinary rendition, the Patriot Act, and American reservations about the International Criminal Court. While Ignatieff identifies three variants of exceptionalism in American rights legislation—exemptionalism, double standards, and isolationism—he also demonstrates the active role played by the United States in international human rights legislation, even at times when such legislation imposed restrictions on the country. He takes pains to point to the nonpartisan nature of such efforts, represented by FDR as well as Ronald Reagan, even if they preferred to see legislation based on American models: "America teaches the meaning of liberty to the world; it does not learn from others" (Ignatieff 2005, 14). This claim has proved particularly true of the recent Bush regime, which has also extended the city/beacon allusion to hitherto unexplored territory. The obligatory allusion appeared, as one would expect, in President Bush's speech to the nation on September 11, 2001, when he referred to his country as the "brightest beacon for freedom and opportunity in the world" and promised that "no one will keep that light from shining." More recently this somber allusion has turned culinary; a menu for a state dinner in 2006 offered the nation's governors a new dessert, " 'city on a hill' caramel cake."[4] In retrospect the injunction to eat this particular cake accrued an ominously prophetic resonance as the regime left an impoverished country ripe for revolution (even if Marie Antoinette seems an unlikely model for the First Lady). The question may not be whether there will be a revolution but rather whether a nation can have its exceptionalist cake and eat it too.

The fact that apologists for the continued legitimacy of exceptionalist claims and their critics are equally products of the same rhetoric, one that is inevitably caught up with assumptions of patriotism—more often than not confused with nationalism—makes criticism particularly difficult. Noble's observation that "[a]n overarching conceptual framework for a non-exceptionalist history of the United States is not yet in place" (Noble 2002, 35) is corroborated by the most ambitious recent attempt to "explain America to itself and to its foreign observers" (ix), Peter H. Schuck and James Q. Wilson's *Understanding America*, which is subtitled "The Anatomy of an Exceptional Nation." Donald Pease contends that the problem with even the work of the proponents of New Americanist Studies (often accused of anti-Americanism) is that "it is not yet not americanist" (Pease 2006, 101). The word *Americanist* is ambiguous in itself, and Pease's choice not to capitalize it is deliberate; as Daniel Bell points out, it can refer to someone who subscribes to "Americanism . . . the religion of America" (Bell 1975, 206). In other words, exceptionalism will not lose its hold on Americanist Studies until the field has ceased to be coextensive with national boundaries.[5] But, as Pease contends in his most recent book, *The New American Exceptionalism* (2009), exceptionalism since 9/11 is itself no longer coextensive with the nation's boundaries but has become a "state fantasy" of a "Global Homeland" whose most vulnerable citizens are no longer seen as in need of protection but as potential security threats.

In another recent book on the subject, Godfrey Hodgson debunks *The Myth of American Exceptionalism* (2009) by pointing to the European provenance and continued importance of its tenets and by painstakingly tracing the gap between perception and reality throughout American historiography. The fact that Hodgson, a Brit, finds such a project necessary illustrates the tenacity of the myth. It is indeed intriguing to note how many of the most often quoted definers or exponents of exceptionalism are non-Americans, from the Massachusetts Bay Puritans, British subjects whose disagreement was with the Church rather than the Crown per se, to Crèvecoeur, Tocqueville, Chesterton, Myrdal, and Ignatieff . . . and now the editors of this volume. When we organized the conference we were surprised—and slightly annoyed—at the dearth of submissions from an identifiably conservative viewpoint. We tried, without success, to find a voice willing (within our limited means) to defend the premises of exceptionalism. We also found a widespread assumption among American scholars that they would find a sympathetic audience for criticism of exceptionalism in Canada. Canadian scholars, on the other hand, seemed content not to have to question their own country's now rather tainted assumption of a higher moral ground, what with peacekeeping and universal health care as the pillars of its dedication to "peace, order, and good government." Still, we want to emphasize that the essays chosen for inclusion are not interventions in a political debate but rather case studies illustrating both the history and the pervasiveness of the assumptions underlying the political debate about the role of the United States in the world. Our premise is that exceptionalism, whether one calls it an ideology, a myth, a creed, an ethos, or a god-given truth, inflects every discourse involving relations between the United States and its—internal as well as external—others and that even dissenting counterdiscourses rely on the commonality of assumptions underlying the national ethos.

The authors are from the United States, Canada, and Australia, but what they have in common is a desire to understand how and why the rhetoric of exceptionalism has shaped, and continues to shape, the writing of history and culture in the United States. Historically, the essays stretch from early exploration narratives and Puritan sermons and chronicles to postmodern popular culture. Deborah Madsen's inaugural essay brings the two historical moments together by tracing the dependence of recent political rhetoric on the trope of witchcraft, which has come to define our understanding of the heritage of Puritanism but which also inflects the new discourse on global terrorism. The witch is the ultimate "un-American," but the witch is also that which protects those on the inside from invisible dangers. It is perhaps not surprising, then, that the witch returns at times of perceived threats to homeland security, as indicated by Madsen's genealogy from the Puritans to PNAC. The collection ends as it begins, with the Puritans; Matthew Strohack's essay presents a mirror image of Madsen's by way of a study of H. P. Lovecraft's modernist inversion of Puritan tropology in his short stories. This narrative loop closes the collection of essays, but rather than leave the debate with academics, whose work remains within the framework of institutions often caught within, or based on the inheritance of, exceptionalist rhetoric, we have chosen to leave the—always provisional—last word to its original exclusion on American soil. The native Trickster is given voice in Choctaw scholar Terri Baker's afterword, which, as it follows the presumed end and reveals, rather than attempts to resolve, the contradictions and paradoxes that the essays have analyzed, may provide a way out of the inevitable circularity and centeredness of argumentation and perhaps even hold out the possibility of new beginnings.

Following Madsen's transhistorical study, we return with James Allegro to pre-Puritan exploration narratives that construct a cosmography in which America is seen in relation to Asia rather than Europe. All exceptionalist rhetoric focuses on the youth of the "new" world, which is a world of potential and promise, against which the "old" one stands out as tired and stagnant, burdened by tradition. In this early orientalist discourse, however, it is not Europe but Asia that represents the "old" against which America is eventually defined as an exception. Allegro thus situates himself in recent critical debate that questions the Eurocentrism and the Atlantic focus of the discourse of exceptionalism.

Emily García brings us to the founding of the nation, focusing on the imbrications of nationalist exceptionalism with universalism that characterize the writings of Thomas Paine. She traces a narrative in which this intertwining goes back to John Winthrop, distinguishing four key conjunctures of the two aspects: coincidence, confluence, paradox, and contemplation. García thus illustrates how the shifting relationships between exceptionalism, with its inevitable nationalist resonance, and universalism, shape American political rhetoric from Winthrop to the present.

Matthew Brophy takes us into the literary critique of exceptionalism, often associated with Herman Melville but which he shows begins with Washington Irving and which he locates in the genre of the burlesque, a subgenre of satire, which criticizes "the sanctification of violence" that both writers see as an inherent part of the ideology. Through a Foucauldian reading, Brophy points to the sacred status of the American rhetoric of exceptionalism and its inherent kinship with violence, which Melville and Irving critique without, as in traditional satire, proposing a corrective counterideology but rather leaving the reader faced with a moral dilemma. The early critiques of exceptionalism authored by Irving and Melville have since found a place in the literary canon. Yet the satirical burlesque hardly represents American popular culture as does the ever-popular Western with its inevitable association with Manifest Destiny and the frontier myth. Christine Bold's careful and inventive reconstruction of the birth of the Western shows it to have a lot to do with the transatlantic interests of British imperialism. The first popular Western writer, Owen Wister, whose *The Virginian* became a bestseller, and the publishing industry that followed were very much the creation of what Bold poignantly dubs "the frontier club," a group held together by shared "stock" interests, in several senses of the word.

Contemporaneously with the evolution of the "frontier club" on the western front developed the notion of Anglo-American—Protestant—culture as the road to "world salvation," which Nathaniel Cadle sees as presaging current rhetoric about globalization. Reading such writers as Josiah Strong as representing a shift between Winthrop at one end and Ronald Reagan at the other, Cadle points to their early advocacy of an interventionist stance, aided by technological innovation, on the world stage. Among influential intellectuals in this debate at the turn of the last century was also W. E. B. Du Bois, according to whom the foundation of American democracy on racism made the nation the least suitable model for the world. Cadle's reading of Du Bois draws the conclusion that African Americans are the "talented tenth" of the entire nonwhite world and hence best placed to save the world for modernization. As different as they are in focus and motivation, Strong's Christian mission and Du Bois's pan-Africanism share the missionary rhetoric of the United States as the beacon of modernization that is the necessary condition for saving the world.

Crucial to all debates about exceptionalism is the issue of immigration and assimilation, questions dealt with by both Strong and Du Bois and which continue to shape political debate in the present. Considering its foundational structure, which requires a division between "us" and "them" that is almost invariably tainted with a degree of racialism, it is not surprising that exceptionalist rhetoric becomes particularly visible at times of perceived threats to the nation, among which war and immigration loom large. Carl Bon Tempo defines the tenets of exceptionalism in his study of the debate between restrictionists and liberalizers in recent debates about immigration and traces its relationship to contemporary discussions of multiculturalism.

The last four essays turn to popular culture. Anthony Stewart shows how Du Bois's notion of African American exceptionalism has been turned on its head through a reading of Percival Everett's novel *Erasure.* A century after Du Bois's advocacy of the "talented tenth," the relationship between rule and exception has been reversed in white clichéd constructions; the truly exceptional African American—the criminal, the athlete, and the entertainer—has become the model, while the ordinary individual, whose only dream is of a "normal" middle-class life, has come to be seen as exceptional. Furthermore, Everett shows how the African American exception continues to be called into the ideological service of an overriding American exceptionalism dominated by whiteness.

That the critique of exceptionalism has entered the realm of popular culture is also clear in Roxanne Harde's intervention into the debate about capital punishment by way of the songs of Steve Earle. The United States is somewhat of an exception in the Western world as one of very few countries that still practice capital punishment, and Earle questions the compatibility of a practice of legislated murder with a democracy in which each individual shares the responsibility for actions taken in the name of the nation. The analogy between the penal and the military systems drawn by Earle is particularly relevant today. Based on violence and exclusion, judicial power comes close to bringing war home and the link between slavery, the penal system, and the military is such that it casts actors into one of two roles: executioner or victim. Yet it is the kind of activism represented by the likes of Steve Earle that also defines American exceptionalism as the quality that allows, and indeed calls for, individuals to dissent when they perceive that the nation does not live up to its democratic mission.

If Steve Earle holds American exceptionalism to account, so to speak, he also criticizes the sensationalization of crime that shores up capital punishment as a form of redemptive righteousness rather than the vengeance it is. Oprah Winfrey, on the other hand, falls into exactly the trap he warns against, according to Sarah Humphreys's study of her "Watch List" designed to call the nation to act against the problem of child abuse. Oprah's uncritical use of the rhetoric of good and evil, Humphreys shows, leads to a vigilantism that does more to perpetuate the exceptionalist narrative than to prevent crime and which, in the process, also re-victimizes the victims of crime.

Matthew Strohack's return to the Puritan origin of the exceptionalist discourse by way of the stories of H. P. Lovecraft forms an appropriate bookend, bringing us back to the genre conventions of the allegorical origins of the narrative of American exceptionalism but with a twist. Somewhat like Irving and Melville, Lovecraft leaves the reader in suspension rather than proposing an alternative narrative, but it is a suspension associated with horror rather than with burlesque. Although these writers share a certain pessimism, they show that it is in the very nature of the exceptionalist paradigm that once it leaves the realm of easy interpretation, represented by Puritan typology, it leaves the reader/citizen faced with only the promise—or threat—of something else, whose content is for the individual to shape. As Lovecraft's fictions illustrate, it is the shapelessness of that which cannot be interpreted, that which is yet unnameable, that invokes such horror and triggers the yearning for certitude that typological exceptionalism provides. We are back at the double-edged sword of a rhetoric that on the one hand can provide a comforting shelter for those who want to be told what to think, who want to be reassured of being part of a protected "we" based on the exclusion of dissenters and, on the other, opens a space for an ethical encounter with individual responsibility.

The editors want to express our gratitude to the contributors for their professionalism and their patience and to the Social Sciences and Humanities Research Council of Canada for its support of the publication of this book.

Notes

1. It is equally ironic the Obama's support in the arts community is prominently represented by the "Manifest Hope Gallery," a movement that "highlights the central themes of the progressive grassroots movement—Hope, Change, Progress, Unity and Patriotism" (http://manifesthope.com/about.php). The providential associations of the word *manifest* are inevitably tainted with the exceptionalist ethos. The McCain camp, on the other hand, has a solid support base on http://theshiningcityblog.com/tag/macain/.

2. See *American Literary History* 17, no. 1 (2005).

3. The fact that Shafer's collection, to which ours may be seen as a sequel, began as a conference on American Exceptionalism at Oxford reinforces our observation about the long-standing fascination with the topic to non-Americans.

4. See http://www.whitehouse.gov/news/releases/2006/02/20060226-4.html. Unfortunately no picture is available of this intriguing dessert.

5. On the exclusions operated by the adjective *American* see also Janice Radway's presidential address to the American Studies Association, 1998.

Works Cited

Bell, Daniel. 1975. The end of exceptionalism. *The Public Interest* (Fall): 193–224.

Chesterton, G. K. 2009. *What I saw in America?* London: Anthem Press.

Hodgson, Godfrey. 2009. *The myth of American exceptionalism.* New Haven: Yale University Press.

Huntington, Samuel P. 2004. *Who are we? The challenges to America's national identity.* New York: Simon and Schuster.

Ignatieff, Michael, ed. 2005. *American exceptionalism and human rights.* Princeton: Princeton University Press.

Kammen, Michael. 1993. The problem of American exceptionalism: A reconsideration. *American Quarterly* 44, no. 4: 1–43.

Lipset, Seymour Martin. 1996. *American exceptionalism: A double-edged sword.* New York: W. W. Norton.

Madsen, Deborah L. 1998. *American exceptionalism.* Jackson: University Press of Misissippi.

Marx, Leo. 2005. On recovering the "ur" theory of American Studies. *American Literary History* 17, no. 1: 118–34.

Myrdal, Gunnar. 2009. *An American dilemma: The Negro problem and modern democracy.* New Brunswick: Transaction.

Noble, David. 2002. *Death of a nation: American culture and the end of exceptionalism.* Minneapolis: University of Minnesota Press (Critical American Studies Series).

Pease, Donald. 2006. 9/11: When was "American Studies after the new Americanists"? *Boundary 2* 33, no. 3: 78–101.

———. 2009. *The new American exceptionalism.* Minneapolis: University of Minnesota Press (Critical American Studies Series).

Radway, Janice. 1999. What's in a name? Presidential address to the American Studies Association, November 20, 1998. *American Quarterly* 51, no. 1: 1–32.

Schuck, Peter H., and James Q. Wilson, eds. 2008. *Understanding America: The anatomy of an exceptional nation.* Oxford: Clarendon Press.

Shafer, Byron E., ed. 1991. *Is America different? A new look at American exceptionalism.* Oxford: Clarendon Press.

Spanos, William. 2008. *The end of exceptionalism in the age of globalization: The specter of Vietnam.* Albany: State University of New York Press.

———. 2007. American exceptionalism, the jeremiad, and the frontier: From the Puritans to the neo-con men. *Boundary 2* 34, no. 1: 35–66.

1

Witch-hunting

American Exceptionalism and Global Terrorism

Deborah L. Madsen

for Charles Swann

Introduction

There has emerged in recent discussions of U.S. foreign policy a series of rhetorical dependences between American exceptionalism and the idea of global terrorism. President George W. Bush's image of the "empire of evil," to designate nation states that sponsor global political terrorism, is entirely consonant with the ideology of American Exceptionalism that posits the United States as a nation uniquely able, and charged with the mission, to oppose this kind of transcendent political evil. From the colonial founding of John Winthrop's "cittie upon a hill," the understanding of New England's exceptional destiny has depended upon the "visible sainthood" of Puritan leaders who led God's mission into the wilderness of the New World. However, this assumption of sainthood for some relied upon the conviction that others, within the colonial community, were diabolical agents, active agents of Satan, determined to destroy God's New England experiment. Indeed, as Chantal Mouffe has commented in relation to the constitution of the political community as a "social imaginary":

> There will always be a "constitutive outside," an exterior to the community that is the very condition of its existence. It is crucial to recognize that, since to construct a "we" it is necessary to distinguish it from a "them," and since all forms of consensus are based on acts of exclusion, the condition of possibility of the political community is at the same time the condition of impossibility of its full realization. (Mouffe 1992, 30)

I take as my starting point this dark underside of American Exceptionalism—the rhetorical basis for the New World claim to an exceptional and divine status. The witchcraft hysteria of the later seventeenth century is relevant here, representing as it does the attempt to engage a force of supernatural evil (an "empire of evil") that lies outside human comprehension but which threatens the exceptional work of New England Puritanism. Later cultural productions engaging with this relationship between exceptional good and transcendent evil include Nathaniel Hawthorne's nineteenth-century narrative return to New England witchcraft, as well as Arthur Miller's use of the metaphor of the witch-hunt, and the recent film *Good Night, and Good Luck* that deals with the McCarthy-era anticommunist crusade. Popular treatments of witchcraft such as the TV series *Charmed*, and films like *Practical Magic* and *The Blair Witch Project* engage the complex representation of witches as alternatively threats of supernatural evil and also potential protectors against this invisible danger.

By offering a survey of this rhetoric of exceptional or "un-American" evil, from the seventeenth century to the present, in a range of cultural forms, I hope to stimulate discussion of the wider implications of the idea of American Exceptionalism for our thinking about the history and culture of the United States.

Exceptionalism "Then"

Two influential but now discredited views of witchcraft assumed *either* that witches were in fact mentally disturbed persons who could not be diagnosed accurately by primitive early modern medicine, or that witchcraft was a form of genocide practiced against women. In fact, witchcraft was, surprisingly, *not* connected with the perception of mental illness in the New England colonial period. John Demos, in *Entertaining Satan* (1982), and others, note that insanity was accepted as a mental disorder without reference to supernatural causes and that, inversely, witchcraft was not necessarily recognized as a sign of insanity.

Similarly, the idea that accusations of witchcraft expressed widespread misogyny, representing what some feminists have called a kind of genocide or "gynocide," has also been disproved by subsequent researches that show, when taken over a period of centuries, that the number of people executed as witches does not disproportionately include women. Men were executed as witches too; in Salem in 1692, a substantial number of the victims were men. So if witches were neither insane nor the victims of women-hating, what were they?

Increasingly, connections between traumatic experiences and behavior that might lead to accusations of witchcraft are being made by scholars. I am thinking here particularly of Janice Knight's groundbreaking work on Mercy Short who, in March 1690 at the age of fifteen, was taken captive during the French/Sokoki raid on the frontier town of Salmon Falls. She was held captive for nearly eight months. She witnessed the violent deaths of both her parents and three siblings before she was finally redeemed back into the society of Boston. Two years later, in 1692, she was placed under the care of Cotton Mather as he tried to cure her of demonic possession. Mather's account of her afflictions and his efforts to cure her was published as *A Brand Pluck'd Out of the Burning*. Knight's 2002 essay is a wonderfully readable account that makes the case for demonic possession as a kind of captivity, where the conventional description of possession enables the recovery of a history and the articulation of a degree of suffering that otherwise cannot be adequately expressed. Knight observes:

> As with many of the Salem accusers, Short was single, young, female, and powerless, held captive and left orphaned as a result of the war on the Maine frontier. Karlsen reports that of the 21 possessed women we can trace, "seventeen had lost one or both of their parents," most often as a result of the war. . . . Like Short, these girls became refugees, arriving in Salem or Boston, and lacking financial or emotional support, they began a life of servitude. (Knight 2002, 42)

> Living under the governance of a family not their own, these women felt excluded, dependent, and subservient. As with many of these orphans, Short's history of possession seems to replay her feelings of abandonment and isolation, and it returns her to the origins of her plight: the experience of captivity. (ibid., 42)

I have dwelt on this description because it seems to me that what is significant here is the status of Mercy Short, and others who were orphaned as a consequence of frontier conflicts, as *outsiders*: abandoned, isolated, excluded. They were made to feel their dependency upon and subservience to those who had not undergone the traumatizing experience of living out a dramatic failure of social protection.

To an extent, the logic of exceptionalist rhetoric demands that the failure of society to protect becomes a *refusal* of protection. For in order to have "saints," we must have "sinners"; to have insiders, we must have the outsiders who define them by opposition; to have a protected coterie of those who belong, we have to have those who are denied the protection of belonging, whether that protection takes the form of military defense or the legal protection of civil rights.

John Winthrop's 1630 sermon "A Model of Christian Charity," delivered to the passengers of the *Arbella*, probably on the eve of their departure for Massachusetts from Southampton, invokes the now-famous image of the "cittie upon a hill":

> [T]he eyes of all people are upon us; soe that if wee shall deale falsely with our god in this worke wee have undertaken and soe cause him to withdrawe his present help from us, wee shall be made a story and a by-word through the world, wee shall open the mouthes of enemies to speake evill of the ways of god and all professoures for Gods sake; wee shall shame the faces of many of gods worthy servants, and cause theire prayers to be turned into Curses upon us till we be consumed out of the good land whether wee are goeing . . . (Winthrop 2005, 317)

Winthrop's sermon is essentially a blueprint for the conduct of an ideal Christian society, the society that is to be the model for the rest of the world. However, he warns that failure to sustain this Christian ideal will result in the unloosing of un-Christian sentiment: "wee shall open the mouthes of enemies to speake evill of the ways of god" and this will result in the (at least spiritual) exile of these Puritan pioneers. These two warnings—against empowering the ungodly and against risking the loss of the land—are taken up but with rather different emphases by that spokesperson of the third generation of New Englanders, Cotton Mather.

Cotton Mather, in "The Wonders of the Invisible World" (1692), describes the land colonized by New Englanders as originally belonging to the Devil, who is just waiting to claim his lands back:

> The New Englanders are a people of God settled in those, which were once the devil's territories; and it may easily be supposed that the devil was exceedingly disturbed, when he perceived such a people here accomplishing the promise of old made unto our blessed Jesus, that He should have the utmost parts of the earth for His possession. (Mather 2005, 509)

In these terms, the exceptional nature of New England lies in the ability to win back for Christians and for the Christian God, territory that is possessed by Satan. But in order to do this, those visible saints must engage in continuous combat with the invisible agents of Satan, who will use any means to retake what they believe is theirs. Mather declares:

> I believe that never were more satanical devices used for the unsettling of any people under the sun, than what have been employed for the extirpation of the vine which God has here planted, casting out the heathen, and preparing a room before it, and causing it to take deep root . . . (ibid., 510)

It is in the face of the success of the Puritan colonists, then, that the Salem events have been designed by Satan as a last-ditch effort to remove, or "unsettle" the settlers:

> [T]he devil is now making one attempt more upon us; an attempt more difficult, more surprising, more snarled with unintelligible circumstances than any that we have hitherto encountered; an attempt so critical, that if we get well through, we shall soon enjoy halcyon days with all the vultures of hell trodden under our feet. (ibid., 510)

Both Winthrop and Mather express exceptionalist visions of New England, but the terms on which these visions are conceptualized are quite different: Winthrop posits a community of visible saints, where Mather envisions an army of invisible Satanic agents. They are similarly divided on the subject of America's exceptional mission: Winthrop's "errand into the wilderness" versus Mather's continual battle against a supernatural "axis of evil." They agree that the fufillment of the divine mission upon which the New England colonists are embarked will result in a period of unimaginable bliss, but where Winthrop expresses a positive vision based on the realization of an ideal Christian community, Mather bases his vision on the decisive defeat of Satan and his demonic agents. It is Mather's vision that informs contemporary expressions of exceptionalist rhetoric, such as the following:

> States like [North Korea, Iran, Iraq], and their terrorist allies, constitute an axis of evil, arming to threaten the peace of the world. . . . History has called America and our allies to action, and it is both our responsibility and our privilege to fight freedom's fight . . . some governments will be timid in the face of terror. And make no mistake about it; if they do not act, America will. (Bush 2002)

Such proclamations come, of course, from President George W. Bush's 2002 State of the Union address, but this kind of rhetoric characterizes much that is said by this administration. The 2002 address drew to a conclusion with the promise: "America will lead by defending liberty and justice because they are right and true and unchanging for all people everywhere."

In this vision, America is defined by its capacity to triumph over evil, to bring "liberty and justice" to everyone, to make "American" that which we might call "un-American." But what is meant by this term *un-American*? If Americans live in America, do un-Americans live in un-America? Where would we locate this un-America? In a central scene of the film *The Blair Witch Project*, the three students find themselves more than just lost in the woods: they are lost in another "America"—un-America. This is the devil's territory, full of indeterminate threat and a place of fear. Above all, it is a place they stumble into, unexpectedly, though the film works to suggest that this alternative reality, this extra spatial dimension, has been there all along. The emphasis on the map that directs the students' movements underlines this attention to physical and spiritual geography. The history of the Blair Witch, painstakingly built up through the movie and its supporting artifacts, is the history of vulnerable individuals who accidentally find themselves in this parallel dimension of evil.

Of course, this identification of the wilderness as Satan's domain is hardly new: Mary Rowlandson, in her captivity narrative, *The Sovereignty and Goodness of God* (1682)—published ten years before the witchcraft events in Salem—depicts the wilderness as a scene of spiritual desolation, inhabited by Native American Indians who are alternately the agents of a chastizing God or of the Devil. She describes her first night in captivity: "This was the dolefulest night that ever my eyes saw. Oh the roaring, and singing and dancing, and yelling of those black creatures in the night, which made the place a lively resemblance of hell" (Rowlandson 2005, 445). We should remember here Mercy Short's experience of captivity; unlike Mary, who was an adult, Mercy was an adolescent when she was captured; Mary's captivity lasted for nearly three months, Mercy's for nearly eight; Mary was forcibly removed around New England but Mercy was taken as far as francophone Canada in the course of her captivity. Perhaps the most important difference between them is that the conditions of life that greeted their redemption were very different. Mary was finally reunited with her husband and surviving children in Boston where, she says:

> In that poor, and distressed, and beggarly condition I was received in; I was kindly entertained in several houses. So much love I received from several (some of whom I knew, and others I knew not) that I am not capable to declare it. But the Lord knows them all by name. The Lord reward them sevenfold into their bosoms of His spirituals, for their temporals. The twenty pounds, the price of my redemption, was raised by some Boston gentlemen, and Mrs. Usher, whose bounty and religious charity, I would not forget to make mention of. Then Mr. Thomas Shepard of Charlestown received us into his house, where we continued eleven weeks; and a father and mother they were to us. And many more tender-hearted friends we met with in that place. (Rowlandson 2005, 465)

In contrast, Mercy Short was returned to Salem as an orphan, reduced to the "poor, and distressed, and beggarly condition" from which Mary's neighbors quickly relieved her. And yet, Mary confesses at the conclusion of her narrative that she suffered the consequences of her traumatic experience, as she lay awake at nights fearful that God might see fit to punish her again by removing her from the protections and comforts of colonial society.

Mary lives in fear of experiencing once again the sanctions imposed by the demands implicit in the exceptionalist American mission. As a member of the elect who risked failing to live up to her grand spiritual destiny as part of the colonial mission, she is acutely aware of the exclusion that awaits as punishment. Mercy Short, in contrast, experienced that exclusion from *within* the ostensible protection of Salem society. And Mercy never wrote her story; it was Cotton Mather who told the story of her suffering as a victim of demonic possession: he was able to give this traumatic experience an exceptionalist reading but, unlike Mary Rowlandson, we can never know what Mercy Short told herself about her experience. For Mather, the witchcraft episode was evidence of New England's exceptional status: only in the place where God's saints were actually creating that "city on a hill" would Satan bother to deploy his diabolical spiritual agents. As in Rowlandson's narrative, the degree of spiritual suffering is a measure of the degree of spiritual eminence that had been achieved in the colonies. But this parallel satanic world still exists as a constant threat and continual danger, as Satan seeks to win back what was once his.

Exceptionalism "Now"

A similar sense of a parallel "un-America" is to be found in the work of Nathaniel Hawthorne. Although he represents a rather different evaluation of New England society, what we do find in *The Scarlet Letter* particularly, but elsewhere in his writing as well, is the suggestion that, unseen in the midst of everyday life, there is another kind of world. Hawthorne's Mistress Hibbins invites Hester to join her in the forest, where she can write her name in the Devil's book, evoking a sense that another community exists just beyond the limits of the town: a parallel "un-America" that exists beside the social world we think we know. The shattering of complacency by the irruption of an alternative America, for which the iconic historical moment is 1692, has been used symbolically to articulate the Red Scare and the McCarthy "witch-hunts."

I want to comment briefly on the film *Good Night, And Good Luck*, which palimpsestically builds on this tradition to suggest that the current "War on Terror" can be seen as our very own contemporary witch-hunt. The movie addresses McCarthy's anticommunist witch-hunt within the context of the role of the media. What the film focuses upon is the effort of "six extraordinary Americans" to challenge the silencing of television, specifically, by the effects of McCarthy's rhetoric and manipulative policies. However, it seems to me that the movie diverts attention away from the ways in which Hollywood is complicit with contemporary witch-hunts, not least in this movie through the subplot that involves the secret marriage of two of the reporters. The husband is reluctant to sign the loyalty oath that will secure his job; at the same time, he has violated the rule that CBS employees must not be married to each other. So he and his wife do in fact have something to hide: they are not Communists but they are disloyal and they are duplicitous. The film is ambivalent on this point, raising but refusing to answer the question: Can we ever assume that anyone is "innocent"?

The more important point that I want to make is that the film works to naturalize the exceptionalist vision of America. Here, McCarthy is represented as an aberration—recall the lock of his hair that waggles before the camera in a hysterically insane way as he rants at the public through the television screen. He is represented as the unfortunate consequence of America's commitment to freedom of speech: the extremist who would deny the freedom of all others. And in contrast to him, we are presented with these "men of integrity" who are prepared to stand up for the American values of truth and justice. Their efforts result in the downfall of McCarthy and the restoration of order, normality, and the American Way. But I want to suggest that in fact the palimpsestic structure of the film presents a very different vision, where hysteria is the American norm and personal integrity is the exception. If not for Edward R. Murrow, this film suggests, McCarthy would have gone on unabated.

Salem, Washington, Guantánamo Bay: scenes where individuals are held accountable for unspecified crimes by private hearsay and secret testimony. Salem in the late seventeenth century was governed in large part by William Hathorne, Nathaniel Hawthorne's ancestor, and the father of Salem's "Hanging Judge," John Hathorne. William Hathorne, a longtime magistrate of Salem and assistant to the General Court at Boston, was notorious as a persecutor of Quakers in Essex County. He operated a system of spies and informers who reported to him individuals who neglected their church and civic duties. Failure to observe the Sabbath, absence from church on fast days and election days, and the like, were reported to William Hathorne who prosecuted such cases vigorously. Perhaps the most notorious case arose from Hathorne's prosecution of a well-known and peaceful Salem family who were imprisoned for harboring Quakers at their home. When finally brought to trial, they were fined not only for the period during which they were guilty of harboring these Quakers but also for the period of their imprisonment while awaiting trial. When they were unable to pay the accumulated debt, Hathorne seized the couple's children, intending to sell them into slavery in the West Indies to offset their parents' debts. Only an intense outcry from the community of Salem, on behalf of the children and the severity of sentence, prevented Hathorne carrying out his scheme (Madsen 1999).

It was in this cultural context that John Hathorne, with Cotton Mather and others, imprisoned and executed the victims of the Salem hysteria. Here, and in the allegorizations of Salem by Arthur Miller in *The Crucible* and George Clooney in *Good Night, And Good Luck*, I think we have to question the extent to which hysteria is represented as something unusual, as opposed to representing the working out of exceptionalist sanctions against those who do not submit to the American Way. What Clooney and Miller, and perhaps even Mercy Short in her own manner, emphasize is the rarity of the individual who will place personal integrity before easy conformity, even at the risk of being demonized, rejected, and excluded.

Other contemporary media "witches" include the heroines of the television series *Charmed* and the characters of the 1998 film, *Practical Magic*, all of whom are ostracized as a result of their special powers, even though these powers are used to fight demonic agents. In the opening minutes of *Practical Magic* we are presented with two scenes: the historical exile of the ancestral witch, Maria, who proves impossible to execute and so is sent into an island exile; we also see a pair of young sisters, her contemporary descendants, being stoned by a group of children who chant malicious rhymes. In these scenes, we are shown that America is not only the world's policeman; America is America's policeman as well. *Practical Magic* is all about exclusion; from the original family curse uttered by the colonial witch Maria as she is banished, to the desire of Sally (Sandra Bullock) to live a "normal" life, as she explains to her aunt:

> Sally Owens: All I want is a normal life.
>
> Aunt Frances: My darling girl, when are you going to understand that being normal is not necessarily a virtue? It rather denotes a lack of courage!
>
> Sally Owens: Well, it's what I want.

In a later scene (which could have come straight out of *The Scarlet Letter*), one of the aunts comments on the hidden sins of their neighbors as the witches pass them on the street. For the witches, normal life means exclusion and hysteria; they define by opposition the "normality" and sense of belonging of the rest of the community. In his 2002 book, *Demon Lovers: Witchcraft, Sex, and the Crisis of Belief*, Walter Stephens argues:

> Witches were imagined as saboteurs or secret agents, and they were discussed to explain why the ideals of Christianity remained unfilled. . . . When faith is impossible, doubt is incarnated as the Devil. But, precisely because doubt is the Devil, God is possible. Thanks to the Devil, God's presence can be inferred even when his works are imperceptible. Very late defenders of witch-hunting phrased this idea with terrifying lucidity: *Nullus Deus sine diabolo.* Without proof of a devil, there can be no proof of God. (Stephens 2002, 341)

Here we have the two "realities" that I mentioned earlier in connection with *The Blair Witch Project.* But now "un-America" exists visibly and necessarily side by side with America. So when a commentator such as Michael Moore asks, "Dude, where is my country?" this is a complex question to answer. Moore's proposition is that America has been hijacked by the Bush administration, which is taking advantage of post-9/11 terrorist hysteria:

> [There is] no terrorist threat, only the terrorizing of the domestic population by the Bush govt . . . just because there are a few terrorists does not mean we are all in some

> exaggerated state of danger. Yet when they speak of terrorists, they speak of them as if they are in the *millions*, that they're *everywhere*, and they are never going away. Cheney has called this a "new normalcy," a condition that "will become permanent in American life." They only hope. . . . Our leaders would have us believe this is a guerilla war, fought by thousands of foreign terrorist-soldiers hidden on our soil. But this is *not* what is taking place, and it is time to do a reality check. (Moore 2003, 96)

Chief among the hijackers of Michael Moore's America are the corporate powers of globalization and international Americanization, especially the organization "Project for the New American Century" (PNAC). One of the fundamental commitments of this project is the belief that "American leadership is good both for America and for the world; and that such leadership requires military strength, diplomatic energy and commitment to moral principle."

The official statement of PNAC principles includes the need to significantly increase defense spending in order to honor the global responsibilities of the United States; to challenge those regimes that are hostile to U.S. interests and values; to promote internationally the cause of political and economic (but not individual) freedom abroad; and finally "to accept responsibility for America's unique role in preserving and extending an international order friendly to our security, our prosperity, and our principles." The "Project for the New American Century" is, fundamentally, about exporting America to "un-America," wherever that might be. Of course this process of exporting America is facilitated by the U.S. military; though since 2003 it is increasingly difficult to obtain clear information concerning military deployments. What a country-by-country accounting of U.S. military installations suggests, however, is that most of the world's nations are in close proximity to a U.S. military presence, which may be seen alternately as protective or threatening.

This extensive global military presence, in conjunction with the ideology of (un-)American exceptionalism, serves to divide up the world in a way that writers such as Thomas Barnett, in his 2004 book *The Pentagon's New Map*, make plain. Barnett, a former professor in the Warfare Analysis and Research Department, at the U.S. Naval War College in Rhode Island, is also a senior advisor to the Office of the

Secretary of Defense, the Joint Staff Central Command, Special Operations Command, and Joint Forces Command. As the map to which his title refers indicates so dramatically, Barnett organizes the world into two parts: the "Core"—comprising the United States and its allies—and the "Non-Integrating Gap" (4). And as we know, what we do with gaps is try to fill them, as quickly and efficiently as possible. In the small print of Barnett's map, we find the following three-pronged strategy designed to extend the "Core" into the "Gap":

1. Work across Core to improve ability to withstand and mitigate 9/11-type "System Perturbations"

   Preserving the Core to grow the Core

2. Discretely firewall off the Core from the Gap's worst exports

   Pandemics, narcotics, terror . . .

3. Shrink the Gap by exporting security to worst "security sinkholes" (306) located there

   Where necessary = regime change + nation building . . . employing forces optimized for both efforts

When the Core finally has obliterated the Gap, through "regime change" and "nation building," America will have become the world. The answer to Michael Moore's question, "Dude, where's my country?" then will become "here" . . . and . . . "here" . . . and "everywhere"! Moore's critique of corporate global America connects with criticisms, made by commentators such as Diane Alden, of Thomas Barnett's vision of a globalized America. She asks:

> When did corporate and collective interests take over the destiny and policy of the United States? Why are the morons we elect to office, the mainstream media and good people NOT screaming bloody murder about this attempt to redefine who we are and what kind of nation we want to be?
>
> Why aren't MORE thoughtful people asking, When did it become our duty or RIGHT to charge around the world bringing "regime change" for any reason? Who in God's name

> thinks in terms of people as "commodities" to be used by rulers and governments for whatever purpose? (Alden 2006)

While I agree with her, my response is that American exceptionalism has always promoted forms of identity that are defined through corporate and collective interests: we need only think of the Puritan "federal covenant," for example. Exceptionalism has always already redefined what Alden terms "who we are and what kind of nation we want to be" and American exceptionalism dictates that it is indeed "our duty or RIGHT to charge around the world bringing 'regime change' for any reason."

We need only look again at that 2002 State of the Union address, where President Bush proclaimed:

> America will lead by defending liberty and justice because they are right and true and unchanging for all people everywhere. No nation owns these aspirations, and no nation is exempt from them. We have no intention of imposing our culture. But America will always stand firm for the non-negotiable demands of human dignity: the rule of law; limits on the power of the state; respect for women; private property; free speech; equal justice; and religious tolerance. (Bush 2002)

It does remain for us, and especially those of us who are not Americans, to ask: the rule of WHOSE law? The power of WHOSE state? Whose private property? WHOSE speech? WHOSE justice?

Conclusion

American Exceptionalism is certainly an ideology of promise and of the American Dream. However, American Exceptionalism is also a punitive ideology of exclusion and demonization. American Exceptionalism signifies inclusion but it is also a powerful rhetoric of exclusion. Exceptionalism defines Americans by contrast with un-Americans; however, those "un-Americans" empower and validate the actions required by American exceptionalism to transform everyone into "American" subjects and everywhere into "America." For those of us who are "un-Americans"—Canadians and Europeans alike—comes the great responsibility to ask the difficult questions. These are questions that should arise from a legitimate and appropriate fear.

Works Cited

Alden, Diane. The empire builders: Leftover leftists rationalizing war? May 11, 2006. http://www.newsmax.com/archives/articles/2006/5/10/155249.shtml.

Barnett, Thomas P. M. 2004. *The Pentagon's new map: War and peace in the twenty-first century.* New York: Putnam.

Bush, George W. 2002. State of the Union address. http://www.whitehouse.gov/news/releases/2002/01/20020129-11.html.

Clooney, George, dir. 2005. *Good night, and good luck.*

Demos, John. 2004 [1982]. *Entertaining Satan: Witchcraft and the culture of early New England.* New York and Oxford: Oxford University Press.

Dunne, Griffin, dir. 1998. *Practical Magic.*

Hawthorne, Nathaniel. 2005 [1850]. *The scarlet letter.* New York: W. W. Norton.

Knight, Janice. 2002. Telling it slant: The testimony of Mercy Short. *Early American Literature* 37, no. 1: 39–69.

Madsen, Deborah. 1999. Hawthorne's Puritans: From fact to fiction. *Journal of American Studies* 33, no. 3: 509–17.

Mather, Cotton. 2005. The wonders of the invisible world (1692). In *The Heath anthology of American literature*, 5th ed., ed. Paul Lauter et al. New York: Houghton Mifflin.

Miller, Arthur. 2006. *The crucible.* In *Arthur Miller: Collected plays 1944–1961.* New York: Library of America.

Moore, Michael. 2003. *Dude, where's my country?* New York: Warner.

Mouffe, Chantal. 1992. Citizenship and political identity. *October* 61: 28–32.

Myrick, Daniel, and Eduardo Sánchez, dirs. 1999. *The Blair witch project.*

PNAC, Project for a New American Century. http://www.newamericancentury.org/.

Rowlandson, Mary. 2005. The sovereignty and goodness of God (1682). In *The Heath anthology of American literature*, ed. Paul Lauter et al., 5th ed. New York: Houghton Mifflin.

Stephens, Walter. 2002. *Demon lovers: Witchcraft, sex, and the crisis of belief.* Chicago: University of Chicago Press.

Winthrop, John. 2005. A model of Christian charity (1620). In *The Heath anthology of American literature*, ed. Paul Lauter et al., 5th ed. New York: Houghton Mifflin.

2

Both East and West

Asia and the Origins of American Exceptionalism

James J. Allegro

In his embarkation poem commemorating Sir Humphrey Gilbert's proposed voyage across the Atlantic, the Hungarian poet Stephen Parmenius described America as a special place unlike any other in the world. "De Navigatione" (1579) called upon Gilbert to seek out a land as distinctive in its climate as it was unusual in its absence of historical conflict: to "Leave the lands / Of Europe, Asia and of Africa," places "less sun would make fortunate," and venture forward in search of a "world which has not felt the weight / Of Babylon, the Persians' might, nor known / Victorious Macedon, and never was / Subdued by Rome" (Parmenius 1972, 85). For the poet, America was a space removed from history, that is, a land untrammeled by the debris of past empires such as Rome or Greece. His poem reflected one strain of writing on the Americas that characterized the New World as a virtuous and unique terrain isolated from the worst injustices of the past.

The origins of an exceptionalist paradigm of American history and society can be traced to the Western European discovery of two previously unknown but significant landmasses in the Western Hemisphere at the end of the fifteenth century. Attempts by late medieval and Renaissance authors and explorers to establish what was special or unique about the Americas in turn derived from a broader and older series of encounters between Europeans and other parts of the globe equally coveted for their historical, spiritual, and economic significance. For instance, the collection of ancient empires spanning the Mediterranean and Indian Ocean rims, such as Persia or Babylon, established the standard through which Parmenius judged America's historical uniqueness; it was the rest of the world, or "Europe, Asia and of Africa" (ibid., 85), through which he established evidence of America's unusual climate.

This chapter examines the influence of these global encounters on depictions of America from the late fifteenth to the early seventeenth centuries. Historians of the "Age of Exploration" rarely place all the spaces of the globe together on the same conceptual map, perhaps reasoning that Western Europe's relatively recent encounter with the Americas signified its incompatibility with other geographical entities possessing a much longer and more complex connection to Europe. As J. H. Elliott observes, "America was peculiarly the artefact of Europe, as Asia and Africa were not" (Elliott 1992, 5). Elliott is correct to identify both Africa and Asia as counterpoints to Europe in late medieval and Renaissance cosmography, but whereas scholars have acknowledged the role of West African society in the cultural and intellectual development of America, particularly as it pertained to the subject of slavery and racism, far fewer have attempted to forge a similar relationship between America and Asia. Asia's significance in Western European cosmography was considerable, and it was described by authors, historians, and travelers as a vast and amorphous entity containing precious minerals, salubrious weather, and coveted religious lore. This chapter draws on theoretical literature spawned by Edward Said's *Orientalism*, and another body of scholarship documenting the New World encounter, to suggest that Western European, particularly English, perceptions of this coveted space and America actually possessed a great deal in common before 1620. It concludes that late medieval and Renaissance travel writing and other sources documenting Asia provided an early and compelling framework for defining the exceptional in America's history, climate, economic potential, and spiritual significance.

The key to uniting the entities of Asia and America in the European mind rests on the assumption that precisely demarcated geopolitical units such as continents can also be imaginary spaces in the minds of those who encounter and describe them. By pointing out Europe's exclusive role in colonizing the Americas, for instance, J. H. Elliott echoes Edmundo O'Gorman's assertion in 1961 in *The Invention of America* that America was an intellectual construct reflecting the priorities and imperatives of its Western European intermediaries rather than a preordained or exceptional entity waiting to be born upon Columbus's arrival. O'Gorman correctly asserted that the two continents lying in the Atlantic Ocean possessed societies as old and as complex as those of the Eurasian landmass from which Columbus, and the numerous other explorers and mariners who followed in his wake, hailed.

O'Gorman's thesis further challenged one form of historical writing on the Americas commonly associated with the work of the late-nineteenth-century historian Frederick Jackson Turner. This interpretation stressed that America's allegedly wide-open spaces provided immigrants with opportunities for social and economic advancement unavailable to them in the competitive environment of Western Europe. As one historian explained, Turner's America was "[a]ltogether more open, more expansive, more equal, more democratic, and more congenial to the aspirations of ordinary free peoples than the societies of the Old World" (Greene 1992, 3). America was more than simply unlike Western Europe, however, since its roomy geography, bountiful opportunities, and very recent discovery by Europe signified it to be historically unprecedented and culturally unique. Critical to the exceptionalist claim, Daniel Bell notes, was an understanding of America as a society "exempt from the laws of decadence or the laws of history" (Bell 1991, 51), that is, a space eternally young in its promise of renewal and redemption.

Whether or not America was actually a historically unique entity was an entirely different matter. As Jack P. Greene points out, criticism of Turner's thesis arose almost immediately on the part of early-twentieth-century historians who placed American history in an imperial framework that accounted for Ireland, Wales, Scotland, as well as Canada, North America, and the West Indies, and progressive historians who pointed out that Old World inequalities did not die with the Atlantic crossing, but instead survived to replicate in modified form (Greene 1992, 3–4). Post–World War II scholars have since added to these claims by stressing the existence of class inequalities in urban centers, harsh systems of labor such as slavery or indentured servitude, and numerous indigenous societies each possessing its own distinctive culture and history.

Most recent scholarship takes issue with the Eurocentric bias implicit in these criticisms by pointing out that the measuring stick for determining the exceptional basis of American history is typically that of Western Europe, particularly Great Britain. These historians instead place colonial American history in a broader Atlantic framework that emphasizes a diversity of indigenous, Western European, and West African influences on the New World encounter. Some go so far as to use the Atlantic as a starting point for constructing a global synthesis of American history. As Allison Games writes, Atlantic history is only "a *slice* of world history," or,

> a way of looking at global *and* regional processes within a contained unit, although that region was not, of course, hermetically sealed off from the rest of the world, and thus was simultaneously involved in transformations unique to the Atlantic and those derived from global processes. (Games 2006, 748)

Attempts to break the seal of Atlantic history have prompted some scholars to focus attention on still other geological and geographical entities to better contextualize North American society. In his essay "Atlantic History from Imperial, Continental, and Pacific Perspectives," for instance, Paul Mapp explores the relevance of entities such as the Pacific Ocean or the North American continent to Atlantic scholarship. In *Turks, Moors & Englishmen in the Age of Discovery*, Nabil Matar triangulates Western Europe and America with the Mediterranean rim by connecting the shifting array of encounters occurring among English, Berbers, Ottomans, Venetians, and others with the language and symbols employed by Europeans to define and appropriate the labor and resources of the Americas. Matar's work stresses the significance of Islam to early modern European society while emphasizing the multicultural origins of the Mediterranean rim. A diverse and difficult to define space encompassing geographical and cultural sites in Africa, Europe, and Asia, the Mediterranean is of particular relevance to those interested in blurring the lines between "East" and "West," or "Orient" and "Occident," originally identified by Edward Said in his landmark work *Orientalism*.

Said, drawing on imperial correspondence, travel literature, and literary sources, argues that the intellectual program of Western European imperialism relied on the creation of the singular archetype of the irrational, deceptive, and immature "oriental," which homogenized the numerous, complex, and diverse societies of Asia to justify the imperial advance of the rational, virtuous, and mature European. Emphasis on Asia's age meanwhile depicted the entity as culturally and morally spent. Said points to British imperial agents who took care in their letters to emphasize the "enormous age of Arab civilization," arguing that their comments, "served to refine the Arab down to his quintessential attributes, and to tire him out morally in the process" (Said 1994, 230). The effect isolated Asia from "the ordinary processes of history" (ibid.) in a manner similar to depictions of America as a timeless space, the difference being that European writers depicted Asia as old and tired, and hence of suspect moral character, while the Turnerian synthesis transformed America into a space of boundless promise and potential.

Said's work has engendered tremendous discussion and debate, one strain of which has criticized the author for embracing the very homogenizing categories he sought to undermine in his analysis. Leela Gandhi accuses Said of defeating the "logic of his own intellectual egalitarianism by producing and confirming a reverse stereotype: the racist Westerner" (Gandhi 1988, 79). In other words, to identify the "East" as a product of a static and homogenizing imperial discourse, Said resorts to similarly static binaries of colonizer and colonized. His failure to "accommodate the possibility of difference within Orientalist discourse" (ibid.) is particularly pertinent to the study of the late medieval and Renaissance period. In *Turning Turk*, Daniel Vitkus argues that the early modern "Orient" was in fact an amorphous category reflecting a shifting balance of power among a diverse array of societies encompassing parts of Europe, the Levant and Middle East, and northern Africa. Like America, then, Asia was a historically constituted reflection of the aspirations and desires of its observers, or as Ian Macleod Higgins writes, it was "the fertile ground of an imagined community's noblest hopes, wildest dreams, and worst fears" (Higgins 1997, 5).

Higgins's claim bears weight for those who would posit that the unique circumstances of Atlantic colonization signified America and Asia as incomparable intellectual constructs. Western Europe certainly possessed a much older relationship to Asia than America, stretching at least as far back as the sixth-century BCE journey of the Greek officer Scylax of Caryanda down the Indus River, and including Herodotus's fifth-century BCE account of Asia in his *History*, Alexander of Macedon's fourth-century BCE march across Egypt, Persia, and India, and the extensive network of trading posts stretching from Rome to China in the first and second centuries CE (Lach 1965, 5–19). However, as Said reminds us, historians should not correlate age with history, but vigilantly separate assertions of historicity from their ideological and political context. America was not nearly as "new" as one would assume, as Western Europeans took an inordinate amount of time to recognize the significance of their discoveries, and even then retreated to preexisting systems of knowledge to make sense of what they saw. Likewise, Europe's relationship to Asia may have been "old," but it was far from static. Europeans projected a range of ambitions onto the "East," appropriating its image to serve their interests, and thereby converting it into their own "peculiar artefact" (Elliot 1992, 5).

In historical perspective, it was Asia, not America, which represented the truly unique space in the Western European mind at the end of the fifteenth century. The shockwaves sent throughout Europe by the Mongol conquests of the thirteenth and early fourteenth centuries vested Asia with a real and immediate presence in European writing that lingered well past the initial discovery of the Americas. Specifically, it facilitated a flurry of contacts between Western European diplomats, merchants, monks, and others and the central and eastern Asian societies with whom they sought to trade, convert to Christianity, or forge diplomatic pacts. During the fourteenth and fifteenth centuries, this network of contacts began to break down with the fragmentation of the initial Mongol conquests and the subsequent growth of other commercial and territorial entities such as the Ottoman Empire and Ming Dynasty. By 1492, the Ottomans had captured Constantinople; Armenia, a bulwark of eastern Christianity, had collapsed; Tamerlaine's conquests had disrupted trade and travel across Persia and Arabia; and the decline of the crusading impulse reflected the increasingly unrealistic prospect that Christendom would ever again lay claim to Jerusalem. Contact with Asia did not disappear entirely, of course, and if anything interest in the complexities of eastern cities, landscapes, and peoples intensified rather than declined during this period. Niccolò dé Conti and others continued their eastern journeys in search of India and China; the locus of the crusading impulse shifted away from Jerusalem toward the former territories of Byzantium, and the birth pangs of a consumer revolution intensified interest in eastern commodities.

Late-medieval readers meanwhile devoured information about eastern cities, landscapes, and peoples, manifest most clearly in the popularity of travel narratives and chivalric accounts such as Marco Polo's *Devisement du Monde* or the Alexander Romances. The most popular of these narratives was undoubtedly the fourteenth-century fictional account of the eastern travels of the English knight Sir John Mandeville. More than two hundred manuscript copies of *Mandeville's Travels* have survived in Irish, English, French, Czech, and other languages. Additionally, the arrival of the printing press to Western Europe during the last quarter of the fifteenth century provided readers with a bounty of information about the known world. Beginning in the early 1480s, English printers such as William Caxton translated and published editions of medieval chronicles and travel accounts of the known world, such as Gautier of Metz's *The myrrour of the world* (1481), Ranulf Higden's *Polichronicon* (1482), and *Mandeville's Travels*, which was published four times between 1496 and 1510.

Asia stood at the center of these sources as the world's largest and most significant cosmographical division. It resided at the top of the tripartite division of the world in most symbolic Christian world maps known as *mappaemundi*. Described by Higden as "moost in quantit[y]" of land, Asia is the dominant regional division while Europe is "lasse [least] / and lyke in nombre of pe[o]ple" (fol. 24^r^). Gautier of Metz echoed a similar refrain in *The myrrour of the world* by asserting that "Asia holdeth and conteyneth as moche space" as the rest of the world combined (sig. E4^v^). An English edition of Bartolomaeus Anglicus's *De proprietatibus rerum* (1495) described Asia as "halfe parte of the londe [tha]t men dwell in / And ye other two countrees conteyne the other halfe" (sig. F4^r^). Residing at the center of this representation of the world was Jerusalem as a symbolic reminder of Christianity's origins and a possible site for the Last Judgment (Akbari 2000, 21–22).

Asia's coveted place in European cosmology likely derived from its association with the Earthly Paradise. The fictional traveler John Mandeville admitted that he had never seen Paradise, which he located in a distant and inaccessible part of Asia separated from the world by a "walle" and residing on the edge of a wasteland of "hylles & roc[k] s where no man may passe" (Anonymous, sigs. S2^r-v^). Paradise was also the repository of precious commodities and temperate weather. Anglicus related that in Paradise there "growth all manere of trees here applies therin the tree of lyf" and was "always full of planetys: wyth flourys & leuyes of good smell / & of lyght bryght shynyng [and] ful[l] of fayrnesse," as well as "Joye & blysse" (sig. H6^r^). Other landscapes and locations in Asia were equally notable for their wealth. Taprobane [i.e., Sri Lanka] was "full of precyous stonys" (Anglicus, sig. J7^{r}). India was the "most wholsom[e] in western wynd[e]" and and possessed sizeable "hylles of gold" (Anglicus sig. J7^{r}).

The coveting of Asia's wealth, climates, and spiritual significance in these sources mirrored the emergence of a new ethos of travel and discovery that would undoubtedly influence Europe's initial encounter with the Americas. As Scott Westrem observes, "the phrase 'new world' was, in fact, a metaphor long before it denoted the Americas" (Westrem 1991, x). Several centuries before mapmakers designated the Atlantic landmasses as a "New World," travelers expressed wonder, confusion, and awe at the customs, speech, and manners which they encountered on their journeys across central Asia. The Franciscan missionary William of Rubruck wrote to France's Louis IX in 1253 of his journey to Mongolia that he felt as if he were "stepping into some other world" (qtd. in Westrem 1991, xi). Others expressed the feeling of revelation through the more immediate and practical language of "rediscovery." The Italian humanist Poggio Bracciolini entitled the 1492 publication of his abridged summary of Niccolò dé Conti's eastern journey *India Recognita* ("The Indies Rediscovered").

The near-epiphenomenal presence of Asia in Western European cosmography and travel literature motivated explorers and mariners such as Christopher Columbus, who famously carried a copy of *Mandeville's Travels* with him on his first voyage, to embark on their famous journeys. The famous period of American history known as the "Age of Exploration" was in part the continuation of a previous pattern of commercial and territorial growth set in motion by European merchants, mariners, and soldiers seeking to intensify their ties to distant eastern kingdoms:

> The discovery of the New World at the end of the [fifteenth] century helps to obscure the fact that Asia, whether it can be defined as India or as the empire of the Great Khan of Cathay, was the main objective of the fifteenth-century expansion of Europe. (Phillips 1998, 230).

Even after the decentralization of the Mongol empire, Western Europeans continued to seek out alliances with the wealthy and populous kingdoms of central and eastern Asia in an attempt to protect and extend Christendom in the face of encroaching Islamic states, as well as to circumvent the heavy taxes incurred by overland trade through western Asia. It was these objectives that scattered Portuguese and Spanish explorers beyond the northern and western coasts of Africa, and English, French, and other mariners deep into the Atlantic. Columbus's initial objective for sailing across the Atlantic was, of course, to find an alternate route to the kingdom of "Great Khan of Cathay." John Cabot likely set out in a westerly direction across the Atlantic to find Asia. Pedro Alvarez Cabral set off on a westward course, becoming the first European to make landfall in South America, before reversing direction and retracing Da Gama's route to India.

Accessing these eastern markets remained an important objective for English mariners well into the sixteenth century. The quest for a northwestern passage to China and Russia motivated the promotional writings and projects of Richard Eden, Sebastian Cabot, Sir Walter Raleigh, and Sir Humphrey Gilbert, among others. Additionally, the identification of a direct sea route to Asia at least partially motivated England's earliest attempts to establish a permanent settlement in North America. In 1587, Richard Hakluyt the Younger dedicated his Latin edition of Peter Martyr's *Decades of the newe Worlde* (1555) to Sir Walter Raleigh, who was then in the process of organizing a second voyage to Roanoke Island. He lauded Raleigh for "open[ing] up countries before unknown and accessible," and expressed the wish that his colonizing enterprises would "[r]eveal to us the courts of China and the unknown straits which still lie hid: throw back the portals which have been closed since the world's beginning the dawn of time" (Hakluyt the Younger 1935, 367).

The earliest printed accounts of the Americas also reflected this preoccupation with eastern peoples and territories. One of the first English books to mention America, Jan van Doesborch's *Of the newe landes and of ye people founde by the messengers of the Kynge of Portygale named Emanuel* (1511), was a compilation of several books documenting the world from South America to the Indian subcontinent. Alongside an abbreviated account of one of Amerigo Vespucci's letters was an account of the German traveler Balthasar Springer's journey to East Africa and South Asia, a description of the legendary eastern kingdom of Prester John, and an account of the ten nations of Christendom (Van Doesborch 1971, xxiii–xxxvii). Asia was also very much a subject of interest for that famous coterie of English editors responsible for translating, disseminating, and promoting much of the information about America available to English readers during the sixteenth and early seventeenth centuries.

Richard Eden's translation of the first three chapters of Martyr's *Decades* (1555) included an extensive appendix of late medieval and Renaissance travel narratives and histories describing far-ranging kingdoms and cultures in Moscow, China, and Indonesia. Richard Hakluyt the Younger divided his paean to English maritime ingenuity into three parts corresponding to three cosmographical divisions of the world. The first book of *The principall navigations* (1598–1600) included information on eastern Africa, the Barbary Coast, and the Near East; the second section focused on northeastern Asia, India, and China, and the third contained information on the Americas.

The legacy of Renaissance travel literature, then, was to fashion all of the previously obscured, never-before-encountered, and newly rediscovered parts of the globe into spaces to be acted upon by the English imagination, whether or not England possessed the capacity to actually control or possess these spaces. Further obstructing historians' capacity to view Asia and America as interrelated intellectual constructs is an inherited set of teleological assumptions regarding the origins of England's expansion across the world beginning in the Atlantic in the sixteenth century and culminating in the Indian Ocean during the first half of the twentieth. Historians correctly view Asia and America as occupying different stages in the evolution of the British Empire, each with their own distinct, separate, and largely incommensurate histories as colonized regions. The differences between the two continents and their historical relationships to England are vast and easy to point out. At the simplest level, British North America comprised a society of immigrants migrating in large numbers with the express objective of permanently adapting their way of life to a new environment, whereas British India was a society in which relatively small numbers of administrators, soldiers, and others temporarily settled in a region to exploit its labor and resources.

Neither of these definitions of colonialism adequately accounts for England's largely ineffectual and incompetent record of imperial expansion prior to the second quarter of the seventeenth century. Before 1620, England possessed neither the resources nor the skills necessary to accomplish any form of colonizing enterprise, and Daniel Vitkus is right to caution scholars against tracing England's phenomenal expansion across the globe (Vitkus 2003, 3–4) to the sixteenth century. In truth, Renaissance England was little more than a second- or third-tier world power when compared to other early modern states such as the Turks, Chi'ing, Mughals, Saffavids, Venetians, or Spaniards. The Ottoman Empire in particular emerged during the sixteenth century as a territorial and commercial force to be reckoned with, having established by the end of the century a significant presence in North Africa, the Middle East, and Eastern Europe. England meanwhile spent the first half of the sixteenth century distracted by a series of religious controversies and internecine conflicts that hampered its expansion beyond the confines of the North Atlantic. Until the 1550s, England struggled to gain permission from the Ottoman Sultan to trade legally in the Levant, and only successfully negotiated its first treaty of capitulation in the 1580s (Inalick 2000, 188–95). The acquisition and execution of eastern trading rights originated out of the efforts of newly formed Muscovy and Levant Companies, moderately successful trading organizations whose desire to capitalize on eastern trade outstripped their capacity to do so until the first third of the seventeenth century. The first English traveler to record his journey to India wrote nearly a century after Vasco da Gama, and even then he would spend the better part of his trip as a prisoner. Ralph Fitch traveled from England to Syria with several others under the auspices of the Levant Company in 1583, whereupon he became the prisoner of the Portuguese viceroy at Goa before escaping and eventually returning to London in 1591 (Andrews 1984, 257–79). He then served as an advisor to the British East India Company, which, although remembered primarily for its role in laying the groundwork for the colonization of India, failed to produce a consistent profit during the first two decades of its inception (Chadhuri, 23–73).

Clearly, England possessed a tenuous diplomatic and commercial position in the eastern Mediterranean and Indian Ocean rims during the Tudor and early Stuart periods, a fact that influenced the way travelers and writers described their encounters with Asia. As Donald Lach writes, Renaissance observers were well aware of their inferior and often dependent status and were "quick to recognize that in some facets of life" the more powerful eastern societies were "more advanced than their own" (Lach 1965, xii). The recognition of this inferior status led to a more ambivalent approach to cultural exchange than that suggested by unitary categories such as "oriental," and English writers in fact described and characterized their Islamic and other neighbors in the Levant through a range of emotions and opinions, including fear, admiration, and jealousy (Vitkus 2003, 11–16). In *The Offspring of the House of Ottomano* (1569?), Hugh Goughe lamented that it was to the "utter decay almost of Christes infallible religion," that the "great Turkes power, and Empire hath spredde itself so farre," and that so many parts of Christian Europe were now "subjecte to his creull tyranny (sig. A4^{r}). Goughe attributed this fact to the Turk's reputation for prowess in battle, as "[T]urkish soldiers in many respectes do surmount the warriors of other nations," because they "obeye, with out grudging or disdain, their Prince and Captaines, which is not observed among us," and "never take flight, but rather assaile and fight more desperately" (sig. A4^{r}).

The hesitant mixture of fear, admiration, and jealousy that characterized England's response to the Ottoman Empire could equally apply to the way in which English writers characterized their encounter with the indigenous peoples of the Americas. Although the diplomatic and military tools for colonization arrived much earlier in America than Asia, England was remarkably incompetent in its earliest attempts to colonize North America. John Rastell's disastrous colonizing venture of 1517 barely made it off the coast of Ireland, John Rut's 1527 attempt to find a northwestern passage to China failed, and Richard Hore's 1536 journey to Newfoundland returned mired in controversy and lawsuits, providing ample supporting evidence for Peter Mancall's claim that the "Europeanization of the Americas was not inevitable," and that the discovery of the New World did not immediately translate into a "yearning to colonize the Western Hemisphere" (Mancall 1998, 26). By 1580 or 1620, England's colonizing aims had improved only by degree. Roanoke Colony had disappeared by 1591, Plymouth Company failed several times before establishing a foothold in New England, the Sagadahoc experiment in Maine faltered, and Virginia's earliest years were plagued by starvation, internal dissension, and general confusion. In 1622, the Powhatan Indians launched a surprise attack on the Jamestown settlement that wiped out nearly one-third of the colony's settlers.

As a result, relations between settlers and the land, not to mention the numerous complex indigenous societies that resided upon it, were far more open and flexible than suggested by simple pictures of colonizer and colonized, or "us" and "them." Bernard Sheehan concludes that the "English vision of the natives had been split from the outset and remained divided throughout the history of the relationship between the two peoples" (Sheehan 1980, 4–5). Karen Kupperman goes much farther by noting that those who never left the confines of England tended to be harsher and more discriminatory in their assessments of Native American society than those who had actually made the journey across the Atlantic: "Colonists, English men and women who actually tried to make a go of establishing themselves in America, could not simply dismiss the American natives as negligible or as cultureless savages—and none did" (Kupperman 2000, 2). Struggling to negotiate an alien environment, the earliest English settlers relied upon, in some instances respected, and in still others stood in awe of those upon whom they depended for food and survival. The result was a picture of cultural exchange in British North America that was similar, at least in its broadest dimensions, to that advanced by Said's critics of the early modern Mediterranean. Native Americans and English colonists interacted with one another in a complex tangle of trade and military posturing that elicited a complex range of emotions and opinions ranging from jealousy to hatred to respect.

This is not to say that the English discarded their imperial ambitions upon arriving in America or the Levant, but rather that they were usually restricted to the realm of motivational rhetoric and grandiose predictions.[1] Richard Eden and Richard Hakluyt the Younger expressed as much frustration as optimism in England's overseas prospects; their editorial efforts represented a promotional campaign of sorts to inspire confidence and competence rather than statements of England's future greatness. Both writers confessed that they wrote in part out of fear that England was losing ground in the Atlantic to the Iberians. Eden expressed the hope in the preface to his edition of Martyr's *Decades* (1555) that England, like Spain, could partake of the "great rychesse that are yearely browght thither from the Indies" (Eden 1971, 54). In the preface to the first volume of the *Principall navigations* (1598), Richard Hakluyt the Younger queried whether or not it would

> be as great a renowne unto our English nation, to have bene the discoverers of a Sea beyond the North cape . . . as the Portugales to have found a sea beyond the Cape of Buona Esperanza, and so consequently a passage by sea into the East Indies; or for the Italians and Spaniards to have discovered unknowen landes so many hundred leagues westward and southwestward of the streits of Gibraltar and of the pillars of Hercules? (Hakluyt the Younger 1935, 434)

Finally, the recognition of England's early and haphazard attempts at colonialism does not invalidate the quest better to understand England's imperial origins. Rather, it reminds us that too much emphasis on the roots of an imperial ideology reduces our capacity to see the early modern world as the messy and complicated entity reflected in the words and thoughts of its inhabitants. Cosmopolitanism and colonialism do not necessarily go hand in hand, and English travelers and writers were worldly long before they could stake an imperial claim to any significant part of the world. At the same time that the Roanoke experiment came to its disastrous end, Stephen Parmenius mounted the claim that it was England's worldliness that in fact suited it to the task of Atlantic exploration. In "De Navigatione," Parmenius wrote of England: "You have traversed / The whole wide world that lies beneath the sun / Both East and West" (Parmenius 1972, 101). In his epistle to Sir Francis Walsingham in the 1589 edition of the *Principall navigations*, Richard Hakluyt the Younger proudly declared that English travelers had journeyed to the "most opposite corners and quarters of the world" (Hakluyt the Younger 1935, 399). Who till now, Hakluyt queried, had witnessed the presence of "English Consuls & Agents [a]t Tripolis in Syria, at Aleppo, at Babylon, as Balsara, and which is more, who ever heard of Englishmen at Goa?" (ibid.).

Depictions of America as an exceptional space emerged from this intertwining of "East" and "West" in correspondence, promotional writing, and other sources. Renaissance Europe's wish to reengage with the wealthy and formidable societies and sites of Asia provided a compelling framework for the construction of America as a both a "new world" and a site of "discovery." For instance, Christian Europe found in America an opportunity to accomplish what it had failed to achieve in Asia, namely, the reclamation of its holy sites and the elevation of Christianity to its rightful position as the world's preeminent religion. According to Djelal Kadir, in *Columbus and the Ends of the Earth*, Western Europeans employed prophetic rhetoric as an ideology of conquest by depicting America as a manifestation of the end time, or the site of the Second Coming of Jesus Christ, and hence the special terrain of God's chosen people on earth. Columbus believed he was still in Asia when he wrote of America as the site of the Earthly Paradise, specifically in Paria, and long after his death Puritan ministers adapted his writings to justify America as the final site for the fulfillment of God's mission. In 1697, the New

England minister Samuel Sewall wrote of how Columbus had described America as "*The Beginning of the East, and the End of the West*," and that if "the *Last Adam* did give Order for the Engraving of his own Name upon this *Last Earth*; 'twill draw with it great Consequences; even as such will, in time, bring the poor Americans out of their Graves, and make them live" (qtd. in Kadir 1992, 36–37).

The Earthly Paradise's salubrious climes further provided writers with a language through which to promote America's unique meteorological and geographical attributes. Associations between America and the Earthly Paradise endured throughout the sixteenth and early seventeenth centuries as part of a broader movement on the part of European explorers to reconfigure their understanding and knowledge of the world's prized locations. Sebastian Münster observed that inhabitants of Calicut on the Malabar Coast of southern India lived "as though they were in an earthly paradise" (Münster 1971, 19). Michael Drayton wrote of Virginia that it was "Earth's onely Paradise," and that sailors could expect their "Hearts to swell" when they encountered the "Lushious smell / Of that delicious Land, / Above the Seas that flowes, / The clear wind throwes" (qtd. in Sheehan 1980, 11). On a more practical level, knowledge of Asia's climates and terrain established a benchmark for identifying and comparing America's environment and resources with the rest of the world. In 1585, Sir Thomas Hariot wrote that America's climate was "answerable" to the "Iland of Japan, the land of China, Persia," the Mediterranean islands of Cyprus and Candi, recently occupied by the Turks, and the southern parts of Greece, Italy, and Spain (Hariot 1952, 383). Hariot also used his understanding of the world's flora and fauna to make sense of America's potentially valuable resources and other entities as "*Tsinaw*, a kind of roote much like unto t[ha]t which in England is called the China roote brought from the East Indies" (ibid., 348).

English writers further bound Asia and America together as potential solutions to the problem of England's surplus labor. Another form of promotional writing argued that the colonization of the Americas furnished a unique opportunity for England to vent its surplus population, in the process providing the working poor with the chance to remake their lives. In his *Discourse of Western Planting* (1584), Richard Hakluyt the Elder depicted America as a "*remedy to all the inconveniences*" presented by the "many thousands of idle persons" in England who, "havinge no way to be sett to worke," have become "very burdensome to the common wealthe" (Hakluyt the Elder 1935, 234). Just as England's poor benefited from the opportunity to remake themselves by migrating to the Americas, the "poore naturall subjectes of this Realme" further benefited from the development of stronger commercial ties between England and "Russia, Barbarie, Turkye, Persia, &c." Hakluyt the Elder also claimed that the growth of global commerce stimulated industry and encouraged full employment (ibid., 238). "[M]ore than hath bene" already "sett on work" in England's cloth trades would result from the encouragement of eastern commerce, and the seemingly boundless market of consumers of northern and western Asia suggested that England's surplus population was in fact its greatest asset, as the "honor and strength of a Prince consistenth," he concluded, "in the multitude of the people" (ibid., 238). The implication was that eastern trade would soon keep the poorest and most destitute of England's masses busy and prosperous with work.

Even the histories of the two entities possessed a shared origin in the Western European mind. Notions of America as "new" and isolated from history, and ideas of Asia as "old" and hyper-historical, emerged during the Renaissance as interrelated strategies on the part of Western European writers seeking to use the past as an ideological weapon in the struggle to impose their imperial ambitions onto the many distant and coveted landscapes of the world. Stephen Parmenius wrote at length of the origins of the "unknown race and people" who occupied the Americas, querying if perhaps they "boast an ancient ancestry / Derived from Pan" who inhabited the idyllic "land of woods and fertile fields" of folklore and legend (Parmenius 1972, 87). It was in places such as these that "the Golden Age began," where men and women lived "in blessedness" until the "corrupted years" had reduced them to ages of "Silver, Bronze and dull / Iron." (ibid.). These were the older spaces of the earth, the morally spent lands of Africa and Asia, where violence and conflict had reigned for quite some time:

> Or so it seems, If I look back beaten on all
> The cities shaken by disastrous wars,
> And kingdoms beaten down on many sides
> By despots: African and Asian lands
> Are crushed by Muslim regiments
> And bow submissive heads. (ibid.)

The poet referred here to the aggressive and successful military tactics of the Ottoman Empire, who had managed to extend its "hateful rule of pagan mastery" into north Africa and eastern Europe, and now stood at the border of Parmenius's homeland of Hungary, which was forced to guard "Her narrow boundaries against the threat" of Turkish invasion (Parmenius 1972, 87).

The ire demonstrated by the poet toward the prospect of an attack on his homeland by an Islamic empire with roots in central and western Asia reminds us that imperial expansion and cultural exchange were not confined to simple or dichotomous borders such as "East" and "West," and that it was the accumulated experiences of the Eurasian encounter that established the outer limits of the new and the old, or the historical and ahistorical, for late medieval and Renaissance authors. The global context in which Parmenius set his poem further reminds us that the revelation of the Americas at the end of the fifteenth century, while unprecedented and perhaps even exceptional, did not occur in a vacuum. The historical forces leading to the discovery and colonization of the Americas by Western Europeans were connected, and in some cases even identical, to those historical forces propelling Portuguese merchants to India and Indonesia, English merchants to the Levant and Moscow, and Spanish or French pilgrims to Palestine and Jerusalem. America was therefore neither unique nor preordained, but rather the byproduct of a vibrant global culture that spanned the markets and bazaars of Goa and Cairo, the cathedrals and mosques of Bethlehem and Istanbul, the longhouses and forts of Iroquoia and Jamestown, and the counting houses and taverns of Venice and London.

Note

1. The exception to the rule of England's imperial incompetence may have been Ireland, where England possessed a long and intricate history of colonization that preexisted and, as Nicholas Canny originally asserted in *Kingdom and Colony*, influenced North American settlement. Recent scholarship also suggests that England's imperial project in Ireland, impeded by the same turn-of-the-seventeenth-century rebellions and administrative challenges that plagued its efforts to consolidate England's northern and eastern borders, may have proceeded at a more fragmentary pace than previously assumed (Lenman 2001; Ellis 1998).

Works Cited

Akbari, Suzanne Conklin. 2000. From due east to true north: Orientalism and orientation. In *The postcolonial Middle Ages*, ed. Jeffrey Jerome Cohen, 19–34. New York: St. Martin's Press.

Andrews, Kenneth R. 1984. *Trade, plunder, and settlement: Maritime enterprise and the genesis of the British Empire, 1480–1630.* Cambridge: Cambridge University Press.

Anglicus, Batholomaeus. 1495. *De proprietatibus rerum.* Westminster: Wynken de Worde.

Anonymous. [1499]. *Here begynneth a lytell treatise or booke named Johan Mau[n] deuyll knight born in Englonde.* Westminster: Wynken de Worde.

Ashton, Peter. 1546. An epistle. In Paulus Jovius, *A shorte treatise vpon the Turkes chronicles.* London: Edward Whitechurche.

Bell, Daniel. 1991. "The Hegelian secret": Civil society and American exceptionalism. In *Is America Different? A New Look At Exceptionalism*, ed. Byron Shafer. Oxford: Oxford University Press.

Bracciolini, Poggio. 1963. The Indies rediscovered. In *Travelers in disguise: Narratives of Eastern travel by Poggio Bracciolini and Ludovico de Varthema*, trans. John Winter Jones, ed. Lincoln Davis Hammond, 1–45. Cambridge: Harvard University Press.

Canny, Nicholas. 1988. *Kingdom and colony: Ireland in the Atlantic world.* Baltimore: Johns Hopkins University Press, 1988.

Chadhuri, K. N. 1965. *The English East India Company: The study of an early joint-stock company, 1600–1640.* New York: Augustus M. Kelly.

Eden, Richard, "Rycharde Eden to the Reader." 1971. In *The first three English books on America*, ed. Edward Arber, 49–60. New York: Kraus Reprint Co.

Elliott, J. H. 1992. *The old world and the new, 1492–1650.* Oxford: Oxford University Press.

Ellis, Steven. 1998. *Ireland in the age of the Tudors, 1447–1603: English expansion and the end of Gaelic rule.* London: Longman Press.

Games, Allison. 2006. Atlantic history: Definitions, challenges, opportunities. *American Historical Review* 111, no. 3: 741–57.

Gandhi, Leela. 1988. *Postcolonial theory: A critical introduction.* New York: Columbia University Press.

Goughe, Hugh. 1569 [?]. To the right worshippeful knight, Sir Thomas Gres[h]am. In *The of[s]pring of the House of Ottomano,* ed. Bartolomej Georggivec. London: Thomas Marshe.

Greene, Jack P. 1992. The intellectual construction of America: Exceptionalism and identity *from 1492 to 1800.* Chapel Hill: University of North Carolina Press.

Hakluyt the Elder, Richard. 1935. Discourse of western planting, 1584. In *The original writings and correspondence of the two Richard Hakluyts*, ed. E. G. R. Taylor, Vol. 2, 211–326. London: The Hakluyt Society.

Hakluyt the Younger, Richard. 1935. Epistle dedicatory to Sir Walter Rale[i]gh by Richard Hakluyt, 1587. In *The original writings and correspondence of the two Richard Hakluyts*, ed. E. G. R. Taylor, Vol. 2, 356–69. London: The Hakluyt Society.

———. 1935. Epistle dedicatory to Sir Francis Walsingham by Richard Hakluyt, 1589. In *The original writings and correspondence of the two Richard Hakluyts,* ed. E. G. R. Taylor, Vol. 2, 396–400. London: The Hakluyt Society.

———. 1935. Preface to the reader by Richard Hakluyt, 1599. In *The original writings and correspondence of the two Richard Hakluyts*, ed. E. G. R. Taylor, Vol. 2, 433–51. London: The Hakluyt Society.

Hariot, Thomas. 1952. A briefe and true report, 1585. In *The Roanoke voyages*, ed. David B. Quinn, Vol. 2, 317–87. London: The Hakluyt Society.

Higden, Ranulf. 1482. *Polichronicon*. Westminster: William Caxton.

Higgins, Iain Macleod. 1997. *Writing east: The "Travels" of Sir John Mandeville.* Philadelphia: University of Pennsylvania Press.

Inalick, Halil. 2000 [1992]. *An economic and social history of the Ottoman Empire. Volume I: 1300–1600.* Ed. Halil Inalick and Donald Quataert. Cambridge: Cambridge University Press.

Kadir, Djelal. 1992. *Columbus and the ends of the earth: Europe's prophetic rhetoric as conquering ideology.* Berkeley: University of California Press.

Kupperman, Karen Ordahl. 2000. *Indians and English: Facing off in early America.* Ithaca: Cornell University Press.

Lach, Donald F. 1965. *Asia in the making of Europe, Volume I: The century of discovery.* Book 1. Chicago: University of Chicago Press.

Lenman, Bruce. 2001. *England's colonial wars, 1550–1688: Conflicts, empire, and national identity.* New York: Longman.

Lowe, Kate. 2005. The stereotyping of black Africans in Renaissance Europe. In *Black Africans in Renaissance Europe,* ed. T. F. Earle and K. J. P. Lowe, 1–16. Cambridge: Cambridge University Press.

Mancall, Peter C. 1998. The age of discovery. *Reviews in American History* 26, no. 1: 26–53.

Mapp, Paul W. 2006. Atlantic history from imperial, continental, and pacific perspectives. *William and Mary Quarterly* 63, no. 4: 713–24.

Matar, Nabil. 1999. *Turks, Moors, and Englishmen in the age of discovery.* New York: Columbia University Press.

Metz, Gautier. 1481. *The myrrour of the world.* Westminster: Willam Caxton.

Münster, Sebastian. 1971. Treatyse of the newe India. In *The first three English books on America*, ed. Edward Arber, 3–42. New York: Kraus Reprint Co.

O'Gorman, Edmundo. 1961. *The invention of America: An inquiry into the historical nature of the New World and the meaning of history.* Bloomington: Indiana University Press.

Parmenius, Stephen. 1972. De navigatione. Trans. and Ed. David B. Quinn and Neil M. Cheshire. In *The new found land of Stephen Parmenius: The life and writings of a Hungarian poet, drowned on a voyage from Newfoundland, 1583*, trans. and ed. David B. Quinn and Neil M. Cheshire., 74–105. Toronto: University of Toronto Press.

Phillips, J. R. S. 1998. *The medieval expansion of Europe.* Oxford: Clarendon Press.

Said, Edward W. 1994. *Orientalism.* New York: Vintage Books.

Sheehan, Bernard. 1980. *Savagism and civility: Indians and Englishmen in colonial Virginia.* Cambridge: Cambridge University Press.

Van Doesborch, Jan. 1971. Of the newe landes and of ye people founde by the messengers of the Kynge of Portygale named Emanuel. . . . In *The first three English books on America*, ed. Edward Arber, xxiii–xxxvi. New York: Kraus Reprint Co.

Vitkus, Daniel. 2003. *Turning Turk: English theater and the multicultural Mediterranean, 1570–1630.* New York: Palgrave Macmillan.

Westrem, Scott D. 1991. Introduction: "From worlde to worlde." In *Discovering new worlds: Essays on medieval exploration and imagination*, ed. Scott D. Westrem. New York: Garland Publishing.

3

“The cause of America is in great measure the cause of all mankind”

American Universalism and Exceptionalism in the Early Republic

Emily García

Introduction

In a collection on American exceptionalism, an essay on American universalism might seem out of place. In a sense, the concepts seem contradictory: the first considers the United States unlike all other nations, the second asserts no difference between one nation and all others. However, despite and at times even because of, this contradiction, the two ideologies have coexisted in American literature and culture for centuries. In this chapter I examine how the dualism of American exceptionalism and universalism appears first in Puritan New England and is later reiterated in the revolutionary and early republic periods.

I trace American exceptionalism-universalism through four key moments in its development: coincidence, confluence, paradox, and contemplation. "Coincidence" marks the appearance of universalism and exceptionalism without contradiction, where the relation between the terms is not intended to serve any specific purpose. "Confluence" marks the intentional reiteration of exceptionalism-universalism in revolutionary rhetoric. "Paradox" marks the intentional foreclosure of further revolution through a purposeful sedimentation of the idea in which universalism is actually nationalism. "Contemplation" marks moments in which the two ideals and the relationship between them are examined rather than merely reiterated; these moments seek a temporary return to the pre-paradoxical moment to imagine other possibilities. Reading American exceptionalism-universalism through these four stages offers new insights into the rhetoric of American exceptionalism. Ultimately, it asks that as critics we maintain the contemplative stance first developed in Crèvecoeur, that we continue to consider how the more limited, exceptionalist universalism might be replaced with a more genuine concern for the universal.

Coincidence: Exceptionalism and Universalism in Winthrop

In looking for the earliest instances of American exceptionalism, scholars unanimously point to John Winthrop's sermon delivered en route to founding the Massachusetts Bay Colony in 1630, "A Modell of Christian Charity."[1] In particular, they cite the last few pages of the sermon and Winthrop's image of New England as a "city upon a hill" as founding what Sacvan Bercovitch calls the "jeremiad" that informed American politics for centuries to come. The exceptionalist valence of the image is well known: that America's singularity as exemplar afforded it a privileged position in God's providence. For an analysis of the co-presence of American exceptionalism and universalism in the nation's founding documents, a brief reconsideration of this famous early exceptionalist text is necessary. A closer examination reveals that New England's exceptionalism is attended and perhaps even superseded by its universalism. The oft-quoted image appears in a passage in which Winthrop describes the rewards that await the colonists' virtuous cohabitation and success:

> [W]hen hee shall make vs a prayse and glory, that men shall say of succeeding plantacions: the lord make it like that of

> New England: for wee must Consider that wee shall be as a Citty vpon a Hill, the eies of all people are vppon vs; soe that if wee shal deale falsely with our god in this worke wee haue vndertaken and soe cause him to withdrawe his present help from vs, wee shall be made a story and a by-word through the world. . . . (Winthrop 1931, 295)

Reading the sermon as exceptionalist, scholars have focused on the image of the "city upon a hill" and the implication that New England is removed from and above the rest of the world. But this city, Winthrop makes clear, will be a model upon which others will shape themselves. The idea that future "plantacions" will ask to be made in the image of New England, if carried out, would undermine the very uniqueness that exceptionalism claims. Furthermore, Winthrop assures his listeners that this example will reverberate "through the world"; it bears universal significance for any and all future nations. Of course, the idea that it is New England in particular that bears this weight renders it exceptional, but it is exceptional precisely in its universal significance and the universal interest it presumably inspires. It is exceptional only because the "eies of all people" are on it.

Throughout the sermon Winthrop cites "providence" as on the side of New England, but the very occasion for the speech suggests Winthrop himself feels insecure about the colony's success. The emphatic call to unity and admonition against individualism is made in response to Winthrop's fears that those on board the *Arbella* will rebel against the colony's purpose. He opens with the following remark: "God Almightie in his most holy and wise providence hath soe disposed of the Condicion of mankind, as in all times some must be rich some poore, some highe and eminent in power and dignitie; others meane and in subieccion" (Winthrop 1931, 282). Later, Winthrop develops this point and compels, through a vivid metaphor of the human body, listeners to accept their station in life and live compassionately with others: "Ye are the body of Christ and members of [youre?] parte" and "All the partes of this body being thus vnited are made soe contiguous in a speciall relacion as they must needes partake of each others strength and infirmity, ioy, and sorrowe, weale and woe" (ibid., 289). The implication here is communal investment but also acceptance of one's place, particularly if one is poorer than the next person. That the speech is delivered when the colonists have hardly left England further suggests Winthrop's anxieties about cohesion and unity.

These are logical concerns for separatists who, in their decision to board the *Arbella*, have practiced exactly the kind of dismemberment against which Winthrop preaches. The resort to providence and to future universal admiration is meant to counter their current anxieties about political and spiritual discord. Thus, the appeal to universalism serves to pacify fears that stem from the more detrimental aspects of the colony's exceptionalism. Though both exceptionalism and universalism are prevalent in Winthrop's sermon, we might consider them as merely "coincidental." They are working in relation to each other, but one idea is not used in the name of the other in the way we see in the founding documents. They are "coincidental" because, ultimately, they both stem from Winthrop's vision of Puritan theology and do not contradict each other or comprise an intentional paradox. For that, we have to wait until the rhetoric of independence and national foundation.

Confluence: *Common Sense* and American Exceptionalism-Universalism in the Age of Independence

In *Common Sense*, Thomas Paine intentionally yokes the ideologies of American exceptionalism and universalism to make a strong case for independence. *Common Sense* is best known for popularizing and inspiring the cause of American independence, but it is equally significant for being one of the first popular articulations of American exceptionalism-universalism.

Scholars have considered the evocation of universalism in *Common Sense* as evidence of Paine's indebtedness to Enlightenment notions of sympathy and reason. In her reading of the influence of Enlightenment, and particularly Scottish, philosophy on Paine, Elizabeth Barnes argues that Paine's invocation of "plain arguments" and "simple facts" implies "that there exists a natural, universal 'character of man' to which Paine may appeal" (Barnes 1997, 29). Following Barnes's reading of sympathy to different ends, John Highman contends that in the early national period "nationalism and a proto-universalism fertilized one another," but he misinterprets the connection when he states that "sympathy for the suffering of humanity everywhere was readily experienced as a natural extension of patriotic feelings" (Highman 1993, 198). Highman's reading is determined by the nineteenth-century emphasis of his essay and the importance he ascribes to *Common Sense* philosophy, which lead him to reverse the causal relation. Paine employs universalism *in service to* patriotism, not as an extension of it. Rather than appeal to a universal that already exists, *Common Sense* constructs the universal on its own terms in order to promote independence.

Readings of *Common Sense* that mark the performative elements of the text are useful here, even if they leave questions of universalism and exceptionalism undeveloped. For example, Edward Larkin's *Thomas Paine and the Literature of Revolution* argues that Paine "did not merely 'secure the trust' of an already-existing audience, he invented a public that he could then claim to represent in his writings" (Larkin 2005a, 24). Similarly, Nancy Rothenberg asserts that Paine constructs a "hypocritical" position in regard to his audience, for the act of publication necessitates the adoption of a hierarchical position that contradicts the pamphlet's revolutionary claims. In supporting his argument, Paine "must make an epistemological claim to know that all men must be equal if liberty is to prevail, a claim which in itself creates a privileged position disallowed by the claim, for if everyone knew of this principle of equality, there would be no need to argue for it" (Rothenberg 1992, 345). Larkin and Rothenberg highlight that much of the work of *Common Sense* lies in the performance of the common, even as the text pretends to appeal to a common that exists outside of it. The performance underwrites Paine's rhetoric of political independence and is popularized through his best-selling pamphlet.

David C. Hoffman claims that while Paine's rhetoric evokes universal and ageless truths, the appeal and success of the pamphlet had much to do with the time and place of its publication: the pamphlet was published on the day that King George's incendiary speech on the colonies appeared in the *Pennsylvania Evening Post* and was printed in one of the larger cities of the colonies and home of the Continental Congress (Hoffman 2003, 377–78). Hoffman's comment alerts us to how *Common Sense* negotiates the relationship between the particular and the general. One of the pamphlet's strengths is its ability to frame current political questions as timeless battles between control and freedom. In so doing, the pamphlet marks one of the earliest, and certainly the best known, confluences of universalism and exceptionalism.

It is well known that Paine first published the pamphlet anonymously in order to prevent censure, but from the beginning the writer relates this anonymity to the very notion of common sense. The four-paragraph introduction begins with the sly acknowledgment that "[p]erhaps the sentiments contained in the following pages, are not *yet* sufficiently fashionable to procure them general favor" (Paine 2003, 5; emphasis in original). The "*yet*" in this line cannot be overstated—it is the author's guarantee that his opinions *will be* "fashionable," will garner "general favor"; it is simply a matter of time. If one sense of "common sense" implies self-evident truths, another implies beliefs widely held by a general audience, one that cuts across personal or political differences. The first sentence of *Common Sense* invents this audience and calls it into being. The text presents itself as the repository of general feeling rather than as one person's argument. It is this performance that lies at the heart of the text's meaning and makes its anonymous publication more than just convention. The anonymity is itself part of the pamphlet's thesis. Significantly, the "general favor" is not named as American, colonial, republican, or any other particular kind. No limits are imposed on the general agreement that is sure to pass. It could be universal.

In another move that at once supports and performs the pamphlet's thesis, Paine equates the patriotic cause with the universal subject of freedom. Appearing on the first page of the introduction, the equation forms the basis of *Common Sense*:

> The cause of America is in great measure the cause of all mankind. Many circumstances hath, and will arise, which are not local, but universal, and through which the principles of all Lovers of Mankind are affected, and in the Event of which, their Affections are interested. (Paine 2003, 5)

The cause Paine speaks of here, of course, is the colonies' independence from Britain. But Paine's framing of this cause makes it transcend national boundaries. The implications are dual: that the call for American independence is part of a larger Enlightenment conversation about freedom and independence in the abstract, and that American independence is of universal interest, that it will benefit all Mankind. This pamphlet well known for calling America as a nation into being also evokes a universal polity and, most importantly, makes the two indistinguishable from the very beginning.

Another crucial implication here is that whoever is against American independence is not a "Lover of Mankind" but is ideologically outside of and against universal interest. Two paragraphs after the pamphlet introduces itself as the harbinger of ideas that will no doubt procure "general favor," this "general favor" is defined as no less than universal interest. As Paine states in the rest of the introduction, Britain's policy against the colonies has violated the "natural rights of all Mankind" and the colonies' self-defense and independence are "the Concern of every Man to whom Nature hath given the Power of feeling" (Paine 2003, 5). The statement reiterates the position that those who are against independence stand against the interest of mankind; once again *Common Sense* equates America with the universal. The sentiment is repeated throughout *Common Sense*, as in the point that "[i]t is repugnant to reason, to the universal order of things to all examples from former ages, to suppose, that this continent can longer remain subject to any external power" (ibid., 25). Some might read the point as merely indicative of Paine's hyperbolic rhetoric, but we see more of the pamphlet's significance when we recognize its performance and iteration of American universalism.

The universalizing element of *Common Sense*, traditionally overlooked by scholarship on the text, is of great significance to the work. First, it makes a powerful case for independence by framing it in universal terms. Second, and more of interest to our purposes here, it heralds American universalism even before the nation has itself come into being. *Common Sense* not only makes a persuasive argument for independence, it performs and popularizes the earliest instance of American universalism. Contrary to popular readings of American universalism that register it as a part of nineteenth- or even twentieth-century forms of American imperialism, my reading of Paine illustrates how American universalism is present even before the moment of national foundation, in the call for revolution.

However, since the pamphlet aims in particular at the independence of these thirteen colonies from British control, it registers American universalism in confluence with American exceptionalism. American exceptionalism is the underside of Paine's argument. "America" here signifies these specific colonies on the eastern seaboard of North America. Even though he makes strong arguments against metropolitan control of locations an ocean away and of the British imperial system in particular, the causes of Jamaica, Bermuda, Canada, or other British American colonies are suspiciously missing from this universal cause. This implies that it is only these thirteen colonies that are the cause of all mankind, and as such renders them exceptional. Whether they are exceptional because their cause is universal or whether their cause is universal because they are exceptional seems beside the point. The American exceptional-universal is a trope Paine utilizes to make a convincing argument for independence.

Common Sense is regarded by many as the first American best-seller and, by some standards, one of the best-selling publications of all time. Robert Ferguson reminds us that the pamphlet's initial circulation "reached between 120,000 and 150,000 copies" at a time when "the largest colonial newspapers and most important pamphlets had circulation under 2000" (Ferguson 2000, 466). The pamphlet's sale record, combined with its reproduced and shared circulation in other forms, such as newspapers and libraries, indicates that it reached a large share if not majority of the reading public within a short period of time. Such success indicates two points about the pamphlet's evocation of American universalism-exceptionalism: it disseminates the sentiment throughout the colonies at the time of independence, but the preexisting sentiment might also have influenced the success of the pamphlet and the call for independence. After all, who, precisely at a time of increasing violence and fear, would not want to identify with a sentiment that at once linked them with all mankind and rendered them essentially unique in the eyes of providence? I mark Paine's rhetorical strategy in *Common Sense* as a "confluence" precisely because *Common Sense* strategically brings universalism and exceptionalism together for rhetorical and political ends. They do not merely happen to coexist; they combine to form an ideological impetus for independence that is difficult if not impossible (at least rhetorically) to argue against. In *Common Sense* American exceptionalism-universalism works in the name of revolution, but ten years after the pamphlet's publication the dual concept will be put toward a very different, in fact contradictory, end: that of national foundation.

Paradox: Exceptional Universalism in the U.S. Constitution

In the past two decades, scholars have reexamined traditional views of the Constitution as the ideological heir to the Declaration of Independence and of the federal nation as the natural outcome of independence. The scholarship runs from the presumed uncovering of elite conspiracies to careful reflections on the inherent contradictions of representative democracy, but it all contributes to a necessary examination of the decade between independence and founding (see, for example, Fresia 1988 and Jensen 1948). Rather than read the Federalists as direct successors to Paine, scholars such as Ed White note that it is the Constitution's "appropriation of the 'rhetoric of the Revolution,' but reworked, redirected, and refined within an institutional frame," and not a continued call for independence, that founds the nation (White 2005, 163). For White, Jensen, and others, the Constitution's framers appropriate this rhetoric in order that "faction . . . be integrated into the system" rather than continue to threaten the political and economic safety of the United States (ibid., 165). Furthermore, such a system is designed to prevail for posterity, in that it "foreclose[s] the development of an American intellectual tradition in which differing ideas of politics would be intimately and genuinely related to differing social interests" (White 2005, 163; see also Paine 1997, 562). Such foreclosure bears consequences not only for future American citizens, however. The Constitution's appropriation of revolutionary rhetoric, in particular its presumption to speak for "we the people," embeds the exceptionalism and universalism of Paine's call for independence into a paradox that rhetorically excludes subject positions external to its own.

The Constitution's performance of American exceptionalism-universalism lies predominantly in its subject position, announced by the document's famous first three words. Here the framers revise the more concrete opening of the Articles of Confederation—"We the undersigned"—into a decidedly more open-ended subject position, "We the people of the United States." Strictly speaking, the "we" here refers to something narrower than "the people"; in actuality it can only refer to the document's signers, who represented a political minority at the time. They were a slim majority of those who attended the Convention, as several attendees refused to sign while others left the Convention in frustration. Furthermore, Convention attendance far from represented "the people," given that delegates were chosen from the ruling parties and many Anti-Federalists decided (quite fatefully) to make known their opposition by boycotting the Convention (see Ferguson 2000). The rhetorical strategy through which this unrepresentative but powerful group manages to speak for "the people" relies on American exceptionalism-universalism.

Given the founders' admitted investment in rhetoric, scholars have rightly paid attention to the Constitution's performative language. The document's opening phrase has been read in two ways: either as reiterating the subject position that the Declaration "both announces and brings into being" (Lee 1995, 269) or, as Michael Warner reads it, a "sovereign interpellation" in which "the people are always coming across themselves in the act of consenting to their own coercion" (Warner 1990, 112). In reading the phrase as a "sovereign interpellation" rather than mere representation of the people and in bringing attention to the text's "coercive" qualities, Warner highlights the contradiction inherent in the document's opening line. In claiming to speak for the people, the Constitution effectively renders them mute because, as Warner reminds us, there is "no legitimate representational space outside of the constitutive we" (ibid.). Warner's reading astutely points to the performative paradox that informs the nation's founding and offers a useful framework for examining the Constitution's paradoxical iteration of universalism.

The Constitution's rhetorical position had immediate political consequences for the young nation. "We the people" presumes to speak for all the people of the United States, of the present and future. It is not fixed in a particular time or geographic location. As in the Articles of Confederation, the "United States" here signifies whatever states have entered into a contract of union. Presaging the expansion of the United States by future annexation, the framers do not name particular states. As Edward Larkin reminds us, it is only in the years following ratification that "United States" comes to signify something akin to a nation or country. Hence, "the people" can and will be expanded to include others as necessary.

The inclusion of others is crucial here for the Constitution's deft ability to foreclose future dissent. There is a certain universalism in its claim to speak for "we the people" in this abstract sense, and in claiming to speak for all it also claims to speak once and for all, foreclosing—at least rhetorically—the possibility of outside resistance. This is particularly deft in a document that allows rhetorical license for the mainly Federalist framers to found the kind of centralized, national government that the majority of Americans at the time opposed. The decades following the War of Independence were rife with political turmoil and continuous revolutionary activity, both of which caused the republic's elite to fear "mobocracy."

As is the case with *Common Sense*, the universalism of the United States as determined in the Constitution renders the United States as exceptional as well. If the Constitution makes first claim to speak for the people, other founding documents must only be speaking for someone else. I do not mean to raise suspicions here about the Constitution's ultimate inability to found a republic or democracy or to accuse the founders of purposeful sleight of hand. Rather than take such a judgmental position (which inevitably leads to either pessimism or optimism about freedom and other notions too expansive to examine here), I want only to pay attention to the way the language works at the moment of federal constitution, in particular to note that the convergence of a universal cause with that of the independent states that stems from Paine's Enlightenment revolutionary argument here reaches, or rather is rendered as, an impasse. The subject position of "We the people" may come from real fears about opposition, but it also performs a rhetorical sleight of hand wherein "the people" are seen as, ultimately, speaking to themselves. Robert Ferguson argues that the Constitution "fixes all previous aspects of revolutionary activity, especially the disruptive or chaotic parts, into a text for all to read" (Ferguson 2000, 144). Such inclusion of revolutionary activity into a legible text attempts to make sense of this past but also, ultimately, to contain it and control it through the process of making it visible on its own terms. As such it also looks towards the future. The implication of the Constitution's speaking both to and for all is that only the Constitution can do so, offering an exceptionalist-universalist rhetoric that presumes itself impossible to contest.

The performance of "we the people" and its attendant paradoxes bear significance to the early republic's relationship with other nations. The idea that the cause of America is the "cause of all mankind" underwrites the nation's actions in the hemisphere. For example, it forms the grounds of American expansion into and intervention in the Spanish colonies and Spanish American republics. It also motivates the early nation's actions across the globe. A mere seven years after the Constitutional Convention, for example, Congress passed the "Act to Provide a Naval Armament" (1794) in order to fight the obstructions against U.S. trade over the Atlantic caused by the "Algerine" pirates in the Mediterranean Sea. In his novel *The Algerine Captive* (1797), Royall Tyler illustrates how the institution of a standing military and naval intervention in North Africa are deemed to be in universal interest. His protagonist Updike Underhill charged the United States to "nobly reduce [the Algerines] to reason and humanity" (Tyler 2002, 159), and argues that in doing so the United States will solve not just its own problems with the Algerians but those of Europe as well. In his book published several years before the Constitutional Convention, Michel-Guillaume St. Jean de Crèvecoeur offered a warning against these more sedimentary versions of the paradox by inviting readers to contemplate rather than take for granted the relationship between exceptionalism and universalism.

Contemplation: Rethinking American Exceptionalism-Universalism Through Crèvecoeur's *Letters from an American Farmer*

Even if they are unfamiliar with the author's name, readers often feel a sense of recognition upon reading the most-often cited portions of Crèvecoeur's *Letters from an American Farmer* (1782). Most, if not all, of the ideals that U.S. Americans typically ascribe to their country—whether as reality, dream, or illusion—are found in *Letters*. Like Winthrop's "city upon a hill," the American farmer's examples of self-sufficiency, industry, freedom, and progress—and the promise that these are available to immigrants from all over the globe—have informed American self-identity for centuries. Taken at face value, James's earlier letters espouse American exceptionalism, and nationalist scholars from the mid-twentieth century onward have held the book as evidence of these beliefs. However, critics have overlooked the ways *Letters* complicates these early versions of American exceptionalism with forms of universalism.

Recent critics have rightly revised the reception of the *Letters* as an "exceptionalist text," noticing how certain passages in the book question the more optimistic ones (Larkin 2005, 54). For example, Edward Larkin adapts recent analyses of eighteenth-century cosmopolitanism in literary and cultural studies to argue that the exceptionalist reading is complicated first by Crèvecoeur's British loyalism and second by his identification with cosmopolitan notions of personal and political identity (ibid., 57, 68). However, the relationship between cosmopolitanism and exceptionalism need not be antithetical, as Ezra Tawil convincingly argues in his article for the same issue of *Novel* in which Larkin's reading of Crèvecoeur appears.

In his reading of Crèvecoeur's contemporary, Charles Brockden Brown, Tawil convincingly argues that Brown's "early version of literary exceptionalism" is rooted in European thought, though he admits that Brown's combination of exceptionalism and cosmopolitanism is paradoxical (Tawil 2006, 105). In Brown, according to Tawil, European aesthetics of the sublime connects the two. In Crèvecoeur, the notion of the universal, which is conversant with but still distinct from the cosmopolitan, provides an ideological counterpoint to the text's exceptionalist moments. Through them, Crèvecoeur illustrates how certain manifestations of universalism are at their core exceptionalist and offers a powerful critique that, when read carefully, inspires a contemplation of the dualism rendered static and unquestionable in the Constitution.

We get our first glimpse of universalist rhetoric in the book's preface, which frames the text as a response to the French Abbé Raynal's *Histoire des deux Indes* (1770).[2] This dialogical framework is mirrored in the narrative itself, which is framed as the American farmer James's correspondence with the English gentleman Mr. F. B. On both levels, Americans connect with Europeans in a literary manifestation of the eighteenth-century republic of letters to reveal the universal ideals on which such connections are based and, ultimately, to examine how these ideals inform and also undercut the exceptionalist ideals that are articulated as well.

The preface begins: "Behold, sir, an humble American planter, a simple cultivator of the earth, addressing you from the farther side of the Atlantic and presuming to fix your name at the head of his trifling lucubrations" (Crèvecoeur 1981, 37). The initial greeting accomplishes several things: it names Raynal's *Histoire* as the intellectual predecessor of *Letters* and establishes a connection, albeit fictional, between Raynal and Crèvecoeur. It also presents the author as a "humble American planter," cloaking it in the conventional humility of eighteenth-century prose. Through its performance of an address to Raynal, it also imagines a correspondence between Raynal and Crèvecoeur. Thus, it also marks Crèvecoeur's self-introduction into the republic of letters in which Raynal is an important figure.

Crèvecoeur explains his right to enter into this sphere by citing "a secret communion among good men throughout the world, a mental affinity connecting them by a similitude of sentiments" and reckoning that, as someone who shares Raynal's sentiments, he shares this communion (Crèvecoeur 1981, 38). While this transnational affinity might be regarded as simply Crèvecoeur's cosmopolitanism, Crèvecoeur himself is careful to name it as universal: he thanks Raynal for giving him his first glimpse of the "relative state of nations" and exemplifying "that universal benevolence, that diffusive good will, which is not confined to the narrow limits of your own country, but, on the contrary, extends to the whole human race" (ibid., 37). The preface frames *Letters* as an addition to this conversation, written in this very same spirit of "universal benevolence."

While the author's preface is careful to mark the text's place in a universal conversation, the narrator's opening remarks negotiate more clearly between universal and local interest. Like Crèvecoeur, James addresses a transatlantic reader, in this case the "first enlightened European" he has met (Crèvecoeur 1981, 51). Mr. F. B. had paid a visit to James's farm during a tour of the colonies and, upon his return to England, asks James to supply further knowledge about America through letters. Letter I begins with a question that echoes the humility of Crèvecoeur's preface: "Who would have thought that because I received you with hospitality and kindness, you should imagine me capable of writing with propriety and perspicuity?" (ibid., 39). Such lack of confidence about measuring up to the task, James states, stems from insecurity about his merit as a writer and about the subject matter itself. He worries that "this local and unadorned information" will not meet Mr. F. B.'s expectations (ibid., 40). However, as is the case with Crèvecoeur's preface, the very act of addressing the European reader in a sense renders these worries false. After all, it is precisely this kind of information that Mr. F. B. seeks, for he has specifically called on James for the task. The act of writing here, and the narrative that ensues, forges a connection between the American and European and between the local and universal that levels discrepancies between them. The act of James's writing, even though it results from Mr. F. B.'s order, affords this "simple citizen" and "cultivator of the earth" a place in the republic of letters (ibid., 50). The negotiation of the local and universal, of unadorned and intellectual, is particularly significant given the implied thesis of James's narrative, at least as it commences.

Both Crèvecoeur's preface and James's oft-quoted initial description of America in Letter III portray America as asylum. In the preface, Crèvecoeur praises Raynal for having seen North America in its "true light" and rightly portraying it as "the asylum of freedom, as the cradle of future nations and the refuge of distressed Europeans" (Crèvecoeur 1981, 37). In response to the question "What is an American?" James's Letter III claims that in "this great American asylum, the poor of Europe have by some means met together, and in consequence of various causes" (ibid., 68). America is an asylum, James tells us, because the poor and struggling of Europe can come here to make a name for themselves; it is the country for those who previously "had no country" (ibid., 68). Through the image of the asylum, America is figured as the place wherein, to reverse Paine's argument in *Common Sense*, the cause of mankind is the cause of America.

In this letter, the connection between universalism and its attendant exceptionalism is rendered immediately. In the paragraphs following the above discussion, James defines an American as the "new man" who exhibits "that strange mixture of blood, which you will find in no other country" (Crèvecoeur 1981, 69). It is precisely in its mixture of other nations that America is unique. Such a reading of America is not new to twenty-first-century readers, but it was still fairly new in 1783. I would argue that it only really begins to take shape in the universalist revolutionary rhetoric popularized by Paine. However, though Crèvecoeur's *Letters* proclaims this ideal quite vocally, it does not do so without qualification and, more importantly, contemplation. The last of the *Letters* is titled "Distresses of a Frontier Man," and James's distresses stem in large part from the dissolution of his optimism in the face of the realities of colonial life, particularly violence and slavery.

The optimism of James's perspective in his earlier *Letters*, the one that echoes that which Crèvecoeur's preface ascribes to Raynal, begins to unravel practically as soon as it is introduced. In Letters IV through VIII James offers Nantucket as a complementary ideal to the agrarian farm. As in the abstract America, the inhabitants of Nantucket find that hard work and a communal rising against their hardship will eventually allow for subsistence and survival. Such possibilities, James tells us, are a stark contrast to the circumstances they encountered in Europe: "The great number of European emigrants yearly coming over here informs us that the severity of taxes, the injustice of laws, the tyranny of the rich, and the oppressive avarice of the church are as intolerable as ever" (Crèvecoeur 1981, 106). These sentiments seem only to echo the exceptionalist claims made earlier, but James's commentary begs for a careful reading. In an astute contemplation of the fact that America's prosperity results from that of those who have suffered elsewhere, James concludes: "This country, providentially intended for the general asylum of the world, will flourish by the oppression of other people" (ibid., 106). The tone here remains exalting, but the sentiment is rather critical in its irony. James alludes to the fact that America will grow on the basis of immigrants who are fleeing oppressive governments at home, but the statement points to the more chilling aspects of American exceptionalism-universalism. First, it implies that some crisis or oppressive circumstance must always exist in order for America to thrive, a thought that almost paints America as parasitically reliant on the oppression of others. This is the opposite of "the cause of America is in great measure the cause of all mankind," but it is the logical outcome of exceptionalist universalism. Thus, Crèvecoeur reminds us of the reactionary potential of American exceptionalism-universalism in that it regards only its own cause as universal.

Letters from an American Farmer is still known in some circles for its early articulation of the American dream, but these other passages in the text mark it as more analysis than panegyric. By examining how James moves from the earlier optimism to the later "distress," Crèvecoeur invites his readers to contemplate the more negative aspects of their hopes and dreams. The final Letter illustrates how the violent underside of American prosperity, first witnessed in the horrors of Southern slavery, has finally reached James's own backyard in the Revolutionary War. It is this violence and the attendant realization that "the innocent class are always the victims of the few" that leads James to question his previous assumptions in fear and isolation (Crèvecoeur 1981, 204). It forces him to ask: "What is man when no longer connected with society, or when he finds himself surrounded by a convulsed and half-dissolved one" (ibid., 201). This "convulsed and half-dissolved" America is far from the happy prospects he thought evident on his farm and elsewhere; it problematizes the exceptionalism seen in earlier passages.

Conclusion

If my reading here has highlighted the universalist implications of American exceptionalism, it has also highlighted the exceptionalist nature of universalism, at least as it has been proffered in nationalist rhetoric from the ratification of the Constitution to the present. Both Paine and Crèvecoeur offer different approaches to the yoking together of these ideals, but Crèvecoeur most notably offers a critique of them and their significance in American thought. Though Crèvecoeur's *Letters* offers a critique of eighteenth-century Euro-American thought, its contemplative stance is useful still today. What would James make, for example, of President Bush's claim in his State of the Union address on January 31, 2006, that "for people everywhere the United States is a partner for better life"? What would he think of Bush's decision to withdraw the United States from the Kyoto Protocol or the U.S.'s repeated criticism of the United Nations? My purpose in naming these contemporary examples is not to criticize them but to note how they illustrate that the United States' definition of universalism is still quite exceptionalist.

The presence of exceptionalism alongside several of the key instances of universalism explains, at least in part, the limits to certain renderings of universalism that, in fact, are not truly "universal." This does not suggest, however, that what Immanuel Wallerstein calls "universal universalism," as opposed to European universalism, might not or cannot exist.[3] Indeed, Judith Butler, whose work in queer theory and political philosophy informs the reading I have offered here, articulates quite effectively the reasons why a critique of what she calls "culturally viable" universalisms should not render universalism obsolete. For Butler, the problem with universalism emerges "when the meaning of 'the universal' proves to be culturally variable, and the specific cultural articulations of the universal work against its claim to a transcultural status" (Butler 2002, 45). However, as Butler claimed in the earlier work *Bodies That Matter*, "This is not to say that there ought to be no reference to the universal or that it has become, for us, an impossibility" (Butler 1993, 45). Indeed, one intention I have for my reading of American exceptionalism-universalism is that it contribute to recent discussions in academic and popular discourse that look toward the possibility of a universalism that makes no exceptions, but rather seeks through contemplation and conversation to develop a transcultural understanding of the universal.

Notes

The author wishes to thank John Leavey, Susan Hegeman, Julian Wolfreys, Álvaro Félix Bolaños, Ed White, Julie Kim, Danielle DeMuth, Daniel McClure, and Deborah Madsen for their comments and suggestions on this essay.

1. Historians and critics differ on whether the speech was written and/or on board the *Arbella* or whether it was delivered, as Ivy Schweitzer suggests, "probably at Southampton . . . on the eve of their departure" (Schweitzer, 441). Scholarly consensus on Winthrop's sermon as a root of American exceptionalism is wide-reaching. For two influential discussions, see Madsen and Bercovitch. For a more recent approach to the question, see Spanos.

2. Abbé (Guillaume-Thomas François) Raynal (1713–1796), *philosophe*, best known for *L'Histoire philosophique et politique des établissements et du commerce des Européens dan les deux Indes* (1770). This encyclopedic work of geographic description and political philosophy, attributed to Raynal and less often Denis Diderot, serves as a well-known and extensive counterpoint to James's own "personal" narrative. Srinivas Aravamudan offers a nuanced analysis of the *Histoire* and Raynal's significance as author in "Progress through Violence or Progress from Violence? Interpreting the Ambivalences of the *Histoire des deux Indes*," in *Progrès et violence au XVIIIe siècle* (Paris: Champion, 2001). For more on the complexities of authorship and authority in the text see Ottmar Ette's "La

vuelta al universo en nuestro piso: Lectores y lecturas en la 'Histoire des deux Indes,'" in *Del tiempo y las ideas*, ed. Agustín Mendoza (Buenos Aires: Fondo de Cultura Económica, 2000).

3. In *European Universalism* Wallerstein examines "the universalism of the powerful [that] has been a partial and distorted universalism," which he calls "European universalism." To this, Wallerstein counters "genuine universalism" which he calls "universal universalism" (xiv).

Works Cited

Aravamudan, Srinivas. 2001. Progress through violence or progress from violence? Interpreting the ambivalences of the *Histoire des deux Indes*. In *Progrès et violence au XVIIIe siècle*, ed. D. Dawson and V. Cossy. Paris: Champion.

Barnes, Elizabeth. 1997. *States of sympathy: Seduction and democracy in the American novel.* New York: Columbia University Press.

Bercovitch, Sacvan. 1978. *The American jeremiad.* Madison: University of Wisconsin Press.

Butler, Judith. 1993. *Bodies that matter: On the discursive limits of "sex."* New York: Routledge.

———. 2002. Universality in culture. In *For love of country: Debating the limits of patriotism*, ed. Martha C. Nussbaum, 45–52. Boston: Beacon Press.

Coviello, Peter. 2002. Agonizing affection: Affect and nation in early America. *Early American Literature* 37, no. 3: 439–68.

de Crèvecoeur, Michel-Guillaume Jean. 1981. *Letters from an American farmer and Sketches of eighteenth-century America.* Ed. Albert E. Stone. New York: Penguin.

Davidson, Edward H., and William J. Scheick. 1991. Authority in Paine's *Common Sense* and *Crisis Papers*. *Studies in the Humanities* 18, no. 2: 124–34.

Ette, Ottmar. 2000. La vuelta al universo en nuestro piso: Lectores y lecturas en la "Histoire des deux Indes." In *Del tiempo y de las ideas*, ed. Agustín Mendoza. Buenos Aires: Fondo de Cultura Económica.

Ferguson, Robert A. 2000. The commonalities of *Common Sense*. *William and Mary Quarterly* 58, no. 3: 465–504.

Fresia, Jerry. 1988. *Toward an American revolution.* Boston: South End Press.

Greeson, Jennifer Rae. 2003. From colonial planter to American farmer. In *Messy beginnings: Postcoloniality and early American studies*, ed. Malini Johar Schueller and Edward Watts. New Brunswick: Rutgers University Press.

Highman, John. 1993. Multiculturalism and universalism: A history and critique. *American Quarterly* 45, no. 2 (June): 195–219.

Hoffman, David C. 2003. Paine and prejudice: Rhetoric leadership through perceptual framing in *Common Sense*. *Rhetoric & Public Affairs* 9:3 (Fall): 373–410.

Jensen, Merrill. 1948. *The Articles of Confederation: An interpretation of the social-constitutional history of the American Revolution, 1774–1781*. Madison: University of Wisconsin Press.

Larkin, Edward. 2006. The cosmopolitan revolution: Loyalism and the fiction of an American nation. *Novel* 40, no. 1–2: 52–76.

———. 2005. Inventing an American public. *Early American Literature* 33, no. 3: 250–76.

———. 2005a. *Thomas Paine and the literature of revolution*. Cambridge: Cambridge University Press.

Lee, Benjamin. 1995. Performing the people. *Pragmatics: Quarterly Publication of the International Pragmatics Association* 5, no. 2: 263–80.

Madsen, Deborah L. 1998. *American exceptionalism*. Edinburgh: Edinburgh University Press.

Paine, Thomas. 2003. *Common sense*. In *Common sense and other writings*, ed. Gordon S. Wood. New York: Modern Library.

Parrish, Susan Scott. 2006. *American curiosity*. Chapel Hill: University of North Carolina Press.

Rothenberg, Molly Anne. 1992. Parasiting America: The radical function of heterogeneity in Thomas Paine's early writings. *Eighteenth-Century Studies* 25, no. 3: 331–51.

Schweitzer, Ivy. 2005. John Winthrop's "model" of American affiliation. *Early American Literature* 40, no. 3: 441–69.

Spanos, William. 2007. American exceptionalism, the jeremiad, and the frontier: From the Puritans to the neo-con men. *Boundary* 2 34, no. 1: 35–66. Tawil, Ezra. 2006. "New forms of sublimity": *Edgar Huntly* and the European origins of American exceptionalism. *Novel* 40, no. 1–2: 104–24.

Tyler, Royall. 2002. *The Algerine captive*. Ed. Caleb Crain. New York: Modern Library.

Wallerstein, Immanuel. 2003. *The decline of American power*. New York: New Press.

———. 2006. *European universalism*. New York: New Press.

Warner, Michael. 1990. *The letters of the republic: Publication and the public sphere in eighteenth-century America*. Cambridge: Harvard University Press.

White, Ed. 2005. *The Backcountry and the city: Colonization and conflict in early America*. Minneapolis: University of Minnesota Press.

Winthrop, John. 1931. A modell of Christian charity. In *Winthrop papers*. Vol. 2, 282–95. Boston: Massachusetts Historical Society.

Wood, Gordon S. 1991. *The radicalism of the American revolution*. New York: Vintage.

4

Burlesquing America's Errand

Savage Satire in Irving's *History of New York* and Melville's *The Confidence-Man*

Matthew Brophy

The notion that America has a sacred mission to spread democracy and freedom throughout the world has its roots in John Winthrop's assertion that "providence" had ordained the Massachusetts Bay Company to found a colonial government that was "both civill and ecclesiasticall," with the implication that both the act of building this civilization, and the state that would be its result, were manifestations of God's will (Miller 1956, 5). By the nineteenth century, this "errand into the wilderness" had transformed into the teleology of "Manifest Destiny," with the persistence of the underlying assumption that the work of building a Christian democracy gave white Americans a divine entitlement to their land. John L. O'Sullivan, who coined the phrase, cited "the God of Nature" as the source of legitimacy for American expansion (qtd. in Weinberg 1935, 62). These two manifestations of American exceptionalism—the Puritan "errand" and the Jacksonian "Manifest Destiny"—share not only an allusion to a divine covenant between God and America, but also an implicit rationalization for the massacring of indigenous peoples. This sanctification of violence becomes a central target of both Irving's and Melville's burlesques and a crucial point of attack for their critique of American exceptionalism. The desired effect of their respective critiques is to split the fused "secular and sacred" symbol of America, by showing an American history (and present) that is decidedly unholy and unexceptional.

The genre of burlesque, with its propensity for ridicule and profanity, proves suitable for discovering this "ugly" America. According to Martin Roth, the function of traditional satire is "to posit a rational or absolutely moral norm in terms of which the grotesque or the ridiculous is to be measured" (Roth 1976, 5). For our purposes, we will define burlesque as a subgenre of satire, in which the grotesque and ridiculous are exposed *without* explicitly positing a moral norm. In other words, traditional satire exposes the "grotesque and ridiculous" of one ideology to assert another, while burlesque satire shows the "grotesque and ridiculous" to be omnipresent. While traditional satire can potentially fit Sacvan Bercovitch's mold of the jeremiad, by criticizing a "false America" against an assertion of a "true America," burlesque satire resists the latter gesture. The burlesque does not morally re-center its reader, nor does it reaffirm nationalist or theological narratives; the American reader is not told how she has strayed from her errand, but rather the errand itself is shown to be "grotesque and ridiculous." Roth points out the "danger" of the form as perceived by some Americanist critics, because the genre is an "international tradition," which disrupts the "territorial agreements" of "critical nationalism" (ibid., 6). Critics whose orientation is to define what is uniquely American about American literature tend to find disfavor in the burlesque not only because it is not a uniquely American form, but also because it attacks the religiously held symbolism of American exceptionalism—the notion that secular America is sacred. Irving's and Melville's burlesques create worlds of "elemental flow and continual recombination," which disrupt the providential narrative of America's progress on the frontier (ibid., 7).

The function of Irving's and Melville's burlesques is analogous to what Foucault suggests to be the purpose of "effective history," or "genealogy," that is, to introduce "discontinuity into our very being." For Foucault, genealogy sets out to disrupt the theological tradition of history, which "aims at dissolving the singular event into an ideal continuity—as a teleological movement or a natural process" (Foucault

1984, 88). Reading Irving and Melville under this framework, we can see their burlesques as genealogical disruptions of a nineteenth-century theological American historiography. Both writers perform the three oppositional modalities (parodic, dissociative, and sacrificial), which Foucault credits with the potential for such a disruption (ibid., 93). The intended effect of these three modalities is to call into question constructions of American reality, American identity, and American history.

Looking at the first modality, the parodic, we see Irving and Melville both undermining the perceived reality that European Americans possess a divine (or natural) entitlement to North American land. Irving's *History* parodies the arbitrary centering of America in certain theological histories of New England. By centering the Dutch colonists, as opposed to the English, Irving frames the Yankees as the "villains" of his *History*, who spoil destiny rather than fulfill it. Irving's invented historian, Diedrich Knickerbocker, characterizes the Yankees as insatiable imperialists: "[T]hey have facetiously received the nickname of THE PILGRIMS: that is to say, a people who are always seeking a better country than their own" (Irving 1984, 162). Exposing the term *pilgrims* as a euphemistic signifier, Irving implies that the movement westward is only nominally motivated by religion, but is better characterized as a pathological desire to acquire more land. For Melville, too, the "devout sentiment" that underwrites American nation building is pathological, as he reveals in his chapter "The metaphysics of Indian hating" (Melville 2002, 155). The discourse of settlement as a national crusade is exposed as a justification for racially motivated killing.

As for the dissociative modality, this is at the very heart of Melville's *Confidence-Man*. Identity, according to Foucault, is a weak construction, "which we attempt to support and to unify under a mask . . . itself only a parody" (Foucault 1984, 94). Melville's protagonist, the shape-shifting confidence-man, has no stable identity at all but only an assortment of masks. Moreover, he is a master at exposing the masks of those he encounters, such as the Yankee mystic Mark Winsome, whom many scholars believe to be a parody of Emerson. Moving through Melville's novel, several iconic American "types" come to be revealed as fraudulent characters. The confidence-man, for example, claims to be a philanthropist, yet sounds more like a cannibal: "Served up à la Pole, or à la Moor, à la Ladrone, or à la Yankee, that good dish, man, still delights me" (Melville 2002, 133). In Melville's satire of Emerson, the transcendentalist comes off as a "pedantic hobby-horse," a standard figure of burlesque (Roth 1976, 104). In Irving's text, we have the figure of the great American historian (Knickerbocker) and the great American political leader (Stuyvesant) dislodged from a sacred, iconic status. Knickerbocker (whom Roth reads as a stand-in for New England historians such as Thomas Prince) and Stuyvesant (whom several critics read as a stand in-for Thomas Jefferson) consistently appear ridiculous to the reader, under the weight of Irving's irony, as they revel in delusions of grandeur.

The third and final modality, the sacrificial, opposes the idea of "history as knowledge" (Foucault 1984, 93). In composing de-centered narratives that self-consciously draw attention to their own artifice, Irving and Melville both construct conspicuously nonobjective texts. To see how this works in Melville, consider how his story of Colonel Moredock, the pathological Indian killer, is really a parody of a nonfiction account of Moredock by James Hall in his *Sketches of the West.* Moredock's story is paradoxically a fiction within a fiction, but also hauntingly real. The metafictional form of the attack not only indicts the reality of Moredock's violence, but also undermines the textual authority of such "philosophical" justifications for racially motivated killing. In other words, Melville's fiction comes off as more "true," or at least more honest, than James Hall's history, without any claim to historical knowledge as such. Similarly, Irving's *History*, though based on many historical events from New York's colonial past, does not pretend to be an objective, historical text. Despite the fact that the Library of Congress places Irving's *History* on the same shelf as other, "legitimate" histories of New York, it is nevertheless clearly a mock history that is, in fact, antihistorical. Through his ironic spokesman, Knickerbocker, Irving praises the historian as possessing power superior to that of a tyrant: "The tyrant may oppress while the object of his tyranny exists; but the historian possesses superior might, for his power extends beyond the grave" (Irving 1984, 242). History, according to Irving, has the potential to be transcendentally oppressive.

Burlesque tropes such as lying travelers, comic philosophers, and mock dissertations allow Irving and Melville to construct parodic, dissociative, and sacrificial texts, and to destabilize the dominant metaphysical discourse of American exceptionalism. As Cecilia Tichi points out, the language of this discourse—as Melville heard it in his life, and amplified it in his parody—is "horrendously corrupted and debased" (Tichi 1972, 643). Tichi, too, uses the term *burlesque* to describe Melville's "verbal irony" (ibid., 645) when satirizing the self-righteousness of his age. Now we will look at how Irving and Melville specifically attack the presumptuous claim, on the part of their contemporaries writing in the tradition of the Puritan jeremiad, of access to "eternal Providence." The posturing of these writers as America's prophets and epic historians proves to be not only hubristic and silly but also insidiously propagandistic, as they become apologists for America's violent past and catalysts for a violent future.

Burlesquing America's "Prophets"

Sacvan Bercovitch notes that the "deep, stubborn optimism" of American exceptionalism can be traced back to the seventeenth-century New England Puritan rhetoric that combined "the role of visionary with that of social critic" (Bercovitch 1978, 55). It is precisely this role—that of American "Prophet"—that Irving and Melville attack in their respective burlesque portraits of Diedrich Knickerbocker and Mark Winsome. According to Roth, Irving's parody is based on writers such as Thomas Prince, author of *A Theological History of New England* (Roth 1976, 115), while several critics such as Egbert Oliver and Elizabeth Foster argue that Ralph Waldo Emerson is the inspiration behind Melville's Yankee mystic. Common to both "prophets" is a teleological sense of history, stretching back to the Creation and looking optimistically and proleptically into the future. The purpose of the American "prophet" is to be a missionary for the Puritan errand, that is, "to bring history itself to an end" (Bercovitch 1978, 12), a rather presumptuous and potentially apocalyptic goal, it would seem. For Irving and Melville, the goal is to destroy the "prophet" before the "prophet" destroys the world.

Before we hear a word of Diedrich Knickerbocker's *History,* we are introduced to him as an eccentric and reclusive "scholar" who never paid his rent. He vanished after the writing of his work, but reemerged after its publication, which brought him provincial fame among "the literati of Albany" (Irving 1984, 14). We are told of his death, but also that his fame, paradoxically, allowed him to enjoy "in advance [his] own immortality" (ibid., 16). Then, the *History* begins:

> "To rescue from oblivion the memory of former incidents, and to render a just tribute of renown to the many great and wonderful transactions of our Dutch progenitors, Diedrich

> Knickerbocker, native of the city of New York, produces this historical essay." Like the great Father of History, whose words I have just quoted, I treat of times long past, over which the twilight of uncertainty had already thrown its shadows, and the night of forgetfulness was about to descend forever. (Irving 1984, 17)

His purpose, as he claims, is to "rescue" the Dutch past of New York from "oblivion," but Irving hints that Knickerbocker's real goal is to rescue *himself* from oblivion, and to write himself into history the way he writes his name into Herodotus's quotation. One might think that he succeeds, since he enjoyed his immortality "in advance," but it does not take long to see that for what it is—nonsense. Knickerbocker's immortality, like his history, is a myth. The passage also reveals Knickerbocker's metaphysical sense of time, in that he attempts to project himself into the future by imposing himself upon the past. As for rescuing history from the "twilight of uncertainty," it is undoubtedly a chivalric endeavor, but if Knickerbocker treats history the way he treats the Father of History, one can expect a violent imposition of self onto fact.

Knickerbocker again reveals the vanity and absurdity behind his metaphysics by claiming that "cities *of themselves*, and, in fact, empires *of themselves*, are nothing without an historian" (Irving 1984, 19). As Roth points out, Knickerbocker writes "as if the act of the mind were prior" (Roth 1976, 117) to all other reality. The claim strikes the reader as ridiculous, but there is also an element of truth behind it. While the historian does not create the empire, he does create the *myth* of the empire, and the power of that myth can radically impact the material reality of an empire's people, as well as direct the political future of the empire. This is the darker side of Irving's burlesque, which emblematizes Knickerbocker as a manufacturer of American myth. Knickerbocker's vision borders on apocalyptic:

> It is the patient narrator who records [empires'] posterity as they rise—who blazons forth the splendor of their noontide meridian—who props their feeble memorials as they totter to decay—who gathers together their scattered fragments as they rot—and who piously, at length, collects their ashes into the mausoleum of his work, and rears a monument that will

> transmit their renown to all succeeding ages. (Irving 1984, 19)

Granted, Knickerbocker is speaking generally here, and not specifically about America, but it is still quite clear that the act of writing history, for him, anticipates an *end* to that history. For Knickerbocker this is particularly poignant because his New York, or at least the New York of his ancestors—New Amsterdam—has already met its end, and it is precisely that end which his narrative sets out to meet. The thrust of Irving's critique is that a teleological history does not end in glory, or fulfillment, but in ashes.

Once Knickerbocker satisfies his desire (for the time being) for self-aggrandizement, he turns to the beginning of New York's history, which, fittingly for him, is the creation of the world. After paraphrasing a variety of creation myths, he makes the following remark:

> It has ever been the task of one race of philosophers to demolish the works of their predecessors, and elevate more splendid fantasies in their stead, which in their turn are demolished and replaced by the air castles of a succeeding generation. Thus it would seem that knowledge and genius, of which we make such great parade, consist but in detecting the errors and absurdities of those who have gone before, and devising new errors and absurdities, to be detected by those who are to come after us. (Irving 1984, 32)

This passage seems particularly Ovidian, with its emphasis on cycles of demolition and invention, and as such it subverts the exceptionalist myth that America represents the providential fulfillment of history. Despite Knickerbocker's odd claim that "devising new errors and absurdities" is an act of genius, he has nevertheless stumbled onto a bit of wisdom, namely, that his generation's beliefs are just as absurd and erroneous as any other generation's. The passage also has a metafictional quality to it, as one can see in it a description of Irving's own work. The "genius" of the burlesque, after all, is quite literally in "devising new errors and absurdities" in order to demolish those in the world around us.

While Irving uses Knickerbocker to parody the theological trend to link the "creation" of America to Christian grand narratives, Knickerbocker does not restrict himself to Christian mythology. Rather, in an attempt to show off his erudition, he paraphrases myths from a plurality of cultures, making his privileging of "the account handed down to us by Moses" seem quite arbitrary. One such non-Christian myth reads as follows:

> The negro philosophers of Congo affirm, that the world was made by the hands of angels, excepting their own country, which the Supreme Being constructed himself that it might be supremely excellent. And he took great pains with the inhabitants, and made them very black and beautiful; and when he had finished the first man, he was well pleased with him, and smoothed him over the face, and hence his nose, and the nose of all his descendants, became flat. (Irving 1984, 29)

The phrases "negro philosophers" and "black and beautiful" must have been jarring to Irving's antebellum white readers, not to mention a creation myth that posits the *first* man to have been a *black* man. Irving holds this myth up as an ironic reflection of the Puritan "City on a Hill," implicitly suggesting the essentially fictive nature of both. Just like other peoples, Irving suggests, we are only the elect according to our own mythology.

One final passage from Knickerbocker that reveals his intensely metaphysical sense of being is his account of reading Erasmus Darwin:

> Little did I think at such times, that it would ever fall to my lot to be treated with equal discourtesy, and that while I was quietly beholding these grave philosophers, . . . they would on a sudden turn upon me and my readers, and with one hypothetical flourish metamorphose us into beasts! (Irving 1984, 41)

This passage, even more than the last, is explicitly Ovidian, and evokes again the power of narrative to transform reality. For Knickerbocker, who lives completely in his mind, reading Darwin is experientially equivalent to being transformed (or having his *being* transformed) into an animal. Not only does the passage show Knickerbocker's reduction of all reality to conceptual reality, but it also shows his susceptibility to and anxiety about "other" theories, particularly those that threaten his sense of his own immortality, that is, his sense of himself as an

American prophet. To read Darwin is to lose one's humanity, and thus to lose one's place in the great chain of being, and, of course, also to lose one's identity as an American. Ironically, this keeps Knickerbocker from seriously considering the only theory he mentions which is actually based on facts. Continuing to read Knickerbocker as a stand-in for a New England theological historian, or American "prophet," one can see Irving's critique of such a Puritan tradition as being more concerned with justifying its own superiority by means of mythological invention than with accurately representing the past.

Turning to Melville, we find a parody of another American "prophet," the Yankee mystic Mark Winsome. As mentioned earlier, several critics have pointed to the likelihood that Melville's depiction of Winsome is a thinly veiled critique of Emerson, or if not Emerson personally, at least the ideals of Emersonian self-reliance. As Bercovitch notes, Emerson came to be emblematic of the dual function of the American jeremiad: "[N]o one more virulently denounced corruption in America, and no one more passionately upheld the metaphysics of the American system" (Bercovitch 1978, 182). While Bercovitch credits Emerson with being a "severe critic," he also emphasizes his compulsion to "[reaffirm] the basic tenets of the culture" (ibid., 184). The portrait Bercovitch gives us is that of a tragic, conflicted figure, one who masked his own pessimism because of his fear that "if America failed, then the cosmos itself—the laws of man, nature, and history, the very basis of heroism, insight, and hope—had failed as well" (ibid., 190).

As we will see, Melville's portrayal of Winsome is not as kind as Bercovitch's portrayal of Emerson. Where Bercovitch sees tragedy, Melville sees hypocrisy. Some critics, such as Egbert Oliver, find "warmth and humour" (Oliver 1946, 72) in Melville's critique of Emerson, but it seems that Oliver is trying a little too hard to make Melville and Emerson friends. Elizabeth Foster, in her introduction to the 1954 edition of *The Confidence-Man*, characterizes Melville's critique as "severe" and "sweeping," which seems more accurate. Another difference between Oliver's and Foster's readings is that Oliver sees Winsome's disciple, Egbert, as representative of Henry David Thoreau, whereas Foster sees Winsome and Egbert as a splitting of the "two sides" of Emerson.

In the spirit of Irving's attitude toward Knickerbocker and the historians for which he functioned as a parodic construct, Melville attacks Emerson's epistemological presumptuousness. Melville wrote in an 1849 letter: "I could readily see in Emerson, notwithstanding his merit, a gaping flaw. It was, the insinuation, that had he lived in those days when the world was made, he might have offered some valuable suggestions" (qtd. in Oliver 1946, 61). Once again, this criticism could just as easily be applied to Irving's Knickerbocker, who actually does "create a world," by means of cosmogony, and concludes that "the creation of a world is not so difficult a task as . . . first imagined" (Irving 1984, 31). The hubris that Irving burlesques in Knickerbocker is the same Yankee hubris that Melville objects to in Emerson's metaphysics.

Oliver notes Melville's frequent description of Mark Winsome as "cold," such as in the way he sits: "purely and coldly radiant as a prism" (Oliver 1946, 65; Melville 2002, 192). Winsome sees life completely in abstract terms: "The data which life furnishes, towards forming a true estimate of any being, are as insufficient to that end as in geometry one side given would be to determine the triangle" (Melville 2002, 193). This remark reflects a discrediting of the knowledge of direct experience ("data which life furnishes"), and by deferring to a geometric analogy to make the point, it is implied that abstract (or metaphysical) "data" are superior. This privileging of metaphysics reflects Emersonian ideals of individualism, in which "the relation between man and man is important only in its bearing on the relation between man and God" (Foster 1954, lxxvii). As Melville recognizes, only those who live privileged lives such as Emerson can afford to be governed by such self-reliance. Emerson's downplaying of man's duty to man reveals his own elitism, and his admitted anxiety about the masses: "[C]alamity is the masses; I do not wish any shovel-handed, narrow-brained, gin-drinking mass at all" (qtd. in Foster 1954, lxxxi). We see this side of Emerson in Mark Winsome's disdain for the "haggard, inspired-looking man" who comes along "peddling a rhapsodical tract" which turns out to be "quite in the transcendental vein" (Melville 2002, 194–95). Winsome will not read a word of this man's pamphlet, no matter how similar it might be to his own philosophy, simply because he is a "scoundrel," by which he means dirty and poor. Winsome criticizes his fraudulence, for having "sense" while "seeming to be a madman," and Melville's critique of Winsome (and thus Emerson) seems to be a similar charge. It is Winsome, more than the beggar, that is a fraud; he appears to have "a beautiful soul—one full of all love and truth" (ibid., 190), but he is, in fact, a misanthropic snob. Melville's reader is led to reject transcendentalism just as the cosmopolitan rejects Egbert's story of China Aster as indicative of an "inhuman philosophy" (ibid., 223).

Burlesquing the Errand in the Wilderness

Bercovitch defines the Puritan errand as "the church's gradual conquest of Satan's wilderness world for Christ" (Bercovitch 1978, 12), and shows how the rhetoric of the Puritan errand in the New England wilderness transformed into the rhetoric of nineteenth-century American expansionism, that is, into the "errand" of Manifest Destiny. This shift invested the symbol of the frontier as the setting "for the quintessentially American drama of destined progress" (ibid., 164). According to Bercovitch, this was more of an "amplification" of the Puritan errand than a changing of it. Instead of being a regional concept, it was now a national one, but the essentially sacred sense of the errand was preserved. The movement westward, according to the exceptionalist discourse, was providentially ordained, and this belief served as a foundational justification for all the (Indian) blood that was shed as a means to the fulfillment of that errand. Such violent ideological hypocrisy is the target of the most "savagely" satirical passages in Irving's *History* and Melville's *Confidence-Man.*

To read Irving's text in this way, as I do, is to read it against his own stated intentions in his introduction to the revised 1848 edition, which came out three years after the phrase "Manifest Destiny" emerged in American political discourse. He offers an apology for the profanities of his text, stating that his "presumptuous trespasses into this sacred, though neglected, region of history have met with deserved rebuke" (Irving 1984, 5). He insists repeatedly that his comic history is not meant to be transgressive, but is "good-humored" in nature (ibid., 6). Like critics such as Donald Ringe, Robert Ferguson, and William Hedges, I read this profession as a kind of "mask," which Irving wore to protect himself from censure. While there is much good-humored wit in Irving's text, it is unmistakably—and deliberately—haunted by the shadows of American history. The promise of "good-humored"—as opposed to subversive—humor not only protects the author, but it sets a trap for the reader, which Irving springs at the end of Book One, with Knickerbocker's attempt to justify the extermination of Indians. At this point, the reader's laughter turns to shame and repulsion. The specter of race and genocide haunt Irving's text and prevent it from being, as he claimed, a work to be "thumbed and chuckled over by the family fireside" (ibid., 6).

Rooting American history in Christian mythology presents problems for Irving's Knickerbocker, the first being the lack of a biblical ancestor for American aborigines. While Asians, Africans, and Europeans can be traced back to the sons of Noah, the lack of a fourth son threatens the American Indians with "logical annihilation" (Irving 1984, 39). Irving means this absurdity to clash with his reader's knowledge that Indians, in the early nineteenth century, faced the possibility of *actual* annihilation, not because of the lack of a Western theory explaining their origination but because of the existence of a Western theory that constructed them as subhuman and irredeemably savage. Knickerbocker, however, remains blind to this contradiction, arguing for the necessity of Indians' existence in one chapter, and the necessity for their extinction in the next. The comical absurdity of trying to argue a people into existence is sharply undercut by the shameful, insidious argument that denies a people's right to exist.

It is at this moment, in the last chapter of Book One, that the laughter stops. Knickerbocker calls into question the right of "the worthy people of America" to "enjoy the soil they inhabit," by posing the following question: "What right had the discoverers of America to land and take possession of a country, without first gaining the consent of its inhabitants?" (Irving 1984, 44). By invoking the "worthy people of America," and alluding to their "unsullied consciences," Irving entraps his readers within the moral dilemma at hand. No longer can one laugh comfortably at Knickerbocker's fallacies and equivocations, because one's right to be standing where one stands has been called into question. Whereas a moment ago Irving invited us to ridicule Knickerbocker's vanity and illogic, we must now shamefully listen as he offers an apology for genocide *on our behalf.*

Knickerbocker identifies "DISCOVERY" as the "first source of right" by which the European settlers acquired North American land. Of course, to invoke "discovery" one must establish that the land was uninhabited by human beings, which Knickerbocker does by referring to the Indians as "certain animals, that walked erect on two feet, had something of the human countenance, uttered certain unintelligible sounds, very much like language, in short, had a marvelous resemblance to human beings" (Irving 1984, 44). To support this dehumanization, Knickerbocker defers to the authority of the "zealous and enlightened fathers" of "monasteries and bishoprics," implicating the church in the crime (ibid.). Knickerbocker goes on to quote several sources on the inferiority of the "two-legged race of animals" concluding with the following quotation: "In a word, these unhappy mortals may be compared to children, in whom the development of reason is not completed" (ibid., 45). By referring to the Indians as "children," Knickerbocker reveals that, somewhere along the line, he forgot that he was building a case not just for *inferiority*, but for *extermination*. Thus, he has unwittingly implicated his readers in mass infanticide.

After the secondhand accounts of Indians, Knickerbocker adds his own observation, "that [the Indians] were of a hideous copper complexion—and being of a copper complexion, it was all the same as if they were negroes—and negroes are black, 'and black,' said the pious fathers, devoutly crossing themselves, 'is the color of the Devil!,' " ending once again with Christian rhetoric to put his argument beyond reproof (Irving 1984, 45–46). Irving's satire suggests that the real reason that the European colonizers were unable to recognize the humanity of the Indians is that the Indians were not white. It had nothing at all to do with "Indian inferiority," and everything to do with a blinding racism informed by Christian symbolism.

Satisfied that he has established "right by discovery," Knickerbocker proceeds to argue "right by cultivation," arguing that people who "disdain to cultivate the earth . . . *deserve to be exterminated as savage and pernicious beasts*" (Irving 1984, 46). Knickerbocker says this is a "law of nature" and once again points to God for validation: "Heaven intended the earth should be ploughed and sown, and manured, and laid out into cities" (ibid.). Irving's burlesque comes across in his juxtaposition of the sacred and scatological (heaven and manure), implying that the absence of the latter is somehow an offense to the former. Knickerbocker himself admits that the "savages . . . drew all the benefits from the land which their simple wants required," but concludes that the Europeans are superior for having a greater number of wants (ibid., 47). Avarice, then, equals greatness? Once again, Knickerbocker's logic defeats itself.

The third "right" Knickerbocker outlines is the "right acquired by civilization," in which he argues that the colonizers acted as *benefactors* to the Indians by bestowing upon them such gifts as alcohol, medicine, and Christianity. Knickerbocker even goes so far as to claim that the diseases introduced by the Europeans were also benevolent, in that they gave the Indians the chance to practice European medicine (Irving 1984, 45). The introduction of Christianity at first seems unnecessary (God forbid!) because the Indians "neither stole nor defrauded; they were sober, frugal, continent and faithful to their word; but though they acted right habitually, it was all in vain, unless they acted so from precept" (ibid., 48). According to Knickerbocker, and according to the American errand, the *moral* worth of the Indians is meaningless without "the precept," that is, a Western metaphysical narrative, behind it. The American continent is *destined* to be conquered by Christ, and there is no place on that continent for a non-Christian people, no matter how morally they may act. To be non-Christian in the face of the American errand is to side with the enemy—the devil—and to open oneself up to annihilation. Knickerbocker describes the "Christianization" of the American wilderness as a crusade: "whole troops of fiery monks and furious blood-hounds—purified [the Indians] by fire and sword, by stake and fagot; in consequence of which indefatigable measures the cause of Christian love and charity was so rapidly advanced that in a few years not one-fifth of the number of unbelievers existed in South America that were found at the time of its discovery" (ibid., 49). This is undoubtedly the darkest, most "savage" point of Irving's burlesque, made so by his association of the American errand ("the cause of Christian love and charity") with what can no longer be regarded as anything other than genocide. This brings Knickerbocker to his final "right" of European entitlement, which he alternately calls "RIGHT BY EXTERMINATION" and "RIGHT BY GUNPOWDER" (ibid., 50). According to American exceptionalism, the fact that the Indians *were* "exterminated" is proof enough that they *should have been.* Destiny is destiny, according to American metaphysics, and whatever happens to fulfill that destiny—even genocide—is as it should be.

Irving's satire reveals, as Robert Ferguson wrote, "a nation of swindlers and belligerents beneath America's pious myths" (Ferguson 1981, 38). Ferguson credits Irving with the courage to produce what he claims is "the first American book to question the civic vision of the Founding Fathers," and to do so at a time when anyone who challenged this orthodoxy was labeled a fool, a knave, or a traitor (ibid., 30, 36). Irving's irony is not antidemocratic, anti-American, nor anti-Christian, but rather he uses it to consistently point at "the gap between what is and what ought to be" (ibid., 37). This gap—between the Christian democratic rhetoric of America and the often brutal and oppressive practices of nation building—reveals a hypocrisy more appalling than comic.

Melville's telling of the story of Colonel Moredock, by way of the "metaphysics of Indian-hating," is a burlesque just as dark as Irving's of the American errand's Christian killer. Many critics have identified this section as the novel's crux, but readings of it, going back to those of John

W. Schroeder and Roy Harvey Pearce, show a history of interpretative problems. The story of Colonel Moredock is told to the confidence-man (in the guise of the cosmopolitan) by a "stranger" (later called Charlie Noble) who heard the story years ago from a Judge James Hall, and attempts to reproduce it in the judge's own words. As previously mentioned, the "distance" between the story and its source immediately calls into question its authority (and authorship), and as critics who have compared Melville's portrait of Moredock to Hall's have noted, the tone is quite changed. Foster notes a shift from Hall's "humane" treatment of the Indian, to Melville's "sub-human" or "extra-human" symbolism (Foster 1954, lxvii). But to accept the symbolic significance of the Indians as "evil" or "devils," and to attribute this to Melville's treatment of Indians, is to fundamentally misread Melville's burlesque. As Tichi reminds us, "Melville insists . . . that the language of narration is not the language of the narrator" (Tichi 1972, 642). The problem with reading the Indians as "devils" can be seen in Schroeder's conclusion that Moredock is the moral hero of the novel, that he has "succeeded in locating Evil in its real home; there is no distortion in his vision of reality" (Schroeder 1951, 379). Such a reading, as Hershel Parker points out, misses "the ironic inversion of accepted values which is the basis of Melville's gigantic satire" (Parker 1963, 166). Melville's alterations from Hall's source are not meant to reflect a positive symbolism of the American frontier, but a grotesque (and burlesque) amplification of the Christian mythology informing the American errand. As Richard Drinnon points out, Melville's appropriation of Hall's text is meant as an attack on Hall himself, as a "peddler of the national moral swindle" (Drinnon 1980, 213).

Roy Harvey Pearce, in his response to Schroeder's misreading of Moredock, rightly states that "there is nothing but distortion in the Indian-hater's vision of spiritual reality," and that his ideology is just as perverse as that proffered by the confidence-man: "The issue of blind confidence and blind hatred is in the end identical" (Pearce 1952, 942). One can find evidence that the confidence-man and Colonel Moredock represent two sides of the same, demonic coin in the simple observation that they have the same initials: C. M. The two figures represent "two possible extreme attitudes toward the natural world" (ibid., 943): one sees no evil, while the other sees nothing *but* evil, but both are manifestations of a blinding, errand-driven American discourse. The fact that two antithetical views of reality are both contained in and produced by the same discourse reflects back on the contradictions and hypocrisy of American metaphysics. The errand discourse, as seen in Melville's parody, generates a compulsion for *philanthropic violence*, a paradox that can only be resolved by dehumanizing the target of that violence.

While Irving's attack focused more on the capacity of American exceptionalist discourse to justify violence, Melville focuses more on the capacity of that discourse to precipitate violence. This causal relation is reflected in Melville's prefacing of Moredock's story with the "metaphysics of Indian-hating" and the articulation of the Indian-hater *par excellence*. It is the discourse—the American mythic rendering of Indians as devils—that creates the Indian-hater, and thus the violence that he produces:

> Accordingly, if in youth the backwoodsman incline to knowledge, as is generally the case, he hears little from his schoolmasters, the old chroniclers of the forest, but histories of Indian lying, Indian theft, Indian double-dealing, Indian fraud and perfidy, Indian want of conscience, Indian blood-thirstiness, Indian diabolism. . . . In these Indian narratives and traditions the lad is thoroughly grounded. . . . The instinct of antipathy against an Indian grows in the backwoodsman with the sense of good and bad, right and wrong. In one breath he learns that a brother is to be loved, and Indian is to be hated. (Melville 2002, 146)

Melville's burlesque clearly demonstrates that the *narratives* of Indian hating, and not actual encounters with Indians, constitute the generative force behind the perpetuation of hate. Moreover, as Pearce points out, the necessity of such hatred is "subsumed under the dogma of Christian, civilized progress," that is, under the dogma of the American errand (Pearce 1952, 944). Yet Melville is clearly undermining the hypocrisy of Christian-sanctioned violence, because as Pearce states, "Hatred is hatred; and Melville will not let us see it as anything but hatred" (ibid., 948).

Melville, however, is not simply attacking the hatred of Moredock, but the culture that produced him and wishes to glorify him. We see this in the anecdote concerning Moredock's being "pressed to become candidate for governor" (Melville 2002, 155) of Illinois. Ultimately he decides not to run, because he feels it would be an "impropriety" for the governor to occasionally take a few days off for "shooting at human beings" (ibid.). At this point, Melville's irony seems unmistakable. Why else would he remind us that the Indians Moredock kills are human beings? After all, the dominant American discourse of Melville's time did not consider them to be so. Certainly the Illinois electorate, or at least a substantial component of them, did not consider Indians to be human beings, for they were eager to canonize Moredock as their heroic leader. Moredock's reservation about running is not that he may be vilified on moral grounds, but simply that Indian killing might be an "impropriety" for a governor. While everyone knows that the American errand has its bloody side, it is important to maintain the veneer of Christian philanthropy. It is precisely this veneer that Melville shatters with his burlesque, antiheroic rendering of Moredock and his implicit indictment of writers such as James Hall who celebrate such racial hatred.

Conclusions

Irving's *History* and Melville's *Confidence-Man* are both severely critical burlesques of the mythology behind the American errand and the violence of American expansion in the early nineteenth century. It is somewhat surprising, then, that while Irving's book was applauded as "an immediate success" after its publication in 1809, Melville's novel was virtually ignored by American readers after its publication in 1857 (Roth 1976, 114; Foster 1954, xxxv). As William Spanos notes, "[T]he custodians of the American Cultural Memory went all out to annul [Melville's] witness against America" (Spanos 2000, 271). Irving's novel, being much easier to read, was certainly accessible to more readers, but even after the Melville "revival" of the early twentieth century, *The Confidence-Man* was still rarely praised, and usually thought of as the work of an embittered, despairing mind, or at best, a "magnificent failure." Only in the last half-century have a handful of critics begun to laud it as one of Melville's great works. The difficulty in reading *The Confidence-Man* has to do not only with the complexity and ambiguity of the text itself, but also with a dominant culture of readers who are unwilling to accept (or unable to perceive) narratives that disturb the fundamental symbols of American exceptionalism. While Irving's *History* is similarly disruptive, readers were able to read the text (wrongly) as a satire of a "false America"—an America outside the dominant Anglo-Protestant definition of America. Such readers conclude that

Knickerbocker's failings do not apply to the "true America" and so one can laugh at him (or pity him) from a safe distance. Such a reading still predominates among certain critics today, such as Martin Roth, who sees Irving as distinguishing between "the irrational movements of the mind" inherent in a "Dutch-American voice," and the positive Yankee democracy of "time and work and talk" (Roth 1976, 143). According to this (mis-)reading, the Indians disappeared because they were Indians, just as the Dutch disappeared because they were Dutch, but the Yankees are destined to persevere. In light of my analysis, however, which has shown the implicit critique of a Puritan theological historiography in Irving's text, it seems more likely that Irving uses Knickerbocker, and the Dutch settlers, as a link between "Indian" and "Yankee"—the Dutch Americans being a people who were both colonizers and colonized—to show the Yankee reader that just as the Indian America disappeared, and the Dutch America disappeared, so too, one day, will the Yankee America disappear.

The power of the burlesque is in its ability to ridicule and reveal the absurdities in a given discourse, but the irony with which Irving and Melville make their attacks can often precipitate misreadings, especially with American readers who are so accustomed to Emersonian sermonizing and the tradition of the American jeremiad. The burlesque, unlike the jeremiad, does not assert a positive norm after it dismantles its negative target. The form requires a *thinking reader* to respond with something other than despair, bafflement, or simplification. By subverting the myth of the American errand, Irving and Melville show us an America that is *not sacred*, but rather profoundly (and profanely) violent. It is up to the reader to reinvent America in secular terms, with a future that is, as of yet, undetermined. When critics have, in the past, negatively referred to *The Confidence-Man* as "savage" and belittled Irving for not having a "uniquely American vision," they were objecting to the fact that both writers rejected the symbol of America as sacred, just as they both refused to sermonize in their art.

Irving's *History*, as Hedges suggests, "detaches the links in the great chain of being from one another and throws them into a single heap," and in so doing undermines legitimating narratives for imperial conquest (Hedges 1965, 79). Melville's *Confidence-Man*, as Richard Drinnon observes, anticipates the fact that "when the metaphysics of Indian hating hit salt water it more clearly became the metaphysics of empire-building" (Drinnon 1980, 215). The sanctification of an imperial

America rested on the sanctification of racial hatred and avarice, and thus to challenge this "pious" patriotism, one must critique America on the frontiers of race, religion, and commerce. By linking Irving's and Melville's deployment of burlesque narratives to their capacity to generate counterhegemonic texts, I hope to flag the coincidence between a non-nationalist generic form and anti-imperialist politics. William Hedges notes Irving's overt borrowings from European satirists such as Rabelais and Cervantes, and William Spanos suggests (albeit anachronistically) that Melville's art has more in common with the ideas of European poststructuralists than nationalist critics of American culture (Hedges 1965, 65; Spanos 2000, 202). Hence, I mean to suggest that the work Foucault calls upon "effective history" to perform—the introduction of discontinuity into one's very being by undermining theological historiographies—has been implicitly theorized and executed by burlesque satirists for centuries. While the radical elements of Irving's and Melville's work have been largely neutralized by critics who have domesticated our image of Irving and Americanized our image of Melville, it should perhaps be the "errand" of New Americanist scholars to recover and revalue the "savage" censure these two writers leveled at American state and "civil" practices.

While Melville's dissenting voice has taken a prominent position in the estimation of many New Americanist critics, little attention has been given recently to Irving, either for his own achievement or for his influence on Melville. One notable exception is James C. Keil's account of Melville's extensive "poaching" from Irving's *History* during the writing of *Moby-Dick.* Keil claims that in *Moby-Dick,* "Melville made frequent use of the words, ideas, tone, narrative technique, and structure of Irving's *History*" (Keil 1995, 14). As a primary example, Keil goes on to make a convincing argument that Melville's Ahab was based on Irving's depiction of Peter Stuyvesant. Despite Melville's early criticism of Irving, in 1851, as "imitative," Melville's debt to Irving is profound, and Melville himself eventually recognized this. In February 1890, not long before his death, he wrote a little tribute to Irving called "Rip Van Winkle's Lilac," in his manuscript *Weeds and Wildings.* Melville addresses Irving's spirit in the piece's prologue, and imagines him with "those mellowing Immortals who as men were not only excellent in their works, but pleasant and love-worthy in their lives" (Melville 1963, 322). To conclude, as Melville does *The Confidence-Man,* with a rather unsatisfying prolepsis ("Something further may follow of this Masquerade"), I will say that much is still to be discovered (or recovered) about Irving, his influence on Melville, the relationship between the two New York writers, and their shared critique of early American culture (ibid., 251).

Works Cited

Bercovitch, Sacvan. 1978. *The American jeremiad.* Madison: University of Wisconsin Press.

Drinnon, Richard. 1980. *Facing west: The metaphysics of Indian hating and empire building.* New York: Schocken.

Ferguson, Robert A. 1981. "Hunting down a nation": Irving's *A history of New York. Nineteenth-Century Fiction* 36, no. 1: 22–46.

Foster, Elizabeth S. 1954. Introduction. In Melville, *The confidence-man: His masquerade.* New York: Hendricks House.

Foucault, Michel. 1984. Nietzsche, genealogy, history. In *The Foucault reader,* ed. Paul Rabinow. New York: Pantheon.

Hedges, William L. 1965. *Washington Irving: An American study, 1802–1832.* Baltimore: Johns Hopkins University Press.

Irving, Washington. 1984. *A history of New York.* Ed. Michael L. Black and Nancy B. Black. Boston: Twayne.

Keil, James C. 1995. Melville's "American Goldsmith": *Moby-Dick* and Irving's *A history of New York. Melville Society Extracts* 102: 13–16.

Melville, Herman. 1963. *Poems.* New York: Russell and Russell.

———. 2002. *The confidence-man: His masquerade.* Evanston: Northwestern University Press.

Miller, Perry. 1956. *Errand into the wilderness.* Cambridge: Belknap Press of Harvard University Press.

Oliver, Egbert S. 1946. Melville's picture of Emerson and Thoreau in *The confidence-man. College English* 8: 61–72.

Parker, Hershel. 1963. The metaphysics of Indian hating. *Nineteenth-Century Fiction* 18, no. 2: 165–73.

Pearce, Roy Harvey. 1952. Melville's Indian-hater: A note on a meaning of the confidence-man. *Proceedings of the Modern Language Association* 67: 942–48.

Ringe, Donald A. 1967. New York and New England: Irving's criticism of American society. *American Literature* 38, no. 4: 455–67.

Roth, Martin. 1976. *Comedy and America: The lost world of Washington Irving.* Port Washington, NY: Kennikat Press.

Shroeder, John W. 1951. Sources and symbols for Melville's confidence-man. *Proceedings of the Modern Language Association* 66: 363–80.

Spanos, William V. 2000. *America's shadow.* Minneapolis: University of Minnesota Press.

Tichi, Cecilia. 1972. Melville's craft and theme of language debased in *The confidence-man. English Literary History* 39: 639–58.

Weinberg, Albert K. 1935. *Manifest destiny: A study of nationalist expansionism in American history.* Baltimore: Johns Hopkins University Press.

5

Exclusion Acts

How Popular Westerns Brokered the Atlantic Diaspora

Christine Bold

Prologue

When the popular Western crystallized, at the turn of the twentieth century, it brought together three forms of exclusion, all central to mainstream notions of America's distinctive national identity. The men who made the Western belonged to an Anglo-American elite, fighting to protect its political, economic, and cultural power in the face of labor agitation, economic depression, and changing ethnic and racial demographics. Working through exclusive clubs and cultural organizations, they attempted to control transatlantic investment finance, immigration policy, and the literary marketplace. The popular print Western both facilitated and expressed these dynamics in a reciprocal operation. As a network of powerful Anglo-Americans fueled the success of the Western so it, in turn, supported the exclusionary policies designed to control the Atlantic diaspora in the interests of Anglo-Americanization.

G. Edward White first argued, forty years ago, that the late-nineteenth-century eastern establishment was responsible for transforming the American west into a national icon. Richard Slotkin subsequently analyzed how a broad range of frontier mythologies in this period adapted to justify the violent workings of industrial capitalism. Bringing an archive of personal papers and institutional records to bear on this cultural moment reveals the sleight of hand by which clubmen manipulated class alignments to seize the new tools of mass culture on a transatlantic scale. This chapter makes newly visible how, in whose interests, and at what cost a central trope of U.S. culture was made.

Cast of Characters

I call the network of racially and socially exclusive men's clubs behind the making of the modern Western "the frontier club." This network drew on the most exclusive clubs—such as the Dickey and the Porcellian at Harvard, the Philadelphia and Rittenhouse in Philadelphia, the Somerset in Boston, the Union League in Manhattan, and the Cheyenne Club in Wyoming—to form a transatlantic power base. Its members connected America's "preindustrial eastern upper class" with British aristocracy and metropolitan interests with frontier resources, smoothing the way for European speculators to invest in the "bonanza frontier" of open-range ranching while helping American entertainers to build audiences in Europe (White 1968, 6; Slotkin 1992, 18). (Buffalo Bill gained entrée to London society in 1887, for example, through clubmen [Kasson 2000, 79]).

The Boone and Crockett Club was the key organization connecting these clubs' overlapping memberships to Western writing. Theodore Roosevelt began the club in 1887 to increase Anglo-American influence in the west, and it remains best known for "manly sport" and "game and forest preservation" (Roosevelt and Grinnell 1893, 10). Its leading lights, however, were authors and editors, and the club fulfilled an explicit cultural mandate. Claiming to preserve "the very wellspring of America's unique national character," its book series and exhibitions spawned imitations across the British empire and promoted Anglo-Saxon "gentleman hunter" ideologies intrinsic to popular Westerns (Ward 1980, 384).

The most prominent clubman in terms of popular literary success was Philadelphia gentleman and author Owen Wister. In 1902 Wister

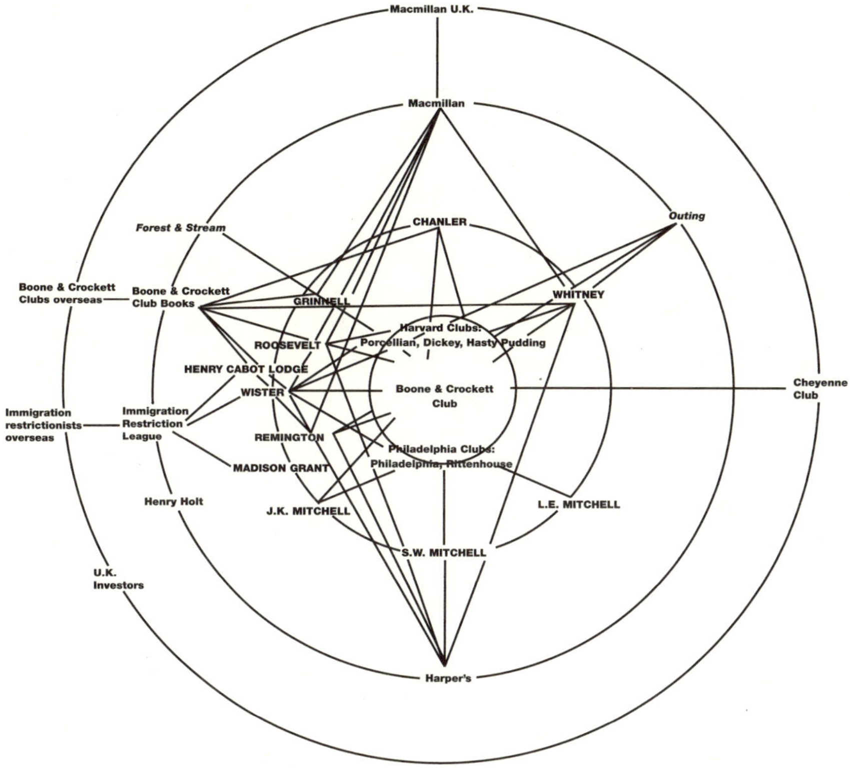

Figure 5.1. The Frontier Club

published *The Virginian*, the best-selling novel whose action—gentlemanly cowboy woos eastern schoolma'am and wins shootout on Main street—is generally credited with crystallizing the modern Western formula. Wister is seen as pulling together the disparate strands of western adventure—from Fenimore Cooper, dime novels, folklore—to create a myth peculiarly suited to America's national image, its international ambitions, and audiences across the globe. Critical tradition has represented the work as an act of individualism as decisive and heroic, in its way, as the skilful gunplay of the lone Western hero.[1] In Wister's own words, "*The Virginian* . . . suddenly created the popular taste which has demanded Western stories ever since" (Wister 1928, xxxix).

Yet Wister could not have conceived of, written, or published his novel without his club network. His clubmates were powerful figures:

Theodore Roosevelt, who became president of the United States in 1901; Henry Cabot Lodge, Republican congressman from 1879, then senator from 1893; Dr. Silas Weir Mitchell, the famous nerve doctor; Caspar Whitney, editor of the sporting journal *Outing*; George Bird Grinnell, leading conservationist and editor of *Forest and Stream* who marshaled the seven-volume Boone and Crockett series into print, 1893–1933; Frederic Remington, western artist and illustrator *par excellence*, and others. Clubmates sent Wister west; framed the region as a personal, financial, and cultural resource; coached his subsequent writing, and gave him an entrée into publishing. Their Western publications fostered Wister's creative process and a receptive audience. So close were the ties that Winthrop Chanler, Boone and Crockett clubmate from the wealthy Astor family, considered Wister's writing "a joint production."[2] Finally, this network of power connected Wister's western vision to burning transatlantic policy debates of the day.

Act One

July 1885, the Cheyenne Club, Wyoming Territory. Several men are lounging on the porch, smoking Havana cigars, sipping 1848 brandy, and discussing stock—livestock. These are the managers of the big cattle companies, come west from Britain and the eastern states. How can they selectively breed European stock to improve their returns? How can they control the open range necessary to their huge profits? For years, they've had free access to the unfenced northern plains, but homesteaders have begun to take advantage of government acts, fencing off quarter sections at a time, blocking access to land and water. The homesteaders simply don't belong on the range. How can the big ranchers elbow them out?[3]

This scene is about brute force and big finance transformed into culture. In 1880, a group of Wyoming cattle barons founded an exclusive social club. They compiled a list of fifty names, approaching them in explicitly anglophile terms. William Sturgis, secretary, wrote to one Harvard alumnus-turned-ranchman, F. O. deBillier: "We purpose having a *good* club on an eastern basis—have limited the numbers to 50 in order to be able to control the social status most satisfactorily." To others, Sturgis described the club as "the Somerset moved West," which "will fill a want long felt by those of us hailing from the East" and provide a mechanism for excluding "undesirables." Sturgis was even blunter in

Figure 5.2. The Cheyenne Club, 1888 (Wyoming Stock Growers Association Records, American Heritage Center, University of Wyoming)

his invitation to Clarence King, the well-known geologist and Boone and Crockett clubman: the exclusive membership list was designed "so that we may keep it full at all times and avoid blackballing too many 'natives.'" Another invitation put it most succinctly: "Trusting you will be 'one of us.'"[4]

Open-range ranching was primarily financed by East Coast and European investors, many with connections in the upper echelons of society, and some ranchers belonged to that social bracket. For example, Theodore Roosevelt and J. P. Morgan—America's biggest financier, whose son was a Boone and Crockett member—invested in the Teschemacher and deBillier Cattle Company, run by Harvard classmates.[5] The rancher Thomas Sturgis—William's brother—was a Boston blueblood come west; when the bubble burst, he returned east, serving for a time under Roosevelt (Gressley 1971, 253–57, 280). Sturgis's Union Cattle Company drew on Boston's financial elite, including Henry Lee Higginson, head of the prominent brokerage firm that first employed Wister (who had access to Higginson through membership in the Dickey [Payne 1985, 34]). Other ranchers were English and Scottish remittance men, younger sons of wealthy families who crossed the Atlantic temporarily to make their fortune.

But the "we" in the making at the Cheyenne Club crossed more class lines than it acknowledged. Some ranchers were middlemen, managers working on behalf of British speculators. In this period, Scotland in particular became the headquarters for an international "client capitalism" (Szasz 2000, 88). While Cheyenne was "overrun with Britishers," most of the aristocrats "stayed home" (Woods 1989, 87, 193). The exclusive society in the making on the plains—"almost a domestic microcosm of the British Empire itself"—served a double function (ibid., 192). It confirmed the superiority of upper-class anglophiles while training aspirants to identify with that class interest.

The Cheyenne Club replicated the forms of privileged British life: cards and billiards, polo and horse racing, tennis, and the most elegant dining available, with European cuisine and an international array of foods and wines shipped out to the barren plains. A fortune was spent on supplies from the famous Park and Tilford of Broadway: Champagne Geisler, Champagne Goulet, Burgundy Chambertin, 1848 Brandy, Jamaica Rum, St. Cruz Rum, Liebfraumilch, Mumms Extra Dry, Delatour Soda, Old Tom Gin, and Reina Vic cigars (the best brand of Manila Cheroots).[6] The club also enforced the strictest protocols of behavior. Elaborate rules governed committee elections, meetings, and minutes. Members were publicly chastised and even expelled for gambling, swearing, fighting (verbally or physically), or exhibiting ungentlemanly demeanor.

All this pomp and ritual facilitated the wielding of real power. The Cheyenne Club was the headquarters of the Wyoming Stock Growers Association, the organization of wealthy cattle ranchers that held sway over the mainly unfenced northern plains. The WSGA controlled ranching practices, land management, cattle branding rules, employment patterns (including blacklists), political power, the banks, the court, and the press. The Cheyenne Club provided the WSGA with the mantle of gentlemanly culture that enabled the cattle kings to roam abroad, variously intimidating and preying on small homesteaders who got in their way. Especially after the disastrous winter of 1886–87—when millions of cattle froze to death on the overstocked plains—a sense of financial desperation joined the cultural insecurity lurking beneath these practices.

The club proved its cultural value at the worst moments of WSGA violence. In 1889, five WSGA members, led by Cheyenne Club stalwart Albert Bothwell, lynched Ellen Watson and Jim Averell, small farmers who dared to stake legal claims on the land seized by Bothwell. The club exerted its influence over the local press to justify the act in the court of public opinion. The Cheyenne newspapers reached for recognizable dime novel conventions to vilify Averell and Watson—"Cattle Kate," they called her—as criminals and degenerates. The *Cheyenne Daily Leader* and the *Daily Sun* claimed that Watson was a prostitute, bank robber, and husband poisoner:

> Of robust physique she was a daredevil in the saddle, handy with a six-shooter and adept with the lariat and branding iron. Where she came from no one seems to know, but that she was a holy terror all agreed. She rode straddle, always had a vicious broncho [*sic*] for a mount and seemed never to tire of dashing across the range. (qtd. in Hufsmith 1993, 11)

Figure 5.3. Ella "Cattle Kate" Watson (Wyoming State Archives, Department of State Parks and Cultural Resources)

Three years later, during the Johnson County War, a much bigger group of WSGA members—about fifty vigilantes, led by Colonel Frank Wolcott—murdered the independent cowboys Nate Champion and Nick Ray. The Cheyenne Club swung into action, celebrating the lynching with a lavish dinner and a silver cup whose engraving reads: "In grateful remembrance of untiring devotion on our behalf during the trying time of the Wyoming invasion of 1892." In both cases, the cattle barons escaped conviction.

But the Cheyenne Club had a much more sophisticated apologist to hand. Sitting, perhaps, among those men on the porch in July 1885 was Owen Wister, who had come west from Philadelphia via a chain of clubmates. The first link was Dr. Silas Weir Mitchell, Wister's cousin and Philadelphia clubmate. Mitchell was a renowned nerve doctor, now notorious for diagnosing Charlotte Perkins Gilman as neurasthenic and prescribing for her—as he did for all women—a "rest cure" of enforced immobility and an injunction against writing. Mitchell also diagnosed Wister as neurasthenic and prescribed for him—as he did for all men—a trip west involving as much vigorous activity and minutely observed

Figure 5.4. The Johnson County War "The Invaders," May 4, 1892 (Wyoming Stock Growers Association Records, American Heritage Center, University of Wyoming)

Figure 5.5. Owen Wister, ca. 1895 (Owen Wister Papers, American Heritage Center, University of Wyoming)

writing as possible (Tuttle 2000; Will 1998). Mitchell billeted Wister with Colonel Wolcott, manager of the VR Ranch (Cobbs 1984, 8). On arrival in Wyoming, Wister was met by another rancher, Richard Trimble, Porcellian clubmate, who escorted him to the Cheyenne Club and spent lavishly on food and drink. Wister was enchanted. He returned to Wyoming repeatedly, becoming increasingly enamored of the Cheyenne Club, which he dubbed "the pearl of the prairies,"[7] and increasingly allied with the cattle kings, many of whom belonged to his Harvard fraternity. He also contributed to the network, introducing, for example, his Philadelphia and Boone and Crockett clubmate, Dr. Charles Penrose, to the club. Penrose subsequently joined the Johnson County posse.

These were Wister's formative years as a writer, and his craft coalesced as he shuttled back and forth across the continent. His eastern club connections gave him privileged access to literary mentors and publishers—to such a degree that the creative effort seems collective. The tenderfoot narrator in *The Virginian* sounds like the first-person narrators of the Boone and Crockett Club stories and the clubmen's private correspondence. Winthrop Chanler (who traded literary critiques with Wister throughout the 1890s) asserted that the Porcellian Club was the true author of Wister's "Evolution of a Cowpuncher."[8] Amos Tuck French—another frontier club stalwart—remarked that one of Wister's western stories "brought back to me a scene at the Porc. When Harry Mudge visited us in '84."[9] Wister confided to his diary not only that he "wrote every word of 'Hank's Woman' over again because of what Harry Mercer [yet another clubmate] said," but also that he "can't remember a single story that has not gained by my adopting the criticism of one of these several *long*-suffering friends and making (often several) changes."[10] He rewrote a scene in *The Virginian* at Roosevelt's behest and for several years collaborated with Remington (Wister 1930, 33–34; Vorpahl 1972). The Mitchell family played a pronounced role. Wister received detailed stylistic commentary from both sons (Langdon, with whom he coauthored a novel, and John, his Boone and Crockett clubmate). Wister was so closely coached by and imitative of their father, Silas Weir Mitchell, that on at least one occasion Mitchell was mistakenly identified as the author of a Wister story. Indeed, Mitchell's medical writings about outdoor life introduced Wister to the frontier as a resource for men. Mitchell also gave Wister his entrée to the Harpers, who published his stories in *Harper's Weekly*, *Harper's Monthly Magazine*, and book form for ten years.[11]

Wister's western club connections gave him materials for his fiction, including settings, anecdotes, and historical incidents. Many western acquaintances were prototypes for his characters: Frank Wolcott for Judge Henry, Richard Tisdale (Cheyenne Club member and Johnson County vigilante) for Balaam, Sheriff Frank M. Canton (WSGA detective) among a whole raft of ranchers, cowboys, and western guides for the Virginian (Woods 1989, 218, n.25). The plains also taught Wister how his class could control a mass market to their benefit. A cartel of owners raked in profits from the comfort of home and club via economies of scale (thousands of cattle roaming the open range), disposable contract labor (cowboys), and middlemen (managers of animal and human resources). The structure closely echoes the power dynamics of emerging mass culture, as analyzed by Richard Ohmann: a corporate ruling class consolidated itself by delegating management of its enterprises to a new "professional-managerial class," which marshaled the swelling industrial working class in the production of mass commodities (Ohmann 1996, 118–19). The mutually reinforcing structures suggest that the steps from robber baron to cattle baron to media baron were small. In the six years between his first Wyoming trip and his first published story, Wister learned to see the west through Cheyenne Club eyes—grafting anglophile rituals onto the western plains, rationalizing the cattle barons' violence, disguising the real status of cowboys, shutting out "the natives," and learning a modus operandi for exploiting cattle, commodities, and people with heroic impunity.

Act Two

May 1894, the Somerset Club, Boston. Several men are lounging in the private dining room, smoking Havana cigars, sipping 1848 brandy, and discussing stock—racial stock. These New England Brahmins are planning an organization to sustain Anglo-Saxon dominance in America. How can they prevent interbreeding between "the native American stock" and non-Anglo Saxons who "dilute the Yankee gumption . . . pollute the Yankee blood"?[12] *How can they control immigration patterns? For years, "British, German, and Scandinavian stock, historically free, energetic, progressive," composed the bulk of the American population. Now "Slav, Latin, and Asiatic races, historically down-trodden, atavistic, and stagnant" are flooding the country (Hall 1897, 395). "New immigrants" simply don't belong in America. How can the Brahmins elbow them out?*

In 1894, three Harvard graduates—Charles Warren, Robert DeCourcy Ward, and Prescott Farnsworth Hall—founded the Immigration Restriction League, working to preserve their own social group by lobbying for tighter regulation of immigration. Census counts since 1870, which indicated declining Yankee birthrates and accelerating immigrant populations, had caused particular consternation. The Anglo-American upper-class establishment feared that their voting power, cultural influence, and control over public lands were threatened by the influx of southern and eastern Europeans.

Whereas some groups argued the anti-immigration case on economic grounds, the league was deeply racialist in its principles. It fomented and profited from the rise of eugenics, claiming a pseudoscientific superiority for Anglo-Saxon heredity and wielding the biological vocabulary of Social Darwinism. Francis Amasa Walker, economist and director of the 1870 and 1880 censuses, whose increasingly race-based analysis partially inspired the league, explicitly paralleled cattle and human breeding to prove Anglo-Saxon superiority: "The climate of the United States has been benign enough to enable us to take the English short-horn and greatly improve it . . . to take the English man and improve him too . . . in rowing, in riding, in shooting, and in boxing, the American of pure English stock is today the better animal" (Walker 1891, 642). A Wyoming cattleman echoed this trope when he nicknamed the Cheyenne Clubmen "Herefords" after the broad white shirtfronts of their formal evening wear (Woods 1989, 147).

The language of "stock," "breeding," and "bloodlines" could equally be used to dehumanize immigrants. Henry Cabot Lodge approvingly quoted one description of Polish immigrants traveling the railroad, packed into "fourth-class cars, like cattle and at live-stock rates" (Lodge 1897, 607). Traveling in steerage across the Atlantic, poor immigrants were treated like animals—penned in holding areas like stock, their bodies poked and prodded for defect and disease—on arrival in America. Scaremongering about floods, waves, and seepage of "aliens" was highly reminiscent of the fear of saturation on the western plains.

At first, the league had an uphill battle. In attempting to change immigration policy, they threatened a cornerstone of America's self-image as a democratic refuge for all. The contradiction between the welcome afforded league members' ancestors and the exclusion they were advocating against newcomers was stark. In 1893, the satirical magazine *Puck* skewered the inconsistency in a cartoon of corpulent dandies—clubmen to a "T" in top hats and frock coats—blocking a poor laborer's access to America's shores. The league had to sustain a persuasive distinction between desirable, northern European immigrants and undesirable immigrants from southern and eastern Europe and from Asia. It had to distance itself from other anti-immigration groups—the virulently anti-Catholic, the pro-labor—so that it could maintain its class privileges. For those and other reasons, it maintained strong transatlantic links with English immigration restrictionists who had brought their ideas to America in the early 1880s and continued to lead the way in integrating restrictionist ideology with social sciences and social work.

Figure 5.6. Joseph Keppler, "Looking Backward," *Puck* January 11, 1893

The Immigration Restriction League—not unlike the Cheyenne Club—was a socially exclusive group ultimately dependent on broad public support for its power. The league's constitution emphasized the need to seize the public sphere: "to issue documents and circulars, hold public meetings, and to arouse public opinion to the necessity of a further exclusion of elements undesirable for citizenship or injurious to our national character" (De C. Ward 1894, 639). They responded to Lodge's urgent call for "an intelligent and active public opinion to which Congress will respond" (Lodge 1891, 612). Prescott Hall used the middle-class *Saturday Evening Post*—which became known as a virulently anti-immigration organ—to claim that the league's existence was proof of "public demand" (Simon 1985, 317). Other members capitalized on the league's academic, social, and business networks to place essays in mass magazines, undertake cross-country speaking tours, and issue pamphlets, on "Immigration Figures for 1903", the "Character of Present Immigration," "Needed Additions to the Excluded Classes," and immigrants' illiteracy.

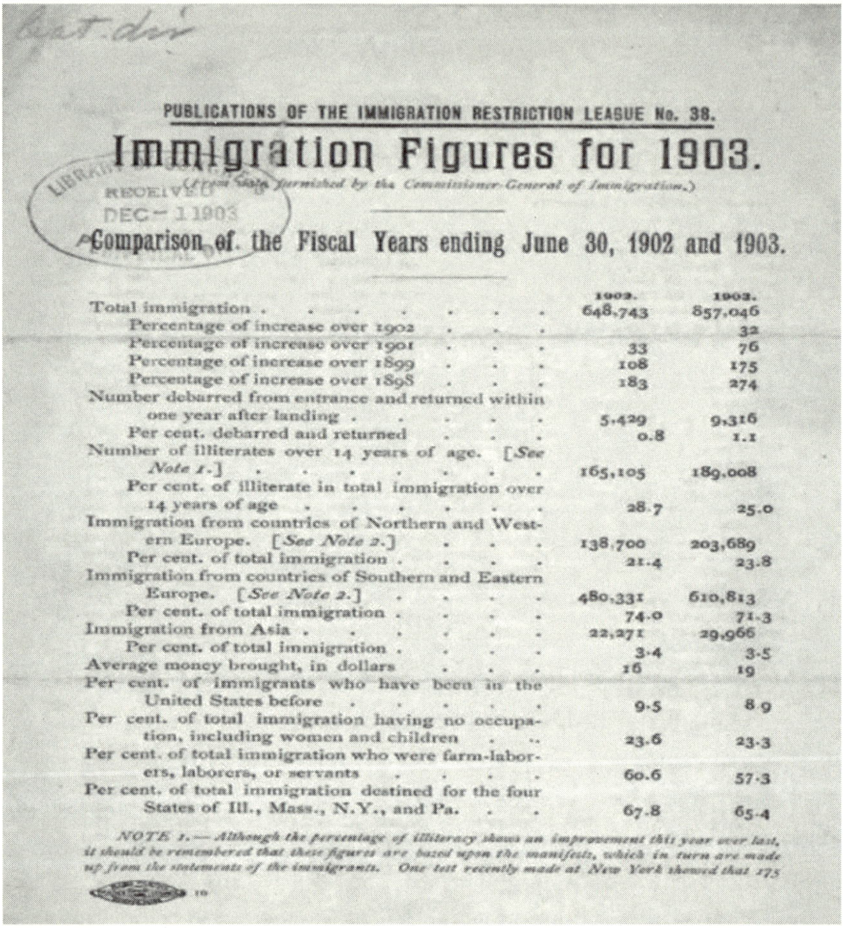

PUBLICATIONS OF THE IMMIGRATION RESTRICTION LEAGUE No. 38.

Immigration Figures for 1903.

(From data furnished by the Commissioner-General of Immigration.)

Comparison of the Fiscal Years ending June 30, 1902 and 1903.

	1902.	1903.
Total immigration	648,743	857,046
Percentage of increase over 1902		32
Percentage of increase over 1901	33	76
Percentage of increase over 1899	108	175
Percentage of increase over 1898	183	274
Number debarred from entrance and returned within one year after landing	5,429	9,316
Per cent. debarred and returned	0.8	1.1
Number of illiterates over 14 years of age. [*See Note 1.*]	165,105	189,008
Per cent. of illiterate in total immigration over 14 years of age	28.7	25.0
Immigration from countries of Northern and Western Europe. [*See Note 2.*]	138,700	203,689
Per cent. of total immigration	21.4	23.8
Immigration from countries of Southern and Eastern Europe. [*See Note 2.*]	480,331	610,813
Per cent. of total immigration	74.0	71.3
Immigration from Asia	22,271	29,966
Per cent. of total immigration	3.4	3.5
Average money brought, in dollars	16	19
Per cent. of immigrants who have been in the United States before	9.5	8.9
Per cent. of total immigration having no occupation, including women and children	23.6	23.3
Per cent. of total immigration who were farm-laborers, laborers, or servants	60.6	57.3
Per cent. of total immigration destined for the four States of Ill., Mass., N.Y., and Pa.	67.8	65.4

NOTE 1.—Although the percentage of illiteracy shows an improvement this year over last, it should be remembered that these figures are based upon the manifests, which in turn are made up from the statements of the immigrants. One test recently made at New York showed that 175

Figure 5.7. Immigration Restriction League pamphlet, 1903 (Library of Congress, Rare Book and Special Collections Division)

In general terms, league publications provided "an educational program for the American public" (according to Barbara Solomon, "very much in the pattern of teaching at Harvard College" [Solomon 1956, 106]). One strategy, particularly germane to understanding constructions of "the popular" in the period, was the attempt to harness the support of the emerging middle class for their cause. Their rhetoric attempted to build an alliance with skilled workers, arguing that the interests of organized labor and upper-class Brahmins were identical. The 1895 annual report of the league's executive committee, for example, appealed directly to skilled workers in terms that elided class divisions within a vision of the national good: "the horde of illiterate, unskilled laborers" from abroad was "a menace to the labor as well as the national interests" (Immigration Restriction League 1895).

Ultimately, however, league publications were drab documents. The league had in its midst a much more dynamic opinion maker. Sitting, perhaps, in the club room that day in 1894 was Owen Wister. Wister belonged to the class most threatened by the movement of new immigrants across the Atlantic Basin. As a Harvard alumnus, he was educated in what became the main breeding ground for immigration restriction, and he maintained strong ties with "blueblooded" Boston families who supported the league's formation. One league backer was Henry Lee Higginson, Boston's most powerful broker, also a cattle investor and Wister's first employer (Solomon 1956, 123). Increasingly, the author entered the league's inner circle, becoming its vice-president in 1903.

Wister's writing trades in ethnic stereotypes that prove Anglo-American superiority, and his early western stories include caricatures of venal Jewish drummers and pidgin-English speakers. His attacks became more virulent with his league service. In 1903, his most explicit anti-immigration fiction to that point, *Philosophy 4: A Story of Harvard University*, appeared in book form. Set during his years at Harvard, this whimsical novella of undergraduates on a spree before their philosophy exam launches a sneering attack on "new" immigrants. The students are celebrated as "old stock" northwestern European immigrants: "Bertie and Billy had colonial names" and "belonged to the same club-table." Oscar Maironi, their tutor of Jewish Italian descent, has parents who "had come over in the steerage." With his "suave and slightly alien accent," "shiny little calculating eyes," and "patient, Oriental" manner, he provokes distrust and is ultimately bested in the exam by his wholesome, boisterous students (Wister 1903, 23, 45, 36, 14, 15, 29). Wister's next novel, *Lady Baltimore*, was a study of Old South manners. It positions colonials who trace their roots to Elizabethan England as the true Americans and takes repeated swipes at newly enfranchised blacks and the North's "pest of Hebrew and other low immigrants" who make up "our sullen welter of democracy" (Wister 1906, 112, 48).

From the 1890s to the 1920s "when restrictionist rhetoric and anti-immigrant sentiment peaked," Wister's Boone and Crockett clubmates contributed equally enthusiastically to the cause (King 2000, 19). Henry Cabot Lodge, a mentor to the Harvard founders of the

Immigration Restriction League, served as the organization's chief congressional spokesman. Theodore Roosevelt's first annual presidential message of December 3, 1901, argued for strengthening the anti-immigration laws against "all persons of a low moral tendency or of unsavory reputation" (qtd. in Garis 1927, 102). Roosevelt further advanced the league's cause when he appointed one of its leaders, Jeremiah W. Jenks, to head the U.S. Immigration Commission and later became honorary president of a fellow organization, the American Defense Society (Slotkin 1992, 190). Madison Grant, another Boone and Crockett clubmate, became vice-president of the league in 1909, worked extensively with Hall and Ward on eugenics committees, and finally whipped up eugenic panic more broadly with his publication of *The Passing of the Great Race* in 1916.

"Between the Acts"

When *The Virginian* was published in 1902, it entered into a cultural environment already thick with mutually reinforcing discourses of privilege and exclusion. The class of transatlantic Anglo-American "old stock" was fighting for its survival in the face of rapid industrial, urban, and demographic change. Aiming to win over public opinion, this class jockeyed for position within emerging international mass culture, learning the techniques and language of market control—whether the market was in cattle, humans, or books. This language Wister absorbed and reproduced in his club dealings, east and west; his negotiations with his publishers, and the details of his writing.

Throughout Wister's Westerns, the action is saturated with the exclusionary logic and language of the frontier club. His first published story—"Hank's Woman" (1892)—showed how new immigrants failed the test of the frontier west. An Austrian-Hungarian woman and a racially blurred American—"little black Hank"—enter into a hellish marriage, ultimately destroying each other over religious differences (Wister 1892, 821). "The Evolution of the Cowpuncher" (1895) used the evolutionary scheme of Social Darwinism to implant Anglo-Saxonism triumphant in the west. The essay—illustrated by Frederic Remington—argues that the cowboy is the direct and last descendant of the chivalric knight of old England, a heritage distinguishing him from what Wister called the

Figure 5.8. Frederic Remington, "The Last Cavalier," *Harper's New Monthly Magazine* September 1895

"dingy whites"—the Jewish peoples, southern and eastern Europeans, and the laboring poor—who had also crossed the Atlantic (qtd. in Guterl 2001, 6).

At times, Wister's fiction served frontier club interests in very specific ways. He rewrote the notorious Cheyenne Club lynchings, justifying the lynchers as honorable men. Wister's host, the bully Colonel Wolcott, for example, becomes the wise Judge Henry in *The Virginian*. One chapter is devoted to the judge's apologia for the lynch party headed by the Virginian on his orders. The judge's task is to persuade Molly, the Virginian's bride-to-be and the face of eastern refinement, who is horror-struck by the news of her fiancé's violence, of the rightness of their actions. Wolcott-cum-Henry insists on a key distinction:

> [I]n all sincerity I see no likeness in principle whatever between burning Southern negroes in public and hanging Wyoming horse-thieves in private. I consider the burning a proof that the South is semi-barbarous, and the hanging a proof that Wyoming is determined to become civilized. We do not torture our criminals when we lynch them. We do not

> invite spectators to enjoy their death agony. We put no such hideous disgrace upon the United States. (Wister 1904, 434)

The emphasis is particularly troubling in light of the fate of Nick Ray, whose burned corpse was displayed after he had been gunned down by Wolcott's posse. Judge Henry leads Molly through a series of specious arguments by which he transforms intimidation by a power elite into a democratic uprising of the people, intent on asserting social order. He concludes that lynching in the west is a case of "your ordinary citizen" taking back the power of the U.S. Constitution, which is rightfully his (Wister 1902, 340). Molly's counterarguments dwindle in the face of Judge Henry's logic. Finally, she has no rebuttal.

Between 1907 and 1911, in response to the Dillingham Commission's study of immigration patterns (inaugurated by Roosevelt), the Immigration Restriction League vigorously lobbied for a literacy test for immigrants. In the same period, Wister published "The Gift Horse" in *The Saturday Evening Post* (July 18, 1908). This story also hinges on the danger of illiterates, with a horse rustler's illiteracy causing cattle barons almost to lynch the eastern narrator by mistake. (Insiders would recognize that the horses have been stolen from the big WSGA ranches, including Wister's home away from home, the VR outfit managed by Wolcott.) When Henry Cabot Lodge campaigned publicly against the railroad barons' pro-immigration stance, charging that they were motivated purely by their greed for cheap labor, he was echoed by Wister's hero. In a scene at the railroad, the Virginian misidentifies some immigrant workers:

> "There go some more I-talians."
>
> "They're Chinese," said Trampas.
>
> "That's so," acknowledged the Virginian, with a laugh. . . . "Without cheap foreigners they couldn't afford all this hyeh new gradin,'" the Southerner continued. (Wister 1904, 181–82)

The joke—which the villain Trampas does not follow—is that Italians and Chinese are all one to the immigration restrictionists and, Lodge charged, the railroad capitalists.

The Virginian, the Southern Anglo-American *par excellence*, demonstrates his heroism by dominating alternative presences on the plains. At the novel's center, Wister underscores the link between his actions and the national good with a series of chapters named "Acts" under the rubric "The Game and the Nation." In the chapter titled "Between the Acts" the Virginian, recently promoted to deputy foreman, pens his mutinous cowboy gang in a railroad car. He declares that he will herd them like steers back to their employer Judge Henry: "Never a calf of them will desert to Rawhide" (Wister 1904, 166). At various moments he shoots down one cowboy and lynches others who refuse to serve the cattle barons' interests; mocks with racist epithets the Jewish drummers and black Pullman porters, as well as Chinese railroad workers; denigrates American Indians as alternately savages and pathetic dependants, and generally rids the west of unwanted categories. Remembering Roosevelt's presidential exhortations to bar from America people "of unsavory reputation," we can appreciate the Virginian's hot defense of his own, to the point of gunning down Trampas over Molly's objections: "What men say about my nature is not just merely an outside thing" (ibid., 475).

Wister drew some other categorical lines with the Virginian. This cowboy's heroic independence separates him decisively from the class of contract worker. The WSGA treated cowboys—especially after the harsh winter of 1886–87—very much as contract labor to be hired and fired at will, taken on for the summer roundups and let go every winter: they "had much more in common with the factory worker than they, or the mythmakers, would care to acknowledge" (Ward 1980, 88). This category of worker was anathema to immigration restrictionists as the role most often filled by unskilled, single men resisting assimilation. Anti-immigration representations of these groups—bands of men roaming around the country, working and bunking together to save their wages for their families in Europe—can sound uncomfortably similar to roaming cowboy bands. Wister's heroization of the independent cowboy—one of the innovations for which the author is generally credited—increased the dissimilarity between the two types. At the same time, his economic positioning of the Virginian reinforces the alliances attempted by the frontier club in its Cheyenne and Boston wings: he is at once skilled worker, ranch manager, business partner, and, throughout, natural gentleman. The Virginian plays out the full spectrum of roles with which readers targeted by the frontier club—the skilled working class, the middle class, the eastern establishment—could identify.

Act Three

November 1896, the Union League Club, New York City. Several men are lounging in the private dining room, smoking Havana cigars, sipping 1848 brandy, and discussing stock—financial stock. Four are Harper cousins, owners of Harper and Brothers Publishing Company. For years, they've struggled to maintain the house's position in the literary marketplace, battling a new generation of entrepreneurs using cut-price methods. Cheap publishers don't deserve to hold sway over a mass readership. How can quality publishers elbow them out?

J. P. Morgan, the fifth man at the meeting, believes he has the answer. The Harpers have approached America's biggest financier to bail them out of insolvency. He agrees on the condition that they convert the seventy-nine-year-old family firm into a joint-stock company, with him as the controlling shareholder (Exman 1967, 173). This arrangement is an uneasy alliance at best. It not only removes control from the Harpers of what has been called "one of the most powerful commercial cultural institutions of the Empire City"—by the 1850s, the largest publishing house in the world (Howard 2001, 6). It also immerses the publishers in competitive capitalism with an explicitness and aggressiveness that they have avoided for years. The Harpers agree.

This scene is about controlling cultural production, a resource every bit as significant in that period as cattle speculation and immigration policy. Culture industries played a major role in the class realignment caused by the crisis in capitalism. Lawrence Levine and Paul DiMaggio have analyzed how class divisions were sharpened through the invention of a cultural hierarchy: "[I]n its American version, [it] emerged in the period between 1850 and 1900 out of the efforts of urban elites to build organizational forms that, first, isolated high culture and, second, differentiated it from popular culture" (DiMaggio 1982, 33). A paradigmatic step in consolidating class solidarity and status was the founding of the Boston Symphony Orchestra in 1881 by Henry Lee Higginson—the same broker, cattle investor, and immigration restrictionist who was Wister's former employer and current friend (ibid.).

In the literary domain, the Harpers were at the heart of this struggle. Earlier in the nineteenth century, the new, lucrative field of mass publishing was controlled by publishers with cultural power and cachet. The Harper brothers participated in the self-described "American publishing fraternity," composed of "reputable publishers" who operated according to "trade courtesy rules" ("International" 1882, 867). A prominent presence in the exclusive club scene of New York, Boston, and Philadelphia, publishers such as Harper, Henry Holt and J. B. Lippincott prided themselves on their gentlemanly practices, brokering deals with each other and their authors in the hallowed precincts of club dining and smoking rooms. As the century wore on, they drew the class line more emphatically, trying to block a new generation of publishers who capitalized on technological and transportation advances to invade the market, using economies of scale to saturate it with cut-price reading material. From 1860, the Beadles undersold the old publishers with dime novels ("A DOLLAR book for a DIME!," their publicity blared); George Munro dominated the market with cheap reprint "libraries" from 1877; and Frank Munsey followed with ten cent monthly magazines. The challenge for the Harpers—analogously to the Cheyenne Club stalwarts and the immigration restrictionists—was to claim class and cultural distinction while winning over a mass audience.[13]

Figure 5.9. Harper Brothers, between 1855 and 1865 (Library of Congress, Prints and Photographs Division, Brady-Handy Collection, LC-DIG-cwpbh-02806)

The Harpers were party to—at times, spearheaded—institutional maneuvers designed to oust the cheap competition. In 1878, Joseph W. Harper initiated a volte-face on international copyright, writing to the secretary of state with a proposed "Harper Treaty" between the United States and Great Britain (Harper 1912, 424–26; Exman 1967, 51–52). In their early days, the Harpers had opposed international copyright, arguing for the gentlemanly practice of voluntary payments to British authors and publishers for early sheets (an arrangement which suited their profit margin). Once reprint libraries entered the scene in 1874, pirating foreign works without recompense and radically lowering prices, Harper vigorously lobbied for Anglo-American copyright, which would force all publishers to pay foreign royalties (Schurman 2002, 98). Under the sponsorship of Henry Cabot Lodge in Congress, that fight was eventually won, in terms reminiscent of the alliances among ranchers and immigration restrictionists. The Chace Act of 1891 rested on agreements among a transatlantic club of "select nations"—the United States, Great Britain, France, Switzerland, and Belgium—as well as another uneasy cross-class alliance, with quality publishers securing the "intelligent cooperation" (in Joseph Harper's euphemism) of unionized printers and typographical workers (Harper 1912, 435).

Then, in February 1895, the literary journal *The Bookman* imitated its English parent by publishing best-seller lists: "Sales of Books During the Month . . . in order of demand." The method by which these monthly lists were compiled immediately benefited the quality publishers. They were based on reports from "leading booksellers" in eighteen cities ("Sales" 1895, 72). The venues and methods on which dime novel and magazine sales most depended—railroad depots, newsstands, subscriptions, and rural commercial travelers—were excluded, as were reprint libraries, cheap editions, and pocket-sized books. As the lists expanded to include thirty cities in the United States and Canada and became the basis for lists of "leaders" and "national best sellers," cheap publications were increasingly blocked from view (Mott 1947, 6). This was another fight over marketplace categories; however shrilly dime novels trumpeted their claim to be "Books for the Million!," the middle-class publishing industry denied them the classification "best-seller." Harper and Brothers, on the other hand, visibly dominated the first best-seller list, with Appleton, Holt, Macmillan, and a string of quality publishers following behind.

In addition to these somewhat circuitous strategies, and for all their moralistic rhetoric, the Harpers systematically horned in on the territory they publicly decried. They began a reprint library (Franklin Square Library in 1878) and a dime series (*Harper's Young People* in 1879, "with the declared purpose of providing an alternative to dime novels" [Howard 2001, 72]). Frank Munsey initiated the "magazine revolution" by dropping the cover price of monthly magazines to ten cents and relying on advertising for income, commodifying readers once and for all (Ohmann 1996; Garvey 1996). The Harpers, too, began to pile on advertising in their periodicals (*Harper's Magazine* went from ten pages of advertisements in 1885 to seventy-five pages in 1890 [Ohmann 1996, 26]).

The Harpers had another gun in their arsenal. Sitting in the same club room ten months earlier was Owen Wister, one of their prized authors, whom they were feting before a distinguished company including William Dean Howells, Mark Twain, and Theodore Roosevelt (Payne 1985, 164–65). Precisely because Wister gained his entrée into publishing through the frontier club, he was attuned to the delicate balance between culture and commerce within the ongoing class struggle. He fitted right into the club culture, conducting business with Henry Mills Alden, editor of *Harper's Magazine*, and J. Henry Harper in the intimacy of their club rooms and homes. In the words of J. Henry Harper, "I always thought of you as one of our family of authors."[14] At the same time, Wister understood the necessity for marketing. In his mythical account of his first act of authorship—set significantly in the Philadelphia Club—he recognized the need to elbow out dime novel versions of the west: "Was Alkali Ike in the comic papers the one figure which the jejune American imagination . . . could discern in that epic which was being lived at a gallop out in the sage-brush?" (Wister 1930, 29). His attitude to the masses on whom his success depended, a mixture of disdain and embarrassment, closely mirrored the Harpers'—as in his uneasily jocular, rhyming preface to *The Jimmyjohn Boss*: "leave the masses,/Read me, and join the small selected classes" (Wister 1900).

Wister was not the only member of the frontier club to enter into mutually beneficial arrangements with the Harper "family." Caspar Whitney "was an important correspondent for the *Weekly*"; when he left to edit the sporting journal *Outing* in 1900—partly as an outlet for his Boone and Crockett Clubmates—he was bankrolled by Fletcher

Harper, among others (Exman 1967, 93; "Outing" 1900). Harpers accepted Frederic Remington's first illustration in 1882, and from 1880 to 1900 frequently published his illustrated magazine writings and six of his books. Theodore Roosevelt and Henry Cabot Lodge made steady contributions to the Harpers' magazine and book publications. In 1913, George Bird Grinnell brokered a deal with them to publish Boone and Crockett volumes.

With Morgan at the helm, however, the fragile balance between commerce and culture at Harper and Brothers could not hold. In December 1899, unable to pay the interest on Morgan's loan, the firm went into receivership. All the Harpers except J. Henry resigned, and Morgan brought in new management from the cheap competition: at first S. S. McClure, doyen of the ten cent magazine revolution, then Col. George S. Harvey, former editor of Pulitzer's sensationalist *New York World*. Practices became at once more commercial and less effective. First to go were the Harpers' trademark handwritten letters. Harvey introduced typewritten form letters, promising "such new methods of vastly greater publicity for books, that the returns promise increased results for both of us."[15] Yet Wister felt that his work was underadvertised and poorly packaged. In 1901, with *The Virginian* nine-tenths completed, he jumped ship to Macmillan.[16]

The transfer to Macmillan was in many ways a sideways move. The publisher claimed a similar middle-class, quality position to Harper's, and its editor, George Brett, was a worthy clubman. But Macmillan was more adept in the new literary marketplace. They understood that novels sold in quantities unavailable to short story collections, particularly since the onset of best-seller lists. Whereas the Harpers repeatedly gathered Wister's work into short story volumes and envisaged *The Virginian* in the same terms, Brett from the first talked up the work as a novel. Macmillan was also more attuned to mass advertising—the key, in Richard Ohmann's analysis, to newly emerging mass culture. They accompanied *The Virginian* with an advertising campaign worthy of their cheap rivals. Wister was both delighted and apprehensive, writing to Brett:

> Last Thursday I was sitting at the extreme back of a railroad car bound for Beverly Farms. In the extreme front somebody opened a newspaper—& I had immediate prolapsis inter. My gracious. I saw THE VIRGINIAN in words so large that many people gave up trying to find seats in the car, thinking they

> were all occupied—It was only your advertisement. . . . I'm getting more & more anxious (as if you didn't know your business!) that you'll get all this money back. It must cost like the devil & all to kick up such a splendid noise. I'm inundated with letters congratulatory & that's all right. But cold hard cash into the publisher's pocket is the other half of my prayer just now.[17]

Macmillan was also more transatlantic in its reach. Whereas the Harpers vaguely promised Wister "some English publisher," Macmillan had a parent company in London, providing simultaneous publication in the United Kingdom and the British Dominions.[18] The move also freed Wister to publish pieces in the *Saturday Evening Post*, a more popular magazine and the journal of choice for immigration restrictionists. Brett knew how to finesse the gap between Wister's cultural aspirations and his audience, gradually persuading the author to disguise his distaste. For a Christmas edition of *The Virginian*, he cajoled Wister into adding a few respectful words: "The book is the best American story that has ever been written and it might not be inadvisable to thank the American public for its very hearty appreciation and for its great good sense and discernment in seeing that fact."[19] With this array of marketing techniques, Macmillan pushed *The Virginian* to the top of the best-seller list—"doing in one week two-thirds of what its three predecessors have done in two, five, and seven years"—and kept it there all year.[20]

Epilogue

April 18, 1924, the United States Congress. Several senators, among them Henry Cabot Lodge, are lounging in a senate antechamber, smoking Havana cigars, sipping 1848 brandy and celebrating the vote on stock—"pure, unadulterated Anglo-Saxon stock," "the same stock as that which originally settled the United States, wrote our Constitution and established our democratic institutions."[21]

This scene marks the passage of the National Origins Act of 1924 with only six dissenting votes. After a series of Exclusion Acts, beginning with the Chinese Exclusion Act in 1882, the National Origins Act definitively entrenched limitations on non-Anglo groups and officially

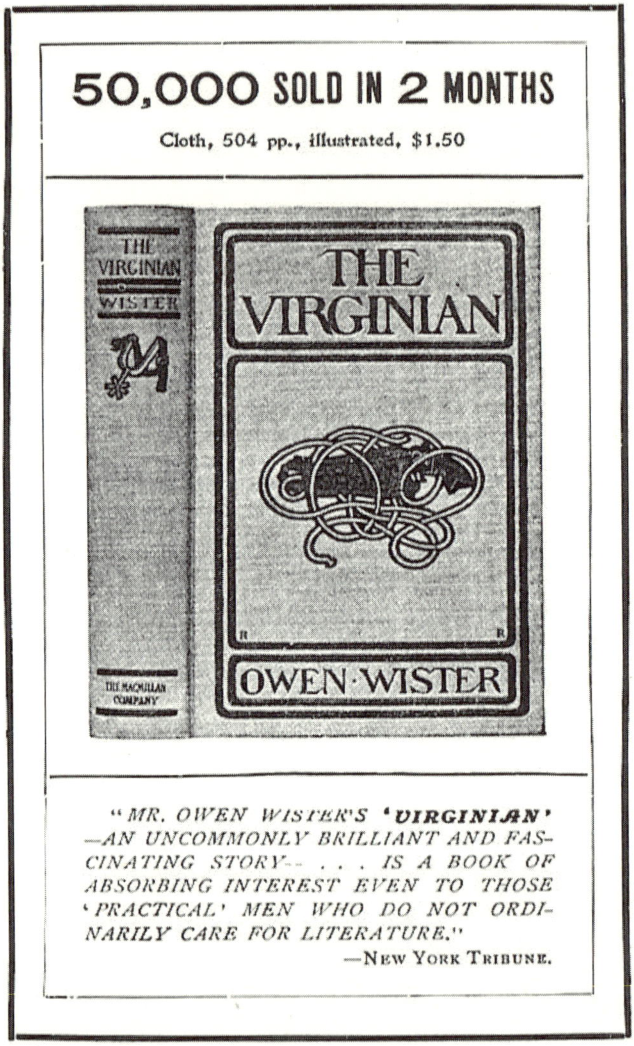

Figure 5.10. Advertising flyer for *The Virginian*, 1902 (Box 79, Owen Wister Papers, Manuscript Division, Library of Congress, Washington, D.C.)

declared Native and African Americans non-people. The Johnson-Reed Act, as it was also known, rolled back the vision of the American population to the 1890 census by establishing entrance quotas at 2 percent of national demographics at that moment; two-thirds of the 150,000 places for immigrants would go to people from northwestern Europe. Using the 1890 census as a base line for quotas, the anti-immigration lobbyists argued, would "Keep America American" (qtd. in Simon 1985, 137). The 1890 census was the very one that Frederick Jackson Turner had enshrined in his frontier thesis at the Chicago exposition in 1893—an iconic moment in the frontier club's founding and in the Western's cultural power. In its final flyer, of June 14, 1924, the Immigration Restriction League saluted the act: "[T]hose still living of the handful of men who, at the call of Mr. Robert DeC. Ward, first met thirty years ago on May 31, 1894 to form the Immigration Restriction League . . . have thus at last seen their belief embodied in what promises to be effective and permanent legislation" (qtd. in King 2000, 206).

This act closed what Michael Rogin calls "the magic circle" of whiteness (Rogin 1996, 56). Popular Westerns drove non-Anglos out of their fictional landscapes. Quality publishers drove competing images of the west out of the international literary marketplace. Transatlantic cattle barons forced competitors off the northern plains. And immigration restrictionists excluded the Atlantic diaspora—the poor and the outcast, the descendants of African slavery, the Asian laborers—from citizenship and livelihood in the United States. The frontier club had learned how to corner the literary marketplace, the cattle range, and the American body politic in one fell swoop. It was its finest hour.

Notes

I am extremely grateful to the Social Sciences and Humanities Research Council of Canada and the American Heritage Center, University of Wyoming, for their generous financial support of this project; to the archivists of the collections named below for their invaluable knowledge and guidance; to Elizabeth Groeneveld for her sterling work as my graduate research assistant at the University of Guelph; and to Ric Knowles for his unfailingly incisive comments on earlier drafts of this essay.

1. For example, Billington 1981, 171; Cawelti 1971, 95; Durham and Jones 1965, 221; Etulain 1973, 35; Evans 2002, 373; Fiedler 1968, 138; Murdoch 2001, 75; Packard 2005, 2, 15; Fanny Kemble Wister 1958, 2.

2. Letter, Chanler to Wister, 14 September 1895, OW Collection, 15.

3. The scenes that open each act are, strictly speaking, fictitious, although they are based on documented evidence of the groups' habits and movements.

4. Wm. Sturgis to F. O. de Billier, 10 June 1880, CC Records, 195, 1; Wm. Sturgis to H. G. Balch, 10 June 1880, CC Records, 195, 1; Wm. Sturgis to Daniel G. Bacon, 10 June 1880, CC Records, 195, 1; Wm. Sturgis

to Clarence King, 12 June 1880, CC Records, 195, 1; Wm. Sturgis to S. F. Emmons, 12 June 1880, CC Records, 195, 1. See also Spring 1961.

5. The Morgan investment in cattle—as, later, in *Outing*—was handled by Robert Bacon, J. Pierpont Morgan Bankers representative and Roosevelt's friend.

6. Order to Mep Park and Tilford, 10 August 1881, CC Records, 195, 1.

7. Owen Wister's Notebook, 3 July 1885, 4, OW Papers, 3.

8. Chanler to Wister, 14 September 1895, OW Collection, 15.

9. French to Wister, 24 January 1898, OW Collection, 20.

10. Owen Wister's Diary, 28 September 1893,, 23, OW Papers, 3.

11. Between Wister and Silas Weir Mitchell, there are lengthy correspondence on stylistic minutiae (SWM Papers, 4.3, 9); distinct echoes between Mitchell's 1879 Yellowstone journal (SWM Papers, 5, 12) and Wister's Wyoming journals a few years later (OW Papers, 3); and Wister's emendations on Mitchell's "Adventure on 5th Avenue," a story reminiscent of Wister's "How Lin McLean Went East" (SWM Papers, 7.4, 17).

12. Prescott F. Hall to the editor, *Boston Journal*, 30 June 1894.

13. Again, a sense of mutually supportive cultural domains is signaled in the Cheyenne Club subscribing only to "quality" periodicals: *Harper's Weekly*, *Harper's Monthly*, and the *Atlantic Monthly* (Subscription Records, 7 June 1882, CC Records, 195, 2).

14. Harper to Wister, 12 November 1901, OW Collection, 22.

15. Harvey to Wister, 27 April 1900, OW Papers, 22.

16. Several members of the frontier club apparently jumped with him. Remington published his seventh book—*John Ermine* (1902)—with Macmillan. Whitney—whom Wister called "your editor Caspar Whitney"—co-authored a book with Wister and Grinnell for Macmillan (Wister to Brett, 2 April 1903, Macmillan Records, 106). By August 1903, Fletcher Harper was off the *Outing* letterhead.

17. Wister to Brett, 2 July [1902], Macmillan Records, 107.

18. Harper and Brothers for E.W.F. to Wister, 2 May 1895, OW Papers, 22.

19. Brett to Wister, 7 April 1911, Macmillan Records, 106.

20. Wister to Brett, 5 June 1902, Macmillan Records, 106. *The Virginian* appears as #1 for 1902 and #5 for 1903 in Hackett and Burke 66, 67.

21. Senator Ellison DuRant Smith, 9 April 1924, *Congressional Record*, 68th Cong., 1st sess., 1924, 65, 5962; Garis 1927, 203.

Works Cited: Archival Sources

Macmillan Company Records, The New York Public Library Manuscripts and Archives Division. Cited as Macmillan Records, Box Number.

S. Weir Mitchell Papers, College of Physicians, Philadelphia. Cited as SWM Papers, Series Number, Box Number.

Owen Wister Papers, Accession Number 00290, American Heritage Center, University of Wyoming. Cited as OW Papers, Box Number.

Owen Wister Collection, Manuscript Division, Library of Congress. Cited as OW Collection, Box Number.

Wyoming Stock Growers Association Records, 1858–1987, Accession Number 14, Series VIII. Cheyenne Club Records, 1880–1947, American Heritage Center, University of Wyoming. Cited as CC Records, Box Number, Folder Number.

Works Cited: Publications

Billington, Ray Allen. 1981. *Land of savagery, land of promise: The European image of the American frontier in the nineteenth century.* New York: W. W. Norton.

Cawelti, John G. 1971. *The six-gun mystique.* Bowling Green, OH: Bowling Green University Popular Press.

Cobbs, John L. 1984. *Owen Wister.* Boston: G. K. Hall.

De C. Ward, Robert. 1894. An immigration restriction league. *The Century: A Popular Quarterly* 49, no. 4: 639.

DiMaggio, Paul. 1982. Cultural entrepreneurship in nineteenth-century Boston, Part 1: The creation of an organizational base for high culture in America. *Media, Culture and Society* 4: 33–50.

———. 1982a. Cultural entrepreneurship in nineteenth-century Boston, Part 2: The classification and framing of American art. *Media, Culture and Society* 4: 303–22.

Durham, Philip, and Everett L. Jones. 1965. *The negro cowboys.* New York: Dodd, Mead.

Etulain, Richard W. 1973. *Owen Wister.* Boise: Boise State College.

Evans, Max. 2002. Afterword. In *The Virginian: A horseman of the plains.* New York: New American Library/Signet.

Exman, Eugene. 1967. *The house of Harper: One hundred and fifty years of publishing.* New York: Harper and Row.

Fiedler, Leslie. 1968. *The return of the vanishing American.* New York: Stein and Day.

Garis, Roy L. 1927. *Immigration restriction: A study of the opposition to and regulation of immigration into the United States.* New York: Macmillan.

Garvey, Ellen Gruber. 1996. *The adman in the parlor: Magazines and the gendering of consumer culture, 1880s to 1910s.* New York: Oxford University Press.

Gressley, Gene M. 1971. *Bankers and cattlemen.* Lincoln: University of Nebraska Press.

Guterl, Matthew Pratt. 2001. *The color of race in America, 1900–1940.* Cambridge: Harvard University Press.

Hackett, Alice Payne, and James Henry Burke. 1977. *80 years of best sellers 1895–1975.* New York: R. R. Bowker.

Hall, Prescott F. 1897. Immigration and the educational test. *The North American Review* 165 (October): 393–402.

Harper, J. Henry. 1912. *The house of Harper: A century of publishing in Franklin Square.* New York: Harper and Brothers.

Howard, June. 2001. *Publishing the family.* Durham: Duke University Press.

Hufsmith, George W. 1993. *The Wyoming lynching of Cattle Kate, 1889.* Glendo, WY: High Plains Press.

Immigration Restriction League. 1895. *Annual report of the executive committee of the Immigration Restriction League for 1895.* Boston.

International copyright: The copyright controversy. 1882. *The Publishers' Weekly* 22 (9 December): 866–69.

Kasson, Joy S. 2000. *Buffalo Bill's wild west: Celebrity, memory, and popular history.* New York: Hill and Wang.

King, Desmond. 2000. *Making Americans: Immigration, race, and the origins of the diverse democracy.* Cambridge: Harvard University Press.

Levine, Lawrence W. 1978. *Highbrow/lowbrow: The emergence of cultural hierarchy in America.* New York: Basic Books.

Lodge, Hon. Henry Cabot. 1891. Lynch law and unrestricted immigration. *The North American Review* 152, no. 414: 602–12.

Mott, Frank Luther. 1947. *Golden multitudes: The story of best sellers in the United States.* New York: R. R. Bowker.

Murdoch, David Hamilton. 2001. *The American west: The invention of a myth.* Reno: University of Nevada Press.

Ohmann, Richard. 1996. *Selling culture: Magazines, markets, and class at the turn of the century.* London: Verso.

Outing in new hands. 1900. *New York Times*, 15 February.

Packard, Chris. 2005. *Queer cowboys and other erotic male friendships in nineteenth-century American literature.* New York: Palgrave Macmillan.

Payne, Darwin. 1985. *Owen Wister: Chronicler of the west, gentleman of the east.* Dallas: Southern Methodist University Press.

Rogin, Michael Paul. 1996. *Blackface, white noise: Jewish immigrants in the Hollywood melting pot.* Berkeley: University of California Press.

Roosevelt, Theodore, and George Bird Grinnell, eds. 1893. *American big-game hunting: The book of the Boone and Crockett Club.* New York: Forest and Stream Publishing Co.

Sales of books during the month. 1895. *Bookman* 2, no. 1: 72.

Schurman, Lydia Cushman. 2002. The effect of nineteenth-century "libraries" on the American book trade. In *Scorned literature: Essays on the history and criticism of popular mass-produced fiction in America,* ed. Lydia Cushman Schurman and Deidre Johnson, 97–121. Westport, CT: Greenwood Press.

Simon, Rita. 1985. *Public opinion and the immigrant: Print media coverage, 1880–1980.* Lexington, MA: Lexington Books/D. C. Heath.

Slotkin, Richard. 1992. *Gunfighter nation: The myth of the frontier in twentieth-century America.* New York: Atheneum.

Solomon, Barbara. 1956. *Ancestors and immigrants: A changing New England tradition.* Cambridge: Harvard University Press.

Spring, Agnes Wrights. 1961. *The Cheyenne Club: Mecca of the aristocrats of the old-time cattle range.* Kansas City: Don Ornduff.

Szasz, Ferenc Morton. 2000. *Scots in the North American west, 1790–1917.* Norman: University of Oklahoma Press.

Tuttle, Jennifer S. 2000. Rewriting the west cure: Charlotte Perkins Gilman, Owen Wister, and the sexual politics of neurasthenia. In *The mixed legacy of Charlotte Perkins Gilman,* ed. Catherine J. Golden and Joanna Schneider Zangrando, 103–21. Newark: University of Delaware Press.

Vorpahl, Ben Merchant. 1972. *My Dear Wister: The Frederic Remington-Owen Wister letters.* Palo Alto: American West.

Walker, Francis A. 1891. Immigration and degradation. *Forum* XI: 642.

Ward III, George Baxter. 1980. Bloodbrothers in the wilderness: The sport hunter and the buckskin hunter in the preservation of the American wilderness experience. PhD Diss. University of Texas at Austin.

White, G. Edward. 1968. *The eastern establishment and the western experience: The west of Frederic Remington, Theodore Roosevelt, and Owen Wister.* New Haven: Yale University Press.

Will, Barbara. 1998. The nervous origins of the American Western. *American Literature* 70, no. 2 (June): 293–316.

Wister, Fanny Kemble, ed. 1958. *Owen Wister out west: His journals and letters.* Chicago: University of Chicago Press.

Wister, Owen. 1892. Hank's woman. *Harper's Weekly,* 27 August: 821.

———. 1895. The evolution of the cow puncher. *Harper's New Monthly Magazine* 91 (September): 602–17.

———. 1900. *The Jimmyjohn boss and other stories.* New York: Harper and Brothers.

———. 1904. *The Virginian: A horseman of the plains.* New York: Macmillan.

———. 1906. *Lady Baltimore.* New York: Macmillan.

———. 1911. *Philosophy 4: A story of Harvard University.* New York: Macmillan.

———. 1928. Preface. In *The Virginian. The writings of Owen Wister.* Vol. 4. New York: Macmillan.

———. 1930. *Roosevelt: The story of a friendship.* New York: Macmillan.

Woods, Lawrence M. 1989. *British gentlemen in the wild west: The era of the intensely English cowboy.* New York: Free Press.

6

America as "World-Salvation"

Josiah Strong, W. E. B. Du Bois, and the Global Rhetoric of American Exceptionalism

Nathaniel Cadle

In 1885, a relatively obscure Congregational minister named Josiah Strong published a remarkable book entitled *Our Country: Its Possible Future and Its Present Crisis.* Originally intended as little more than an extended plea for contributions to the American Home Missionary Society, the text gradually extended into a more complicated treatise on the then-current state of American society and its future role in world affairs. Strong, who fancied himself an intellectual and social reformer, drew—and attempted to synthesize—information from a wide variety of sources: census reports, Papal Encyclicals, the *Encyclopædia Britannica*, Alexis de Tocqueville, articles from *The Nation* and *The Century*, and so forth. Linking the importance of missionary work (including home missions) to U.S. foreign policy and the duty of Anglo-Saxons to spread civilization (that is, Anglo-American culture) throughout the world, Strong produced an instant bestseller. In less than a decade, *Our*

Country sold 175,000 copies in the United States alone, making it one of the most popular books of its time (LaFeber 1963, 73).

Without question, the reason for the book's enormous popularity lay in the careful balance Strong struck between playing to his audience's patriotic belief in America's cultural, economic, and moral supremacy and, at the same time, playing up their fears that alien forces were diluting the national unity that made America's supremacy possible. Half of the book's fourteen chapters are dedicated to describing and deploring seven major "perils" to America's cultural homogeneity: immigration, Roman Catholicism, Mormonism, intemperance/alcoholism, socialism, financial inequality, and urbanization. The other half is a paean to the seemingly limitless economic resources of the American West and moral resources of the Anglo-Saxon race and to the providence that brought the Anglo-Saxon race to the American West. Throughout, Strong insists that America can realize its potential only if its citizens first civilize and Christianize their rapidly closing western frontier, ensuring that the same Anglo-Saxon, Christian culture extends across the continent. Thus, Strong takes a carrot-and-stick approach to his argument, reassuring his readers that America is indeed destined to lead the world yet warning them that the only way to achieve that destiny is to act now.

In essence, Strong places the responsibility for America's continued greatness at the doorstep of his readers, no doubt hoping that the immediate result would be an influx of financial contributions to the American Home Missionary Society. But the length and complexity of Strong's argument—and the fact that he would return twice more to the same themes, in *The New Era or the Coming Kingdom* (1893) and *Expansion under New World Conditions* (1900)—suggest that Strong's aims were more ambitious. Indeed, historian Walter LaFeber claims that Strong wanted nothing less than to influence U.S. foreign policy at the highest levels, citing Strong's later association with expansionist ideologues such as Alfred Thayer Mahan and Senator William P. Frye of Maine (LaFeber 1963, 78).[1] In *Our Country*, Strong repeatedly links domestic issues with global events, and he accepts unquestioningly the central principle of home missions: that "salvation" of the world is inextricably tied to "salvation" of the nation. As a result, he forces his readers to look outward, beyond America's borders, to perceive existing dangers and to glimpse future opportunities. Following the logic of Strong's argument, LaFeber argues:

> American foreign policy makers could only operate from the basic assumption of an ever increasing involvement in world politics. The policy makers had no choice, given the discoveries of steam and electricity and the resulting unity of the peoples of the world. . . . Salvation lay in the fulfillment of the Anglo-Saxon mission to reshape the world in the mold of western civilization. (LaFeber 1963, 76–77)

The use of the word *salvation* in this context is significant and almost certainly intentional on LaFeber's part, for it is precisely this word that drives the rhetoric behind Strong's ideology of global transformation. Unquestionably, this rhetoric echoes that of John Winthrop and the Puritans. In its careful blending of religious and nationalistic language, *Our Country* can take its place comfortably alongside Winthrop's "A Model of Christian Charity" and Ronald Reagan's Farewell Address in the historical trajectory of the rhetoric of American exceptionalism. Yet the particular ideology that Strong espouses, which I term the ideology of world-salvation, is different from Winthrop's in several respects. Perhaps most importantly, Strong's grand mission, unlike the Puritans', is not tied to any one religious group. Indeed, for a minister, Strong's rhetoric is surprisingly devoid of theological particularity. Rather, for Strong, the secular organizing principle of the nation is the key to world salvation. Furthermore, Strong's vision places the United States in a far more active international role than Winthrop ever imagined. As a "city upon a hill," Winthrop's community is essentially passive; his America leads primarily by example. Strong, on the other hand, advocates a more aggressive and interventionist approach to the secular world of international politics. His America harnesses new technologies, pursues far-flung economic interests, and engages in diplomacy—all in an effort to effect what he viewed as change for the better in other societies. In short, the ideology of world-salvation is both global and transformative.

The strand of American exceptionalism found in *Our Country* thus reflects and engages the historical conditions and concerns of late-nineteenth and early-twentieth-century America. As the United States emerged as a world power, through imperial and economic expansion overseas and greater involvement in international diplomacy, American writers, intellectuals, and politicians began interrogating the nature of their national identity, the future of the country, and America's role in world affairs. Like Strong, these writers were responding to and participating in the changes going on within America's social landscape and in the United States' relationships with foreign nations. What Strong provided was a powerful formula for making sense of those changes and carving out a more active and influential role for the United States within the international community. In the following pages, I argue that Strong's ideology and rhetoric of world-salvation offered other writers and intellectuals, including Woodrow Wilson, Frederick Jackson Turner, and Alfred Thayer Mahan, a means of pushing for greater U.S. activity on the global stage. I further argue, however, that world-salvation remained a highly malleable concept; Strong's rhetoric could be—and was—taken up by other writers with divergent political agendas. W. E. B. Du Bois, for example, shared Strong's global perspective but arrived at a different set of conclusions about America's role in the world, acknowledging that the world beyond America also had a role to play in the lives of his fellow African Americans.

The idea of world-salvation turns up repeatedly throughout *Our Country.* It makes its first appearance even before Strong's text begins, in the introduction written by Austin Phelps, a fellow Congregational minister and the former president of Andover Theological Seminary. Phelps, whom Strong admired and quoted extensively, quickly highlights the central strand of Strong's argument: that of a connection existing between national and international well-being or, as Phelps puts it, "the idea of *crisis* in the destiny of this country, and through it in the destiny of the world" (Strong 1885, iii; emphasis in original). A few paragraphs later, Phelps also summarizes Strong's solution for averting this twofold crisis:

> The conflict for *the world's salvation* partakes of the same character [as a military crisis]. And the facts and their corollaries massed together in this book show that nowhere is it more portentously true than in this country. Our whole history is a succession of crises. Our national salvation demands in supreme exercise certain military virtues. . . . The truth [is] that Christian enterprise for the moral conquest of this land needs to be conducted. (ibid., v; emphasis added)

The salvation of America and, by extension, the salvation of the world can result only through ensuring that the "moral conquest" of the United

States gets carried out by Protestant organizations such as the American Home Missionary Society, which provided support for new churches in the western territories until they became financially independent. In his use of militaristic language, which was typical of Protestant leaders of the time,[2] Phelps seems to prescribe a single rule of thumb that guarantees both America's and the world's salvation: the spread of Christian civilization must keep pace with American expansion—and, presumably, vice versa. That is, to ensure America's salvation, Phelps believes that Americans must make the cultural and political identity of the United States synonymous with Christian civilization, and to ensure the world's salvation, they must reshape the world in America's own image.

Thus, in Phelps's introduction, we find the core of Josiah Strong's argument and the starting point of Strong's career as an apologist for American imperialist expansion. Yet what distinguishes this book from other imperialist tracts of the time, such as those of the British novelist G. A. Henty, is exactly what Phelps admires but leaves out of his introduction: all that mass of "facts and their corollaries." It is, in fact, the sheer amount of information that Strong grapples with and attempts to tie together that transforms his treatise from a mere exercise in fundraising into something far more groundbreaking. Despite the dubiousness of Strong's politics, it would be unfair to dismiss *Our Country* as misinformed propaganda from a reactionary figure. On the contrary, as a historical document, *Our Country* remains an intelligent and insightful inquiry into a complex set of social and economic questions that intersected in ways the author himself barely understood. Reading the book today, one is consistently surprised at how closely Strong's study resembles our current understanding of globalization. Likewise, it is possible to find Strong's perceptive observations and incisive correlations echoed in the speeches of Woodrow Wilson, who knew and read Strong's work. In short, the importance of Strong's *Our Country* rests as much upon its lasting impact on Americans' conceptualization of the world as upon its immediate influence on U.S. foreign policy.

Take, for instance, Strong's discussion of immigrants, which is the first and most pressing "peril" he addresses in his book. Although he frets at length over the "noxious" and "profound influence on our national life and character" that a "typical" European immigrant's "meager or false religious training" might exert (Strong 1885, 40–41), he never once entertains the possibility of closing America's borders or establishing immigration quotas. To be sure, he paints a bleak picture of the extent to which immigrants were beginning to transform certain parts of the nation; according to Strong, several cities on the east coast, including New York City, are already "essentially foreign" (ibid., 44). Instead of viewing these immigrants as interlopers, however, Strong portrays them as victims of circumstance or, to be more precise, as the necessary and unstoppable result of historical forces of technology and the global economy. He explains that the mass migration is due to faster and cheaper "facilities of travel," most notably "steam navigation," that reduced the cost of passage from Europe to America by as much as 70–90 percent between 1825 and 1885 (ibid., 38). Strong also links this migration to economic and political conditions on both sides of the Atlantic and, even more perceptively, to how the conditions on one side can affect the conditions on the other. For example, he points to the invention and production of "labor-saving machinery" in America that is then exported to Europe:

> The making of this machinery in the United States increases the demand for labor here, and its exportation decreases the demand for labor in the Old World. That means immigration to this country. We are to send our labor-saving machinery around the globe, and equivalents in bone and muscle are to be sent back to us. (Strong 1885, 39)

Thus, in Strong's opinion, international migration is as much a historical certainty as are the economic realities of production and consumption or the inevitability of technological progress.

But if Strong does not advocate isolationism, then what remedy for this "peril" to American culture does he suggest? His solution is, quite simply, *assimilation*. He writes: "Our safety demands the assimilation of these strange populations. . . . [Either] this in-sweeping immigration is to foreignize us, or we are to Americanize it" (Strong 1885, 45). Coming from an advocate for home missions, such a solution is unsurprising. Once assimilated and Americanized—by which Strong means conversion to Protestantism and adoption of the values of hard work and frugality—these immigrants will become Americans in a way that citizenship alone cannot guarantee. Whether Strong would promote intermarriage as one possible route to assimilation is unlikely; his conception of Americanization is largely cultural. At the end of his chapter on immigration, however, Strong does venture into metaphorical terrain. Comparing the influx of immigrants to a zoo animal being force-fed, he advises that the "only alternative is, digest or die" (ibid., 46). In its emphasis on corporeality, Strong's choice of metaphor is striking. He depicts assimilation as a process of absorption into the larger body politic, though this depiction is neither celebratory nor particularly benign. Seemingly uncomfortable with any degree of cultural diversity, Strong's goal is social and cultural homogeneity. Otherwise, he argues, the nation cannot function coherently on the global stage:

> With the . . . increasing facilities of intercourse, intelligence and influence are less centralized, and peoples become more homogenous; and the more nearly homogenous peoples are, the more do *numbers tell.* America is to have the great preponderance of numbers and of wealth, and by the logic of events will follow the scepter of controlling influence. (Strong 1885, 166; emphasis in original)

In other words, since centers of population and wealth are destined to shift from Europe to America, the United States needs to maintain as culturally homogenous an identity as possible in order to direct its national efforts toward global prominence. By sheer weight of numbers (wealth and population), America can dominate international politics and the global economy.

The importance that Strong places on numbers extends to other facets of his argument. For him, numbers are not just about size and power; they also affect the way we experience the world and our overall quality of life. "To preserve republican institutions requires a *higher average* intelligence and virtue among large populations than among small," he writes.

> The government of 3,000,000 people was a simple thing compared with the government of 50,000,000; and the government of 50,000,000 is a simple thing compared with that of 500,000,000. . . . In the latter there are multiplied relations whose harmony must be preserved. A mistake is farther reaching. It has, as it were, a longer leverage. (Strong 1885, 139; emphasis in original)

What Strong seems to be saying here is that quantitative and qualitative are not discrete paradigms. An increase in the size of any given population entails a simultaneous increase in the number of relations among the individuals who make up that population, and an increase in the number of relations means that society itself becomes more complicated and less predictable. Preexisting models for understanding society cannot sustain themselves when they are unable to account for the new conditions of possibility that a wider range of relations opens up.

Strong was keenly aware of these new conditions of possibility at the close of the nineteenth century. Furthermore, he was aware that new technologies, in particular the steam engine and mass media, were largely responsible for these new conditions of possibility because they were drawing the peoples of the world into closer contact with one another (and thereby multiplying relations). To Strong and others, the advent of these new technologies signaled a new era in human history: "The impetus given to inter-communication of every sort by the application of steam was the beginning of new life in the world" (Strong 1885, 2). Steam power and mass media were working in concert with Christianity to transform the globe and its inhabitants into a unified community: "Christianity is slowly binding the [human] race into a brotherhood. The press transforms the earth into an audience room; while the steam engine, so far as commerce is concerned, has annihilated, say, nine-tenths of space" (ibid., 69). The "new life" that Strong envisions involves a dramatic shift in relations across the board, brought about largely by emerging technologies of travel and communication. Disparate audiences think of themselves as a single community of readers, thanks to a press that can distribute the same information throughout the world simultaneously. And thanks to the message of Christianity, natives of one nation view citizens of foreign countries as brothers rather than rivals. People's relationship with space changes due to the steam engine, which shrinks the world of commerce by making it possible for a single product to appear in any market of the world. Even time itself alters, since people can experience and know more about the world than preceding generations; our lives, Strong suggests, "compress, it may be, years into hours" (ibid., 70).

Communication and the exchange of ideas hold special importance for Strong. After all, for a missionary, Christianity is first and foremost a message to be spread. Strong repeatedly links travel and commerce with communication. For example, he refers to steam ships as "steam communication" (Strong 1885, 4), and *Our Country* opens with a brief history of steam power and its effect on the spread of Western ideas. As noted above, Strong also never advocates an isolationist position. Instead, he promotes what he calls *intercourse.* For Strong, *intercourse* comprises both economic and travel routes, neither of which can be fully separated from the other, as well as the exchange of ideas. "Isolation leads to stagnation," he writes. "Intercourse quickens thought, feeling, action. . . . By bringing the country to the city, the inland cities to the seaboard, the seaports to each other, [steam] has multiplied many-fold every form of intercourse. . . . It has greatly complicated business" (ibid., 69). In this formula, the distances of time and space no longer separate products, people, or ideas; all exist within a web of *intercourse.*

Strong, however, clearly wants the web of intercourse to operate on his own terms, or at least he wants to exploit it for his own purposes. "The elbows of the nations touch," he says. "Isolation—the mother of barbarism—is becoming impossible" (Strong 1885, 14). But he goes on to equate "barbarism" with whatever is non-Christian: "The warm breath of the Nineteenth Century is breathing a living soul under [Asia's] ribs of death. The world is to be Christianized and civilized. . . . Commerce follows the missionary" (ibid., 14–15). In other words, Christianity, civilization, and material and economic progress go hand in hand. And as far as Strong is concerned, only America, with its Anglo-Saxon and Christian heritage and vast economic resources, can adequately embody these three forces and then transmit them throughout the world. In his concluding chapter, Strong assures his readers:

> Our plea is not America for America's sake; but America for the world's sake. . . . If I were a Christian African or Arab, I would look into the immediate future of the United States with intense and thrilling interest; for, as Professor Hoppin of Yale has said: "America Christianized means the *world* Christianized." (Strong 1885, 218)

The same ideology of world salvation pervades the writings of many influential historians and political theorists of the following three decades: Frederick Jackson Turner, Alfred Thayer Mahan, Brooks Adams, Henry Cabot Lodge, and the other men who have become, as Michael Hunt calls them, the "stock figures" in political histories of the era (Hunt 1987, 216, n. 28). Stock figures they may *seem*, but all of them exercised considerable influence over the administrations of Roosevelt, Taft, and Wilson. Mahan and Brooks, for example, often helped shape official U.S. foreign policy, and Turner enjoyed a close friendship with Wilson while also influencing Roosevelt's view of American history through his writing (LaFeber 1963, 80, 71).[3] Naturally, not all of these men (and all of them were, of course, men) agreed upon the exact course America's political leaders should steer for the nation. There were frequent and heated disagreements both between Republican and Democratic factions within the government and, sometimes, within the parties themselves, as the splintering of the Republican Party in 1912 demonstrated. Even Henry Cabot Lodge, whose support for extending U.S. influence abroad was as staunch as anyone's, spearheaded the campaign in the Senate to block ratification of the Treaty of Versailles in 1919–1920 because of his opposition to many of Wilson's aims, and as we see in the writings of W. E. B. Du Bois, the ideology of world salvation itself could transform dramatically when taken up by the writers of an alternative political history.

Nevertheless, what tied these thinkers together was the shared belief that they had entered a "new epoch" in American history and that this new epoch was the result of—and the continued opportunity for—America's greater involvement in world affairs (LaFeber 1963, 95–101).[4] Woodrow Wilson expressed both sentiments quite clearly. In his address to the Senate on July 10, 1919, Wilson proclaimed:

> America may be said to have just reached her majority as a world power. . . . Our isolation was ended twenty years ago [with the Spanish-American War of 1898]; and now fear of us is ended also, our counsel and association sought after and desired. There can be no question of our ceasing to be a world power. (Wilson 1989, 61: 435–36)

And as he continued to urge ratification of the Treaty of Versailles and entry into the League of Nations, he explained in a speech on September 10 of that same year: "We have managed in the process of civilization . . . to make a world that cannot be taken to pieces. The pieces are intricately dovetailed and fitted with one another, and unless you assemble them as you do, the intricate parts of a great machine, the pieces won't work" (ibid., 63: 155). Isolation for the United States has ended, Wilson says, and a return to an isolationist foreign policy would be tantamount to ripping one of the most important gears out of an intricate machine; the world simply will not work properly if America refuses to take part in its affairs.

Such sentiments are also expressed in the writings of Wilson's friend Frederick Jackson Turner. Like Josiah Strong, Turner is most famous today for the significance he placed on the closing of the American west, yet it is important to remember that, in its fullest articulation, Turner's frontier thesis finds its logical conclusion in overseas expansion. In his 1896 essay "The Problem of the West," Turner writes: "For nearly three hundred years, the dominant fact in American life has been expansion. With the settlement of the Pacific Coast and the occupation of the free lands, this movement has come to a check" (Turner 1896, 296). Note that Turner does not say that this movement has come to an *end*, merely to a "check." He goes on: "The demands for a vigorous foreign policy, for an interoceanic canal, for a revival of our power upon the seas, and for the extension of American influence to outlying islands and adjoining countries, are indications that the movement will continue" (ibid.).

In Turner's mind, however, this subsequent movement is not limited to—or even primarily about—people and colonization. He believes that economic routes of exchange must precede other forms of physical movement. In an essay entitled "The Significance of History," originally published in 1891, he writes that

> political relations, in a highly developed civilization, are inextricably connected with economic relations. . . . Reciprocity is a word that meets with increasing favor from all parties. But once fully afloat on the sea of worldwide economic interests, we shall soon develop political interests. (Turner 1968, 23)

In an attempt to refute the notion that the United States is or can remain isolated from the rest of the world, Turner points to America's existing interests in Samoa, Africa, and South America. Clearly, Turner's frontier thesis was never just about domestic concerns; it was a means of revealing the need for new frontiers and of convincing his fellow Americans to think beyond their national borders.

For Alfred Thayer Mahan, the sea formed such a new frontier, and this frontier was omnipresent and could never be permanently closed. Like Turner and Strong, Mahan is remembered primarily for only a small part of his larger argument, though that part exerted a profound influence over U.S. foreign policy and upon the course of American history. In his massive 1890 tome, *The Influence of Sea Power upon History, 1660–1783*, Mahan argued that naval power was the decisive factor in a nation's success in modern war and international politics. Those nations that controlled the major sea lanes and excluded other nations from their use, he explained, were historically the most successful at maintaining a stable economy because they were able to export goods safely abroad and at wielding power over other nations. In practical terms, Mahan's ideas helped convince the U.S. government to invest in building up the navy, a decision that resulted in the famous Great White Fleet as well as in quick naval victories during the Spanish-American War of 1898. Arguably, they also contributed to World Wars I and II, since Mahan's suggestions were followed both by the Germans and by the Japanese, whose own aggressive expansionism brought them into conflict with the United Kingdom and the United States, respectively.

Mahan's argument is somewhat more complex than such a brief summary might imply. For one thing, Mahan's conception of sea power is not unidirectional; he does not suggest that one powerful nation always exerts force over other less powerful nations. Instead, like Turner, he privileges the word *reciprocity* (the principle that exchange between two nations should be open and mutually beneficial). In his 1902 essay "Retrospect and Prospect," Mahan writes: "Reciprocity, increased freedom of movement, is the logical corollary of expansion, which is but increase of scope and power to act" (Mahan 1902, 20). For another thing, Mahan was not quite the glory-hungry saber rattler he is often portrayed as being; his extensive use of militaristic language is a rhetorical device in much the same way that Austin Phelps's or Josiah Strong's similarly militaristic metaphors are. Mahan's battlegrounds are predominantly economic ones, and he states that the primary objective of U.S. expansion should be "to invade *the markets* of the world" (ibid., 19; emphasis added). Even after describing his project as "largely a military history," Mahan avoids depicting the sea as a line of defense (Mahan 1890, 1). On the contrary, Mahan opens his first chapter of *The Influence of Sea Power upon History* with a description of the sea as a wide complex of routes of travel and economic exchange:

> The first and most obvious light in which the sea presents itself from the political and social point of view is that of a great highway; or better, perhaps, of a wide common, over

> which men may pass in all directions, but on which some well-worn paths show that controlling reasons have led them to choose certain lines of travel rather than others. These lines of travel are called trade routes; and the reasons which have determined them are to be sought in the history of the world. (Mahan 1890, 25)

What Mahan describes here sounds remarkably similar to Strong's web of "intercourse." Just as Strong does in *Our Country*, Mahan acknowledges that a multiplicity of relations exist among the nations of the world and that, although these relations seem to operate independently of one another, they intersect in various ways that ultimately produce an overall harmony.

By learning how to control this "wide common"—in a sense, by learning how to play the game of international trade and politics—America can ensure its own safety and prosperity. Elsewhere, in an 1890 essay entitled "The United States Looking Outward," Mahan argues that "to seek the welfare of the country" and "to affirm the importance of distant markets, and the relation to them of our own immense powers of production, implies logically the recognition of the link that joins the products and the markets, that is, the carrying trade" (Mahan 1890a, 817). In other words, maintaining national self-interest means acknowledging and strengthening ties with foreign markets. Such a "view of the relations of the United States to the world [is] radically distinct from the simple idea of self-sufficingness" (ibid.). Thus, Mahan rejects isolationist thinking as wholly untenable now that America has become a mature member of the community of nations. Indeed, Mahan not only agrees with Strong and Wilson that the United States has entered a new era in its history; he characterizes this perceived rupture with the past in far starker and more dramatic terms, comparing it to "the breach of continuity between the middle ages and modern times" (Mahan 1902, 21). The result is that "Whether they will or no, Americans must now begin to look outward" (Mahan 1890a, 822). Echoing Strong's advice to "digest or die," Mahan envisions no other alternative.

That all of the men discussed above were intensely interested in social history goes without saying, as does the fact that most of them were established intellectuals and professional scholars. Wilson and Turner earned PhDs at Johns Hopkins University; Henry Cabot Lodge did the same at Harvard. Both Lodge and Wilson were respected teachers before they entered politics; Mahan taught and served as an administrator at the U.S. Naval War College, and Turner enjoyed a long academic career first at the University of Wisconsin and later at Harvard. Perhaps never before in American history had so many accredited intellectuals exerted so direct and extensive an influence upon official policymakers. Even when, as in Mahan's case, the historical research they undertook was not always particularly reliable, their work was taken seriously by powerful people, and Wilson, of course, remains the only U.S. president to date to have completed a research doctorate. Despite their credentials and sometimes considerable intellectual skills, however, all of them were white men who bought wholeheartedly into what Walter LaFeber and Michael Hunt call the ideology of "Anglo-Saxonism," the belief in the superiority of English-speaking people's civilization and in the duty of English speakers to protect that civilization through the establishment of racial hierarchies that could control other peoples at home and abroad (LaFeber 1963, 99–100; Hunt 1987, 77–91). Consequently, it would be easy to assume that the entire intellectual trajectory outlined above, including the basic rhetoric of world salvation, was similarly committed to that same ideology. But such was not the case. The concept of world-salvation was too powerful not to have a life of its own, and it could be—and was—picked up and used purposively for alternative objectives by a very different type of intellectual.

W. E. B. Du Bois's own standing as an intellectual and scholar was certainly equal to that of any of the other writers discussed so far. Du Bois, too, had earned his PhD from Harvard in 1895, becoming the first African American to do so, and he began teaching at Atlanta University two years later. Over the next decade, Du Bois's writings, including *The Souls of Black Folk* (1903), and political activism, including his involvement in the founding of the NAACP in 1909, would make him one of the foremost black intellectuals of his era. His influence upon U.S. policy may never have been as direct, as consistent, or as extensive as that of his white counterparts, but his interest in and careful examination of global politics was just as strong. And that facet of his work only intensified as he became more and more interested in Pan-Africanism and the role that African Americans could play in that movement.

Du Bois's involvement in the Pan-African movement would lead him in turn to interrogate the ideology of Anglo-Saxonism and the relationship between global capitalism and imperialism. His fullest and most satisfying investigation into these questions probably remains his 1920 work *Darkwater: Voices from within the Veil.* In "The Souls of White Folk," the second chapter of *Darkwater*, Du Bois argues that the colonization of nonwhite territories was implicit in the logic of global capitalism and that World War I was the logical conclusion of the European scramble for those non-white territories. Du Bois writes: "The world market most wildly and desperately sought today is the market where labor is cheapest and most helpless and profit is most abundant. This labor is kept cheap and helpless because the white world despises 'darkies' " (Du Bois 1969, 48). Even more importantly, Du Bois claims, it is precisely this increased contact between whites and nonwhites and the (for whites) economic and political necessity of establishing racial hierarchies to control such contact that gives "modern days" their "newness" (ibid., 42–43).[5] Thus, despite the fact that Du Bois and Josiah Strong might appear irreconcilably at odds, especially in terms of their differing attitudes toward race, Du Bois in fact shares Strong's recognition that there is "new life in the world." Du Bois's vision of this "new life" is far bleaker, though, because he knows it is founded upon the global institutionalization of racism. That is why he rejects Wilson's optimistic pronouncements that America had reached "her majority as a world power" and that "fear of [America had] ended also." "It is curious," he writes in what could be a direct response to Wilson, "to see America, the United States, looking on herself, first, as a sort of natural peacemaker, then as a moral protagonist in this terrible time. No nation is less fitted for this role" (ibid., 50). Far from being a mediator, the United States represented the ultimate failure of democracy, since it had been guilty of institutionalizing racism within in its own borders, not only in far-off colonies.

Darkwater, however, is not Du Bois's only meditation on these problems. He had already conducted a trial run for that work, as it were, in his much shorter but equally trenchant essay "The African Roots of the War," published five years earlier in the May 1915 issue of *Atlantic Monthly.* The essay's central argument is much the same as the one in "The Souls of White Folk": World War I is the direct result of economic competition among the European powers in Africa (i.e., the so-called "scramble for Africa"). Here is how Du Bois words it:

> The present world war is, then, the result of jealousies engendered by the recent rise of armed national associations of labor

> and capital whose aim is the exploitation of the wealth of the world mainly outside the European circle of nations. These associations, grown jealous and suspicious at the division of the spoils of trade-empire, are fighting to enlarge their respective shares; they look for expansion, not in Europe but in Asia, and particularly in Africa. (Du Bois 1995, 647)

What distinguishes "The African Roots of the War" from *Darkwater* is its more optimistic outlook. In the earlier essay, Du Bois acknowledges more fully the potential for resistance that globalization affords oppressed peoples. In order to reach this optimistic conclusion, Du Bois employs not only the rhetoric but also the very phrase *world-salvation* that Austin Phelps used to introduce Strong's *Our Country* thirty years earlier, demonstrating just how powerful and pervasive that rhetoric truly was. Furthermore, in "The African Roots of the War," Du Bois adopts Wilsonian logic and language but only in order to turn Wilson's argument on its head. To begin with, Du Bois accepts completely the supposition that the sovereignty of the nation state is the building block of the international community and that all national communities possess the inviolable right to self-determination. In fact, Du Bois goes a step further and claims that only through belonging to a sovereign nation-state, respected by the rest of the community of nations, can an individual or a people hope to achieve any measure of wealth, respectability, or power in the twentieth century. He observes that the "national bond is no mere sentimental patriotism, loyalty, or ancestor-worship. It is the increased wealth, power, and luxury for all classes on a scale the world never saw before" (Du Bois 1995, 645). Then, making the same appeal to self-determination that white nationalists in, say, Poland or Czechoslovakia were making, Du Bois argues that the privileges of nationhood should be extended to Africa: "The principle of home rule must extend to groups, nations, and races. The ruling of one people for another people's whim or gain must stop" (ibid., 649). Du Bois's appeal would go unheeded, naturally. No one at the Peace of Paris would have taken seriously the suggestion that imperialism in Africa and Asia should end. The fact that France and Britain divided the spoils of the German and Ottoman empires among themselves, even after having informally promised home rule to the Arabs during their insurrection against the Ottomans, lends much credence to Du Bois's claim that the war was about imperial rivalries after all.

Du Bois also shares Wilson's interest in the act of remapping. Whereas Wilson would work to remap the borders of Europe during 1919–1920, Du Bois offers a conceptual remapping of the entire globe in 1915, one that places the continent of Africa at the center of all economic, cultural, and political interests. Quoting the Roman writer Pliny, Du Bois opens his essay with a Latin phrase: *semper novi quid ex Africa* ("everything new always comes out of Africa"). At first, he is referring to the belief that the crucial developments in human history emerged out of Africa, but it becomes clear that Du Bois believes the truth of the quotation continues to obtain. He writes:

> Particularly to-day most men assume that Africa lies far afield from the centres of our burning social problems. . . . In the Dark Continent are hidden the roots, not simply of war to-day but of the menace of wars to-morrow. . . . Nearly every human empire that has arisen in the world, material and spiritual, has found some of its greatest crises on this continent. (Du Bois 1995, 642)

And he continues more emphatically: "Africa is the Land of the Twentieth Century" (Du Bois 1995, 646). What Du Bois means is partly that the vast economic resources of Africa (gold, diamonds, cocoa, rubber, ivory, etc.) offer the rest of the world "boundless chances" to increase its wealth and raise its standard of living (ibid.). In a sense, Du Bois echoes Strong's arguments about the seemingly boundless resources of the American west and then inverts them geographically and racially. According to him, the real center of human civilization is Africa—not just because human civilization began there but because, as Du Bois suggests, Africa can continue to sustain the global economy indefinitely.

By the end of the essay, however, when Du Bois repeats the Latin quotation he opened with, it is apparent that something else new can "come out of Africa," and that new thing is the empowerment of non-white peoples. Perhaps unsurprisingly for Du Bois, this empowerment comes about through a combination of modernization and education. Along with regaining home rule and control over African resources, he writes, "we must train native races in modern civilization. . . . Modern methods of educating children, honestly and effectively applied, would make modern, civilized nations out of the vast majority of human beings on earth to-day." (Du Bois 1995, 649). And who does Du

Bois expect to undertake this training? He asks and then answers that question himself:

> In this great work who can help us? In the Orient, the awakened Japanese and the awakening leaders of New China; in India and Egypt, the young men trained in Europe and European ideals, who now form the stuff that Revolution is born of. But in Africa? Who better than the twenty-five million grandchildren of the European slave trade, spread through the Americas, and now writhing desperately for freedom and a place in the world? And of these millions first of all the ten million black folk of the United States, now a problem, then a *world-salvation* (Du Bois 1995, 650; emphasis added)

Although Du Bois's solution is perfectly clear, the way he presents it is particularly adroit. At the most basic level, he expects his fellow African Americans to take up his call and teach their African comrades how to adapt themselves to modernization. Du Bois's commitment to modernization—and by extension to Westernization—is striking. Much like Strong and Mahan, Du Bois seems to think that there is no alternative to modernization; the conditions of possibility demand it.[6] Thus, he refers to the children of elite Egyptian and Indian families, who were sent to Oxford and Cambridge to learn how to run their own countries based on European models of governance and bureaucracy, and he refers to the governments of Japan and China, which were similarly attempting to modernize. American blacks, the descendants of Africans sold into slavery, are already Westernized, Du Bois points out, and so they should be able to pass that knowledge on to Africans who have not yet modernized. It is difficult not to be reminded of Du Bois's famous "Talented Tenth" here. Just as the most highly educated African Americans (the top 10 percent of their race) bear a duty to lead the rest of the African American community in their struggle for civil rights, African Americans in general bear a duty to lead the peoples of Africa in their struggle for independence. In a sense, then, Du Bois seems to imply that African Americans make up the "Talented Tenth" of the entire nonwhite world.

But exactly how are African Americans supposed to lead their African comrades, especially when Du Bois concedes that they are themselves still "writhing desperately" for their own civil rights and their own "place in the world"? To answer that question, we must turn finally to Du Bois's use of the term *world-salvation.* I suggest that Du Bois's appropriation of this highly charged rhetoric is entirely purposeful. For one thing, he clearly picks up on the missionary work that writers such as Austin Phelps and Josiah Strong had in mind when they talked about *world-salvation.* When Du Bois asks his fellow African Americans to take up the responsibility of educating Africans, he has two methods of education in mind: first, teaching by example, by achieving their own freedom and self-sufficiency; second, teaching by serving as "missionaries" to Africa. Instead of spreading Anglo-Saxon values, paving the way for American economic expansion, or even preaching Christianity per se, Du Bois's missionaries will work towards the goal of achieving Pan-Africanism. Like Strong's *Our Country*, Du Bois's essay contains echoes of Winthrop's "Model of Christian Charity," but both Strong and Du Bois preach a more interventionist message.

Finally, Du Bois also picks up on Strong's goal of reshaping the world, and for Du Bois, world-salvation achieves its transformative power precisely because it embraces and celebrates multidirectional exchange. Here, of course, he falls very much in line with Strong, Mahan, and Wilson. While some of them undoubtedly wanted to reshape the world in the image of America rather than the other way around, all of them recognized that the burgeoning multiplicity of relations in America's new global context made isolation and self-absorption impossible. What distinguishes Du Bois from the other writers, however, is the paramount importance he places on this back-and-forth exchange. For it is only through their attempt to reshape Africa that African Americans can find their "place in the world." That is to say, Du Bois acknowledges that "now" African Americans are simply "a problem," a promise unfulfilled; they cease to be a problem when they become "a world-salvation." Du Bois pointedly refuses to supply a midpoint between "problem" and "world-salvation" because one status ends when and where the other begins. Thus, the act of transforming and empowering others is simultaneously an act of self-transformation and self-empowerment.

Is Du Bois's view of America's role in the world so very different from the one Strong, Wilson, Turner, and Mahan espoused? To some extent, it is. Where Strong advocates assimilation as the solution to America's social problems, Du Bois sees nothing but obstacles to its success. Where Turner and Mahan base their arguments about reciprocity on the assumption that Americans are free to move in any direction,

Du Bois knows that African Americans lack many basic kinds of freedom. And where Wilson optimistically believes that, as an American, he is in contact—and can connect—with all the peoples of the world, Du Bois more skeptically emphasizes the seemingly impassable gulf that already separates white and black Americans. At the same time, however, Du Bois argues that African Americans are indeed capable of representing all of Africa. If Du Bois honestly believes that proposition, then he also might have to accept on behalf of African Americans the role of mediator among the various ethnicities of Africa, as the recent history of Rwanda, for example, drives home. And if Du Bois thinks of African Americans as the "Talented Tenth" of all nonwhite peoples or at least of the descendents of black Africans, then he might also be willing to characterize African Americans as the mediators of the nonwhite world. If so, then what we find in Du Bois's writing is, in a sense, a form of *African* American exceptionalism. What ultimately aligns Du Bois with Strong and the other writers, therefore, is that all of them knew that being American or African American takes on meaning only when understood within a global context.

Notes

1. LaFeber's volume contains one of the first studies of the connection between the ideology of official U.S. foreign policy and the rhetoric of American public discourse. In his second chapter ("The Intellectual Formulation"), LaFeber subjects several of the same figures I am examining here to brief but thoughtful analysis. LaFeber does not, however, examine the writings of Du Bois or consider the multidirectional capacities of the ideology and rhetoric he explores.

2. The formation of the Salvation Army by Edwin Booth in 1865 best exemplifies the militaristic values espoused by Protestant Christians in the mid- and late-nineteenth century. The lyrics for the song most frequently associated with the Salvation Army, "Onward, Christian Soldiers," which metaphorically depicts Christian service as war, were written by Sabine Baring-Gould the preceding year.

3. In some of his academic writings, Wilson responds directly to Turner's ideas and often speaks admiringly of Turner as a fellow historian.

4. This is not to say that what they believed was necessarily true. Some scholars, including Michael Hunt and Amy Kaplan, have made the case that the foreign policies and cultural politics of the era display continuity with preceding periods. See especially Kaplan. Still, I would argue that this belief on the part of Wilson, Strong, and their contemporaries was enough to influence their actions and, more significantly, the rhetoric of their public discourse.

5. This idea is central to Hunt's and LaFeber's discussion of Anglo-Saxonism.

6. Spivak makes a similarly pragmatic claim in "Poststructuralism, Marginality, Postcoloniality and Value." The paradoxical problem of postcolonial identity is to take part in a narrative that has been forced upon you and for which you have no adequate historical point of reference.

Works Cited

Du Bois, W. E. B. 1969. *Darkwater: Voices from within the veil.* New York: Schocken.

———. 1995. The African roots of the war. In *W. E. B. Du Bois: A reader*, ed. David Levering Lewis. New York: Henry Holt.

———. 1996. *The soul of black folks.* New York: Penguin.

Hunt, Michael. 1987. *Ideology and U.S. foreign policy.* New Haven: Yale University Press.

Kaplan, Amy. 2002. *The anarchy of empire in the making of U.S. culture.* Cambridge: Harvard University Press.

LaFeber, Walter. 1963. *The new empire: An interpretation of American expansion, 1869–1898.* Ithaca: Cornell University Press.

Mahan, Alfred Thayer. 1890. *The influence of sea power upon history, 1660–1783.* Boston: Little, Brown.

———. 1890a. The United States looking outward. *Atlantic Monthly*, December, 816–24.

———. 1902. Retrospect and prospect. In *Retrospect and prospect: Studies in international relations naval and political.* Boston: Little, Brown.

Spivak, Gayatri Chakravorty. 1990. Poststructuralism, marginality, postcoloniality, and value. In *Literary theory today*, ed. Peter Collier and Helga Geyer-Ryan. Ithaca: Cornell University Press.

Strong, Josiah. 1885. *Our country: Its possible future and its present crisis.* New York: Baker and Taylor.

———. 1893. *The new era or the coming kingdom.* New York: Baker and Taylor.

———. 1900. *Expansion under new world conditions.* New York: Baker and Taylor.

Turner, Frederick Jackson. 1896. The problem of the West. *Atlantic Monthly*, September: 289–97.

———. 1968. The significance of history. In *Frontier and section: Selected essays of Frederick Jackson Turner*, ed. Ray Allen Billington. Englewood Cliffs, NJ: Prentice-Hall.

Wilson, Woodrow. 1989. *The papers of Woodrow Wilson.* Ed. Arthur S. Link et al. Vols. 61, 63. Princeton: Princeton University Press.

7

American Exceptionalism and Immigration Debates in the Modern United States

Carl J. Bon Tempo

Writing in the *Washington Post* as the debate over immigration policy heated up in the spring of 2006, political commentator Fareed Zakaria asserted: "Compared with every other country in the world, America does immigration superbly. Do we really want to junk that for the French approach?" Zakaria feared that the United States might adopt a European-style temporary worker program that admitted newcomers with needed skills but offered them no path to citizenship or permanent residence. In Europe, such programs had created a restive population of guest workers alienated from their host societies. Instead of the "French approach," Zakaria urged Americans to continue what he believed was a uniquely American approach to immigration that centered on integrating newcomers into society.

The main contention underlying Zakaria's analysis—that the United States' immigration policy was both superb and singular—tapped into a deep historical vein, that of American exceptionalism. One need only look at Emma Lazarus's inscription on the Statue of Liberty for evidence of exceptionalism's deep hold in immigration affairs. The opening lines—"Not like the brazen giant of Greek fame"—distinguish the United States from the rest of the world, a theme that continues with the invocation "Keep ancient lands, your storied pomp!" Instead, Lazurus invites newcomers to escape the troubles of their old lands—political repression and material privation—and come to the "golden door" that promises a new beginning.

American exceptionalism, as Zakaria's comments indicate and the Statue of Liberty symbolizes, has proved an especially potent force in debates about immigration to the United States, never more so than in two key periods in American immigration history. The first moment occurred in 1965, when a bipartisan coalition of immigration advocates, inspired by the African American civil rights movement and concerned about America's standing in the cold war, succeeded in replacing the national origins quota immigration system with procedures that awarded visas on a first come, first served basis without regard to an immigrant's national origins. The 1965 reforms had unintended consequences—mainly, an upsurge in annual immigrant arrivals and a shift in their countries of origins—that over the next four decades created a diverse and multicultural America. The backlash against that multicultural society, as well as the "War on Terror," set the stage for the rigorous immigration debates of 2006, which focused on border security and the status of illegal aliens living in the United States.

Exceptionalist thinking united these two episodes even as the debates tackled very different policy issues and sprang from quite different political, foreign policy, and cultural contexts. Both immigration advocates (called "liberalizers") and immigration opponents (referred to as "restrictionists") endorsed a historical narrative that emphasized the United States' exceptional place in the world. Both camps agreed that the country's political values—equality, liberty, freedom—and its democratic and republican political institutions made the United States unique. Likewise, restrictionists and liberalizers believed the nation's singularity derived from capitalist, free-market economic development that produced an unrivaled bounty shared by large numbers of Americans. Yet, these two important moments also show that exceptionalist rhetoric was by no means static. In 1965, exceptionalism revolved more around political values and traditions—specifically, professions of democracy, individual rights, and freedom, all of which gained added power because of the cold war and the civil rights movement's emphasis on black political rights—while economic concerns were of secondary status. In 2006, exceptionalist thinking took on a different caste. It focused on the United States' unrivaled economic position, although questions emerged as to whether all Americans could still share in that unsurpassed wealth. Just as important, exceptionalism emerged with a distinct racial and ethno-national tinge that decried the supposed debasement of a white, European-based American culture. Such thinking recalled the seemingly vanquished position of immigration opponents of the first six decades of the twentieth century.

These two immigration debates also suggest the importance of a signal distinction that lies at the center of exceptionalism. When it came to the role of immigrants in American society, restrictionists believed immigrants endangered America's exceptional qualities, while liberalizers believed newcomers promoted and protected the nation's unique political and economic achievements. In the former conceptualization, exceptionalism is fundamentally exclusive and defensive, while in the latter it is fundamentally inclusive. This key difference leads to a final proposition: the value and necessity of distinguishing between these two brands of exceptionalism, or what—borrowing from the work of historian Gordon Wood—can be called "hard" and "soft" exceptionalism.

Defining American Exceptionalism

American exceptionalism is the product of both historical figures and scholars of the American past, making it both history and historiography. The Puritan John Winthrop and President Woodrow Wilson embraced exceptionalism, as did chroniclers of American history, most importantly Alexis de Tocqueville, Frederick Jackson Turner, Louis Hartz, and David Potter. Exceptionalism, of course, was, and is, not the sole province of political leaders and scholars; in the twentieth century, immigrants, military veterans, and working class Americans also enthusiastically endorsed exceptionalism, giving it a genuinely popular base of support. All of this is to say that exceptionalism has a deep and long history in American politics, culture, and intellectual life.

Despite this diversity of advocates—and their distinctive characterizations of exceptionalism—it is nonetheless possible to define some of American exceptionalism's basic principles. First, exceptionalist thinking holds that the United States has been doubly blessed geographically, with abundant natural resources and with removal from the political and class conflicts of Europe. This geographical advantage helped produce the second tenet of exceptionalist thinking: America possesses the most developed and advanced political and economic systems in the world. American exceptionalists believe that constitutional government, political liberty and individual rights, and democracy define the United States' political experience, while market capitalism and economic opportunity are central to the nation's economic life and power. Third, the United States is particularly and especially virtuous and innocent, qualities that arise from those economic and political systems that produced a society marred neither by class conflict nor an aristocracy. In some versions of exceptionalist thought, these characteristics are seen as proof of divine blessing. Fourth, the United States has a duty and responsibility to bring these political and economic institutions and ideals to the less advanced and pitiable world; the values and ideals that rest at the foundation of exceptionalism, then, have transformative and redemptive potential. These principles consistently found their way into debates about immigration in the decades after 1965, mainly because they proved to be effective and useful political tools for immigration advocates and opponents to fight and win policy battles over the arrival of newcomers. This is not to say that participants in immigration affairs only cynically professed their exceptionalist beliefs to win their policy agendas, but it is to recognize that exceptionalism was both deeply held and utilitarian.

"The Beacon Light of Mankind": Exceptionalism and Immigration Reform in 1965

The modern era in American immigration history began in 1965 after a bipartisan collection of congressional immigration advocates, with the support of President Lyndon Johnson, eliminated the national origins quota immigration system that had governed immigration to the United States since the 1920s. That system banned immigration from Asia and Africa, and it established strict annual quotas on immigrants from Europe that privileged the admission of northwestern Europeans and discriminated against southern, eastern, and central Europeans. Western hemisphere immigrants were exempt from the quota immigration system. Proponents of the national origins quota immigration system in the 1920s subscribed to exceptionalist principles but saw them in highly racial and ethno-national terms. For these supporters of restrictive immigration laws in the 1920s, the United States' unique political and economic gifts were an exclusive product of northwestern Europeans. This essential racial and ethnic bias, of course, was the foundation of their immigration system.

The post-1965 immigration law proved quite a departure. Instead of country quotas, the new system set up two large annual quotas, one for the Eastern Hemisphere and the other for the Western Hemisphere. The hemispheric caps were of such a size that post-1965 immigrant entry would, according to the law's proponents, not exceed pre-1965 levels of immigrant entry. This prediction ultimately proved false for two reasons. First, loopholes in the 1965 law allowed relatives of American citizens to enter without counting against the caps. Second, as Europe fully recovered from the ravages of war in the 1960s, European immigrants felt less of a pull to the United States, opening up more spaces for non-Europeans under the Eastern Hemisphere quota. Immigrants from both hemispheres were admitted on a first come, first served basis and under a series of preferences that emphasized family reunification and employment skills.

Opponents of the national origins system long had pushed for many of these reforms, but they won them only in the mid-1960s because of a confluence of factors. First, liberal Democrats, the heart of the reform movement, held massive congressional majorities in 1965, the result of President Johnson's sweeping victory in the previous year's presidential election. Second, more and more Americans by the mid-1960s rejected the racist and discriminatory assumptions that lay behind national origins theory, mainly that only persons of certain ethnicities and nationalities could make good Americans, and instead embraced a nascent form of rights consciousness. On this score, immigration reform advocates capitalized on the energy of the African American civil rights movement that asserted that individuals ought to be judged on their merits, accomplishments, and traits rather than on the color of their skin or racial and ethnic ancestry. Finally, cold war foreign policy imperatives led to the destruction of the national origins immigration system. Opponents of national origins argued that in order for the United States to maintain its cold war alliances and its position as an exemplar of democracy and individual rights (in contrast to Soviet totalitarianism), immigration laws had to be cleansed of any evidence of racial or ethno-national discrimination (Tichenor 2002, 196–218).

Opponents of these changes to American immigration affairs—and defenders of the national origins system—couched their objections in exceptionalist rhetoric, just as their predecessors of the 1920s had. Nobody was more convincing than Democratic senator John McClellan of Arkansas. "America cannot survive as the great Nation she is today if we ever so modify and change our immigration policy so as not to protect what we have developed, produced, and now possess" (U.S. Congress 1965, 24555–56), harrumphed McClellan. McClellan continued:

> The Greatness of America just did not happen. This nation achieved its greatness by dedication to the principles of self-government, to hard work, and a strong sense of nationalism. And I say that liberalizing our present immigration policy will only tend to dilute rather than to augment our strength. (U.S. Congress 1965, 24555–6)

McClellan's thinking was laced with exceptionalist rhetoric. The United States' commitment to "self-government"—or as Democratic representative Durwood Hall of Texas reminded his colleagues, "the oldest constitutional republic in the history of known man" (U.S. Congress 1965, 21775)—testified to the nation's unique political identity. Likewise, the United States emerged as a place of inimitable economic blessings. Hall endorsed this premise when he made clear his opposition to immigrant entry because it would "literally skim the cream off the very countries that desperately need the new skills to emerge from the dark ages" (ibid.). Such an assertion made clear that the United States was a marvel of economic modernity and advancement, while the rest of the world muddled along in darkness. For restrictionists, then, all of these unique political and economic achievements signified national virtue and purity that only the national origins quota immigration system might guard.

Racial and ethnonational politics and a defense of "whiteness" very much underlay restrictionists' exceptionalism in 1965. Hall's comments about "the cream" and the "dark ages" unwittingly testified to these concerns. Other restrictionists were less obtuse. Conservative southern white politicians vigorously defended national origins principles—sixteen of the eighteen votes against immigration reform in the Senate came from southerners—which they saw as an ideological partner to a regime of white superiority at home. In defending national origins and in highlighting the United States' exceptional qualities, restrictionists defended a vision of a white and Eurocentric America. Senator Sam Ervin, a Democrat from North Carolina, let slip his discomfort with the possible arrival of people of color under a new immigration system. Ervin lauded Greek immigrants, noting that "Democracy made its first appearance in Greece," and then compared Greek immigrants to potential immigrants from the Congo. "A reporter in the American press," Ervin began,

> who had gone over and appraised the readiness of the Congolese people for self government, wrote back that the people said "We are going to get freedom and democracy. . . . We do not know whether it comes in packages or not, and whether we ought to go to the post office of the express company to get our package of freedom and democracy" (U.S. Senate 1965, 383)

Ervin concluded the story with a question: "Now, you certainly agree with me that people that have that idea of freedom and democracy are not quite as ready to be assimilated into American life as people who come from a civilized nation like Greece or France or England or any other older nations" (U.S. Senate 1965, 383, 389). The message was clear: the arrival of immigrants of color would only debase the United States' exceptional political qualities.

In 1965, exceptionalist thinking was even more prominent among those, especially liberal Democrats, fighting for reform of immigration law. Senator Ted Kennedy, who led the reform effort, linked American greatness with the arrival of immigrants: "Immigration, more than anything else, has supplied America with the human strength that is the core of its greatness. Let us keep the strength renewing" (U.S. Congress 1965, 24229). Like their opponents, liberalizers focused on America's exceptional political system. Democratic senator John Pastore of Rhode Island described the United States as "the beacon light of mankind . . . the hope and envy of the world . . . the bastion of freedom and liberty in an imperiled world today" (ibid., 24563). These assertions of virtue and singularity cannot be separated from the cold war and American foreign policies. Indeed, American diplomatic efforts in the so-called third world throughout this period emphasized these very traits and the attractiveness of the U.S. political system. In this way, immigration liberalizers' pronouncements of the exceptional nature of American politics only reinforced and called attention to the benefits immigration reform would have for the American side in the cold war contest.

Senator Hiram Fong, a Republican from Hawaii, echoed Pastore, but explicitly addressed the issue of race and nationality:

> Our nation is the great pilot demonstration of the most influential principles and ideals in history. Our tenets of equality irrespective of race, creed, or color have inspired freedom-loving people everywhere to look to America as a beacon in their struggle to win freedom and independence. (U.S. Congress 1965, 24468)

Fong's counterpart in the House, Leonard Farbstein, a Democrat from New York, held that immigration reform was motivated by "the belief that men are to be judged on their own merit, as individuals—and not on the basis of their racial ancestry, their skin color, their religion, or their place of origin" (U.S. Congress 1965, 21784). According to Fong and Farbstein, only by eradicating national origins quotas from immigration law could the United States live up to its political values and institutions and protect its exceptional qualities. These comments were especially telling, moreover, because they explicitly rejected the racial and ethno-national overtones present in the exceptionalism of Senator Ervin and Representative Hall. Instead, Fong and his allies construed American exceptionalism "irrespective of race, creed, or color" and their achievement in 1965—the destruction of the national origins system—must be seen as a rejection of the exceptionalist creed offered by supporters of national origins since the early twentieth century.

Supporters of immigration reform also trafficked in the economic dimensions of exceptionalism, but less frequently than the political. Most often, this occurred with a bland endorsement of American economic power, such as Congressman Manny Celler's exaltation: "We have become a great nation. We have the greatest gross national product of any nation that ever existed" (U.S. Congress 1965, 21757). Others avoided such platitudes. Representative Roman Pucinski of Illinois argued that American economic development demonstrated the United States' exceptional nature. Pucinski traced American economic strength to a particular decision: "[R]ather than establish a rigid class structure in this new country, [Americans] set about finding means to work together"

(U.S. Congress 1965, 21796). Pucinski embraced several exceptionalist tenets, the most important of which was that the United States had escaped the feudalism and destructive class rivalries of Europe to build the most powerful economy on earth via the peculiarly American brand of liberal capitalism that stressed cooperation among economic actors. Pucinski's historical interpretation of the American economy was excessively rosy—after all, labor and management relations since the late nineteenth century had been anything but cooperative—but such faults did not blunt the exceptionalist thinking at its heart.

"We Will Drift into Third World Status": Exceptionalism and Illegal Immigrants in 2006

Immigration affairs in 2006 looked quite different than they had forty years earlier. First, and most important, the 1965 reforms ushered in a new era in immigration history. Loopholes in the law (especially those that permitted family members of U.S. citizens to enter without counting against the annual caps) meant that the total number of immigrants entering annually far exceeded the caps established in 1965, producing a surge in newcomers. In the 1990s, for example, nine million immigrants entered, compared with 4.5 million in the 1970s. Moreover, immigrants after 1965 came increasingly from Central America and Asia. By the 1990s, the most newcomers arrived, in descending order, from Mexico, the Philippines, the former Soviet Union, China, and India. This demographic revolution created a more racially, ethnically, and culturally diverse United States. The multicultural America that emerged after 1965 heartened most immigration advocates, but also produced by the 1990s the most vigorous and virulent anti-newcomer movement since the 1920s (U.S. Immigration 2002, 18, 271; Reimers 1998).

These larger changes in immigration patterns served as an important backdrop to, rather than centerpiece of, the 2006 immigration debates. Instead, illegal immigration and border security took center stage in 2006. In the decades after 1965, illegal immigration emerged as an important issue, both locally and nationally. By 2001, estimates held that anywhere between five and eleven million immigrants lived in the United States illegally. The focus on illegal immigrants gave the debates a more populist—and popular—tone than the elite-driven discussions of the mid-1960s, which were strikingly removed from popular political pressures. Moreover, unlike in 1965, when immigration advocates drove and framed the debate, restrictionists were the driving forces behind newcomer politics in 2006. The restrictionist bloc was geographically diverse—centered in the southwest and mountain west, but also strong in states, such as Virginia, that had seen their immigrant populations soar over the previous two decades—and bipartisan, though its most vocal members came from conservative Republican circles. The liberalizer camp had similar diversity, managing to unite rivals such as Republican Senator John McCain of Arizona, Senator Ted Kennedy, and President George W. Bush.

Republicans in the House of Representatives wanted a more aggressive and punitive approach toward illegal immigrants that stressed stricter border security, while President Bush and his allies in the Senate preferred a combination of border security initiatives and mechanisms that would provide illegal aliens with a path toward permanent residence and citizenship. This latter issue proved a major sticking point, and it ultimately doomed comprehensive immigration reform in 2006, much to the delight of restrictionists who vehemently opposed what they called the liberalizers' "amnesty" plan for undocumented aliens. Congress instead passed, and the president signed, a border security measure that ordered construction of a large fence along the Mexico–United States border. These restrictionist victories—the passage of border security legislation and the defeat of efforts to provide illegal immigrants a path toward legal residence—emerged only after months of contentious discussions fired by the approaching midterm elections in which immigration emerged as an important issue. The immigration issue reappeared briefly in 2007, but centrists who crafted compromise legislation could not satisfy immigration advocates and opponents who staked out more intractable positions. Most observers believed by summer 2007 that only the arrival of a new president and new Congress in January 2009 might possibly lead to a new immigration law (Weisman 2006).

Restrictionists and liberalizers in 2006 trumpeted the exceptional nature of America's political system with the usual paeans to the uniqueness of American democracy, liberty, and the protection of equal rights, yet such comments had a perfunctory quality to them (Bush 2008). Instead, exceptionalism—especially for restrictionists—underlay discussions of the United States as a "nation of laws." This formulation grew out of restrictionist objections to so-called amnesty provisions that would have opened a path for illegal immigrants to become citizens. Believing this policy would only reward those who had broken the law by entering illegally, restrictionists launched blistering attacks. Republican congressman John Carter of Texas asked: "Do we really want these law-breakers as new citizens of our great Nation [?]" (U.S. Congress 2006, H5112). Or, as Congressman Steven King, an Iowa Republican, insisted, "We have to enforce laws here in America, and if we don't do that, we won't forever be America" (ibid., H5024). For Carter and King, the amnesty plan was a direct affront to a political and legal system based upon the rule of law, which helped make the nation great. Thus, the amnesty program would only puncture and deflate America's exceptional qualities.

Why this transformation in political exceptionalism? First, and foremost, restrictionists molded exceptionalist principles to fit the policy moment. In other words, stressing that newcomers might damage American legal traditions made sense precisely because the issue under debate was *illegal* immigration. Second, changes in the geopolitical environment since 1965 help explain the absence of professions of the exceptionalist nature of American democracy and liberty. In 1965, the cold war made such statements ordinary, and even necessary, if the United States was going to triumph over Soviet communism and authoritarianism. In 2006, not even the "War on Terror" could revive that same exceptionalist rhetoric, in large part because the "War on Terror" lacked the clear bipolar ideological and political formulation of the cold war.

Strains of economic exceptionalism were much more powerful and omnipresent in the 2006 debates, embraced by both liberalizers and restrictionists. Both groups contended that a powerful economy that spread its wealth to all Americans was a central part of the nation's identity and proof of the United States' unique destiny. But if Americans were still "the People of Plenty," to use the historian David Potter's phrase, the two sides could not agree on the character of that success or whether it was perishing or flourishing. The immigrant advocate and journalist Ruben Navarrette was certain that Americans had displayed an unparalleled work ethic in the past, but he believed that recent immigrants—legal and illegal—were the best exemplars of that work ethic in contemporary America. By harvesting peaches, digging ditches, and working in the meat, poultry, and fish industries, immigrant labor not only kept Americans well fed and well housed but created and perpetuated the nation's historical exceptional material abundance. Immigrants, in other words, kept this principle of exceptionalism alive and well.

For the television commentator and best-selling author Lou Dobbs, who emerged in 2006 as an important restrictionist voice, the situation was not so sanguine. Dobbs thoroughly embraced American exceptionalism, asserting: "Americans are still the richest—in every sense of the word—people on Earth, with more guaranteed freedoms, more wealth, and more opportunity than anywhere on the planet" (Dobbs 2006, 11). Dobbs believed that the Declaration of Independence, the Constitution, and the Bill of Rights were the foundations of a singular American democracy and he repeatedly described the Founding Fathers as unmatched political minds blessed with foresight. Dobbs's exceptionalism, though, found its strongest expression in his interpretation of America's economic history and, specifically, the development of the "middle class." (Dobbs defined the "middle class" in contemporary America as the middle three quintiles of the income structure, those families earning between $26,000 and $150,000 annually; his definition of "middle class," however, lacked historical contingency and paid insufficient attention to culture and consumption.) The American middle class, both past and present, created, fortified, and embodied the values and characteristics that made the United States exceptional. "For more than two hundred years," Dobbs wrote, "the American middle class has been the core of a work ethic, a tradition of values, and a belief that every citizen is an important part of a greater good. This heritage has made the United States a unique nation with shared goals and ideals" (ibid., 9–10).

But the United States' exceptional position, and especially the middle class that produced it, was under assault in 2006. A number of culprits—greedy corporations looking to move jobs offshore, self-serving politicians in the back pocket of those corporations, cultural elites at universities, and "special interest groups"—helped create "The War on the Middle Class," as Dobbs titled his book (Dobbs 2008). Dobbs, though, saved special ire for illegal immigrants. Illegal immigrants drew on local and state services such as hospitals and schools, swamping the social welfare net. Most importantly, they drove down wages by supplying businesses with a ready supply of cheap labor, ultimately destroying the struggling middle class. As Dobbs put it, "immigration strikes right to the heart of the middle class," its economic prosperity and success (Dobbs 2006, 139). (While Dobbs often took care to differentiate between legal and illegal immigrants, he occasionally took to castigating "immigration" rather than illegal immigration.) Given this situation, Dobbs led the charge in 2006 for tougher border security measures and vehemently rejected the possibility of "amnesty" for illegals. To do anything less would be a betrayal of the middle class, and a further attack on America's "unique" political and economic principles. His differences with Navarrette—the two engaged in a running debate and commentary—could not have been starker.

Exceptionalism threaded through not only the economic issues of the 2006 debate, but also the inchoate, but very real, fear that immigrants debased and corrupted American culture. Such concerns were surely on display at Geno's restaurant in Philadelphia, Pennsylvania. Geno's, which serves up a version of the city's famous cheesesteak sandwiches, is a Philadelphia institution. A controversy erupted after Geno's owner, Joey Vento, himself the grandson of Italian immigrants, placed a sticker featuring an American flag and bald eagle in his storefront window that read "This is America. When Ordering, Please SPEAK ENGLISH" (Bahadur 2006). Below the sticker was a sign that read "Management Reserves the Right to Refuse Service," while above the sticker was a long quote from Theodore Roosevelt. In it, Roosevelt asserted that if an immigrant "becomes an American and assimilates himself to us, he shall be treated on an exact equality with everyone else." Roosevelt continued: "We have room for but one language here, and that is the English language," revealing his belief that assimilation—and a place in America—had to involve English language skills. The choice of the Roosevelt passage was interesting, for with it Vento held out the possibility that immigrants could be welcomed in the United States, should they meet certain conditions. In this way, Vento revealed himself to not be an ultra-restrictionist determined to seal shut the open door to the United States.

The subtlety of Vento's storefront declaration was lost—if it was ever recognized in the first place by hungry customers not likely to ponder a long-dead president's thoughts on immigration—as Vento quickly became both a media celebrity and target (Letters 2008). Vento's display troubled immigrant advocates who espoused a faith in cultural and ethnic pluralism that Vento rejected with his Roosevelt citation and his admonition that his customers speak English. But Vento only added fuel to the fire—and gave immigrant advocates reason to disparage him and paint him as a diehard opponent of newcomers—when he asserted in an interview that "A lot of diseases are coming in" with illegal Mexican

Figure 7.1. Sign in the window of Joey Vento's Philadelphia restaurant that ignited a furious debate over immigration and assimilation (Kyle Gradinger)

immigrants. Of the supposed public health threat, Vento noted: "They [the diseases] weren't here before. [Mexicans] play and drink out of the same water" (Bahadur 2006). Immigration advocates labeled Vento a racist and bigot, while skeptics of legal and illegal immigration rallied to his side. Vento's comments, especially his emphasis on language, were revelatory as they made clear his fear—shared with many others—that America's exceptional culture and its sense of nationhood were under assault.

According to opponents of immigration reform and skeptics of current levels of immigration to the United States, the language issue was only one aspect of the coming cultural collapse. Republican Tom Tancredo of Colorado, the leading restrictionist in the House of Representatives, called illegal immigration a "scourge" that paired with "a cult of multiculturalism" would lead to the nation's demise. "We are committing cultural suicide," Tancredo warned, and, "The barbarians at the gate will only need to give us a slight push, and the emaciated body of Western civilization will collapse in a heap" (qtd. in Horowitz 2006, 13). In Virginia, one of the so-called Minutemen, the anti-newcomer organization that took to patrolling the nation's borders and workplaces in an effort to halt illegal immigration, described a local grocery store at which Latinos congregated:

> I started looking at the mess that this 7-Eleven was becoming, the eyesore. People hanging out when there weren't jobs or after they were done looking for work that day. It comes back to their culture. I spent some time in Rio when I was in the Navy. They didn't respect the land in Rio. They urinated on streets, they threw trash, bottles. (qtd. in Leahy 2006)

Underlying such complaints was the proposition that American culture was superior and that it flowed from a distinctly European heritage. This conscious ethno-national superiority found expression in the aforementioned Minuteman's disgust with Latinos and Vento's anger at Spanish-speaking newcomers. Vento's rant, in fact, raised the specter of the need for separate drinking and bathing facilities for whites and nonwhites, a horrible echo of Jim Crow America. Most of the rhetoric and imagery of immigration opponents was not that blatantly evocative of segregation (nor did it recall the Protestant Anglo-Americanism of the early twentieth century, which would have targeted people with last names like Vento and Tancredo). Instead, it recalled the language that many conservatives had developed since the 1970s to critique the minority rights revolution and to express the fears of working and middle-class whites, who linked urban decline, infrastructure collapse, schooling problems, and a growing service sector job market to shiftlessness, laziness, and a lack of respect for the United States among nonwhites.

The commentator and consistent anti-immigration voice Pat Buchanan, though, most clearly identified these concerns in his 2006 book *State of Emergency: The Third World Invasion and Conquest of America*. Buchanan asserted that the immigration problem, both legal and illegal, facing the United States was an ethno-national problem:

> Can anyone say today that we Americans are "one united people"? We are no longer descended from the same ancestors. The European core of the country—almost 95 percent of American as late as 1965—has fallen well below 70 percent and will be less than half the nation by 2050. (Buchanan 2006, 156–57)

Buchanan concluded, "We are entered upon the final act of our civilization. The last scene is the deconstruction of the nations. The penultimate scene, now well underway, is the invasion unresisted (ibid.)."

Buchanan was no mere carbon copy of the immigration restrictionists of the mid-1960s, who tightly linked defense of the national origins quota immigration system with Jim Crow. He did not overtly defend segregation, nor did he disparage blacks as inferior to whites. Buchanan, at times, sympathized with black America, which he noted had prospered the most when immigrant entry was low. Yet, Buchanan also wrote approvingly of race relations before the 1960s, when "[s]egregation persisted, but black folks were as American as apple pie," and he disdained the distinct cultural and racial identity that some blacks embraced after the 1960s (Buchanan 2006, 176–77, 230–31). The differences between 1965 restrictionists and Buchanan (as well as Vento and the Minuteman) were very real, but they all shared a very striking discomfort with a multiracial and multiethnic society that challenged a white, European dominated culture that had made the United States a great nation. Restrictionists, then, almost always defined as European and white the culture that now faced collapse and required protection.

Restrictionists ultimately offered a broad definition of American cultural identity—one that encompassed English language skills, personal cleanliness, fealty to the Anglo-American experience, and a palpable unease with ethnic and racial diversity—and one that was thoroughly based in exceptionalist principles. The "scourge" that would bring on "diseases," "eyesores," and a trashed environment—or, culturally, a trashed identity via the pollution of languages other than English—all presupposed a pure and clean United States unaffected by those very problems that wracked the rest of the world. Or, as Buchanan pithily described the effect of immigration, "Thus, the world's finest five-star hotel, the United States of America, becomes the flophouse for the planet" (Buchanan 2006, 92). Buchanan and Tancredo, likewise, constructed the United States as the last, greatest hope of European culture—or in the latter's case, "Western Civilization"—with the clear understanding of the superiority of that particular culture. Nobody better linked exceptionalism with immigration than J. D. Hayworth, a Republican from Arizona notable for his particularly virulent anti-immigrant politics, who saw immigration advocates as those who "reject the very notion that there is a uniquely American identity, or that, if there is one, that it is superior to any other" (qtd. in Horowitz 2006).

"Hard" and "Soft" Exceptionalism

American exceptionalism—even as its particular principles waxed and waned—was the *lingua franca* of immigration debates in 1965 and 2006, utilized by both immigration advocates and opponents. The common ground between these two groups should not be overstated, however, because of their very different approaches to the place of immigrants in the American nation. As a result, at a very basic level they conceived of American exceptionalism differently, a difference that might best be described as "hard" and "soft" exceptionalism.

The historian Gordon Wood in a 1994 essay for *The New Republic* used the adjectives "hard" and "soft" to describe multiculturalism. "Soft" multiculturalism, in Wood's view, celebrated ethnic, racial, and sexual diversity in American life and honored the idea of a nation made up of immigrants, African Americans, and women (in addition to white men.) Some "soft" multiculturalists saw those groups as assimilating to American life and abandoning their previous identities, while other "soft" multiculturalists emphasized that these groups held on to their distinctive identities as they assumed their place in American society; in the early twentieth century, this latter view was called "cultural pluralism," Wood noted. Wood's larger point, though, was the most important: for "soft" multiculturalists, the United States was multicultural, but that multicultural experience existed underneath the umbrella of the nation. In contrast, "hard" multiculturalism—which Wood saw expressed in the "identity politics" that came to the fore after the 1970s—also celebrated different ethnic, racial, and sex groups, but did not acknowledge any common ground or a place within the larger idea of an American nation. As the historian Gary Gerstle elaborated in 2001, hard multiculturalism had numerous variants, but all at some level rejected the notion of an "American nation" (Gerstle 2001, 349–57). The distinction between "hard" and "soft," then, rests upon notions of permeability and compatibility: hard multiculturalists see the boundaries between nation and group as impermeable and incompatible, while soft multiculturalists do not.

While Wood's analysis addressed an ideology almost exclusively of the political liberal-Left, his concepts of "hard" and "soft" can be imported to the study of exceptionalism, even though—as we have seen—both the political Right and Left have embraced exceptionalism. Immigration opponents believed that newcomers would only debase America's exceptional qualities and characteristics. Thus, they advocated what might best be called a "hard exceptionalism"—one that made no room for newcomers to share in America's greatness and was, inherently, defensive and exclusionary. Hard exceptionalism, then, isolates the United States from the world—in this case, immigrants—because the world seems incompatible with the exceptional qualities at the base of the American experience. Hard exceptionalism does not mean that America's unique qualities and virtue should not be exported, only that they ought not to be risked via the importation of immigrants.

Immigration advocates—as "soft" exceptionalists—operated from a different set of assumptions. In 1965 (and to a lesser extent in 2006, because they had lost the upper hand in immigration affairs), liberalizers utilized exceptionalist rhetoric to argue for a more multicultural and diverse American populace. They urged that the United States ought not to shut itself off from the rest of the world, but should embrace and welcome the rest of the world. No less believers in America's exceptionalism, they believed that newcomers only reenergized America's exceptional qualities. Those qualities were permeable and compatible with immigration. Indeed, liberalizers argued that immigration renewed that exceptionalism.

Liberalizers, as soft exceptionalists, then, offered an alternative to the hard exceptionalism of restrictionists. It is an alternative well worth remembering and protecting, for it demonstrates that exceptionalism need not be the province of isolation and fear, but rather a path to a diverse, hospitable, and—hopefully—tolerant society.

Works Cited

Bahadur, Gaiutra. 2006. Immigration and cheesesteaks. *Philadelphia Inquirer*. 11 June.

Buchanan, Pat. 2006. *State of emergency: The third world invasion and conquest of America*. New York: St. Martin's Press.

Bush, George W. 2008. President Bush addresses the nation on immigration reform (15 May 2006). Online posting. 17 July 2008. <www.whitehouse.gov/news/releases/2006/05/20060515-8.html on July 17, 2008>.

Dobbs, Lou. 2006. *War on the middle class: How the government, big business, and special interest groups are waging war on the American dream and how to fight back*. New York: Penguin Group.

———. 2008. Middle class need to fight back now (18 October 2006). Online posting. 17 July 2008. <www.cnn.com/2006/US/10/10/Dobbs.Oct11/index.html on July 17, 2008.

Gerstle, Gary. 2001. *American crucible: Race and nation in the twentieth century.* Princeton: Princeton University Press.

Hartz, Louis. 1955. *The liberal tradition in America: An interpretation of American political thought since the Revolution.* New York: Harcourt.

Horowitz, Tony. 2006. Immigration—and the curse of the black legend. *New York Times*, 9 July.

Lazarus, Emma. 2008. The new colossus (1883). Online posting. 17 July 2008. <www.libertystatepark.com/emma.html>.

Leahy, Michael. 2006. Crossing the line. *Washington Post*, 19 March.

Letters: A Geno's steak—With plenty of controversy. *Philadelphia Daily News*, 8 June.

Navarrette, Ruben. 2006. Those jobs Americans won't do. *San Diego Union-Tribune*, 3 September.

———. 2006a. A look at two Americas. *San Diego Union-Tribune*, 22 October.

Potter, David. 1954. *People of plenty: Economic abundance and the American character.* Chicago: University of Chicago Press.

Reimers, David. 1998. *Unwelcome strangers: American identity and the turn against immigration.* New York: Columbia University Press.

Tichenor, Daniel. 2002. *Dividing lines: The politics of immigration control in America.* Princeton: Princeton University Press.

Tocqueville, Alexis de. 2000. *Democracy in America.* Indianapolis: Hackett.

Turner, Frederick Jackson. 1962. *The frontier in American history.* New York: Holt, Rhinehart, Winston.

U.S. Congress. 1965. *The Congressional Record.* Washington, DC: Government Printing Office.

U.S. Congress. 2006. *The Congressional Record.* Washington, DC: Government Printing Office.

U.S. Immigration and Naturalization Service. 2002. *Statistical Yearbook of the Immigration and Naturalization Service.* Washington, DC: Government Printing Office.

U.S. Senate. 1965. *Immigration.* Subcommittee on Immigration and Naturalization of the Committee on the Judiciary. 89th Congress, 1st Session.

Washington Post. 2007. Highlights of the House and Senate and border security measures. Online posting. 15 March. <www.washingtonpost.com/wpdyn/content/custom/2006/05/26/CU200605 2600148.html>.

Weisman, Jonathan. 2006. With Senate vote, Congress passes border fence bill. *Washington Post*, 30 September.

Weisman, Jonathan. 2007. Immigration bill dies in Senate; Bipartisan compromise fails to satisfy the right or the left. *Washington Post*, 29 June.

Wood, Gordon. 1994. The losable past. *The New Republic*, 7 November.

Zakaria, Fareed. 2006. To become an American. *Washington Post*, 4 April.

8

Giving the People What They Want

The African American Exception as Racial Cliché in Percival Everett's *Erasure*

Anthony Stewart

American exceptionalism, as the expression is conventionally employed, means *white* American exceptionalism, since the political ability to stand as a beacon to the world has historically resided in the hands of America's white and, for the most part, male, citizens. The men who have shouldered the burden of ensuring the exceptionalism of America have been invoked to represent all the greatness of which America is presumably capable. They have been, and remain, the agents who denied "access for people of African descent to cosmopolitan subjectivity" as well as to "national subjectivity and human subjectivity," as Ifeoma Nwankwo states in *Black Cosmopolitanism.* By contrast, exceptional African Americans have tended to be viewed, for better and for worse, as representing only what *black* Americans are capable of and, perhaps more importantly, are *like.* Moreover, whether as "credits to the race" or as racial clichés, the individuals who are excepted from the African American population as a whole have usually been made subservient to some larger American interest, put to the ideological and, more and more, commercial use of the overarching exceptionalism that defines America.

Percival Everett's 2001 novel *Erasure* is a compelling representation of how this African American exceptionalism is put to work for American cultural, political, and ideological interests through a momentum over which the individual African American has little or no control. In his portrayal of three characters—Thelonious "Monk" Ellison, Van Go Jenkins, and Stagg R. Leigh—Everett presents a complicated narrative that dramatizes the ideological and commercial use to which the (particularly male) African American is relentlessly put in late-twentieth and early-twenty-first-century America. *Erasure* demonstrates how the African American exception has in fact been rendered a racial cliché that satisfies a desire within the larger American culture. Kwame Anthony Appiah's discussion of cosmopolitanism helps to illuminate further how Monk Ellison, the novel's protagonist, wishes to see himself, even though the rest of his society desires to see him otherwise, if at all. By deploying prevailing racial clichés about African American men and then complicating those clichés, Everett demonstrates how the truly exceptional African American citizen is—paradoxically—the individual who simply wants to be an individual, a status much more available to members of America's dominant culture.

Erasure presents three characters who occupy different but significant positions on a continuum of African American exceptionalism. At one end is Thelonious Ellison, nicknamed "Monk." A university professor of English and the author of "[w]idely unread experimental stories and novels" (Everett 2001, 225), Ellison introduces himself as follows: "I have dark brown skin, curly hair, a broad nose, some of my ancestors were slaves and I have been detained by pasty white policemen in New Hampshire, Arizona and Georgia and so the society in which I live tells me I am black; that is my race" (ibid., 1). This self-description, based in familiar phenotype, makes clear that Ellison knows that American society expects its citizens of African descent to wear the markers of difference and endure the consequences of wearing those markers. But he also says this about himself:

> Though I am fairly athletic, I am no good at basketball. I listen to Mahler, Aretha Franklin, Charlie Parker, and Ry Cooder on vinyl records and compact discs. I graduated *summa cum laude* from Harvard, hating every minute of it.

> I am good at math. I cannot dance. I did not grow up in any inner city or the rural south. My family owned a bungalow near Annapolis. My grandfather was a doctor. My father was a doctor. My brother and sister were doctors. (ibid., 2)

Ellison's eclectic list of musical tastes is reminiscent of Langston Hughes's "Theme for English B," whose narrator also feels called upon to explain himself, declaring that his musical tastes run to "Bessie, bop, or Bach" (Hughes, 1310). Ellison's superlative performance at a bastion of American postsecondary education and privilege further signifies how his individual identity frustrates conventional racial assumptions. But his complex individuality only appears to work against him. In a conversation with his agent, after receiving yet another rejection of his work, with the criticism that it is "not black enough," a criticism regularly leveled at his personal manner as well, Ellison asks: "What, do I have to have my characters comb their afros and be called niggers for these people?" (Everett 2001, 43).

Ellison's query reprises a discussion of the privilege to be represented in text on one's own terms, which Everett articulates through the voice of the highly exceptional narrator of his 1999 novel, *Glyph*, four-year-old Ralph Townsend who has a measured IQ of 475. Well into the narrative, Ralph turns his gaze upon his reader, asking: "Have you to this point assumed that I am white?" And he continues: "In my reading, I discovered that if a character was black, then he at some point was required to comb his Afro hairdo, speak on the street using an obvious, ethnically identifiable idiom, live in a certain part of a town, or be called a nigger by someone" (Everett 1999, 54). In *Erasure*, this is exactly the type of character Monk Ellison eventually creates in the novella he writes to protest these same literary conventions. The rest of Ralph's assessment of narrative convention is crucial because he draws attention to how the privilege to take oneself for granted works: "White characters, I assumed they were white (often, because of the ways they spoke of other kinds of people), did not seem to need that kind of introduction, or perhaps legitimization, to exist on the page" (ibid., 54). Ralph briefly gestures here at what Monk Ellison fleshes out over the course of *Erasure*. White characters stand as the default position, determining others' identities by what they choose to call them. Moreover, white characters do not have to worry about becoming representative or rendered racial clichés to nearly the same extent as their black counterparts do. White characters, like white citizens in American society, get to be individuals. They also often serve as the rules that determine the exceptions. This is what Everett dramatizes in *Erasure.* This ontological relationship between interpreter and interpreted maps quite neatly onto the relationships that determine how images of African Americans circulate within American culture at large.

Both Ellison's question to his agent about how these relationships affect the reception of his books and Ralph's elaboration of the answer display the same strategy. In both cases, after acceding initially to the requirements of the image of the black citizen, Everett's characters destabilize this image by revealing the ways in which they are themselves truly exceptional, the ways in which they may be excepted from some of the prevailing stereotypes of the African American subject. Monk provides another such example of his characteristic self-presentation "on a couple of occasions, on a basketball court when upon missing a shot I muttered *Egads*" (Everett 2001, 2). The basketball court satisfies conventional expectations while the anachronistic and generally unidiomatic utterance of "Egads" disrupts them.

Monk's polar opposite in the novel is the clearest expression of what has become a late-twentieth and early-twenty-first-century cliché of the African American man. Van Go Jenkins is the protagonist Ellison creates in the novella he writes in enraged and outrageous protest against the popularity of the runaway national bestseller, *We's Lives In Da Ghetto*, by Juanita Mae Jenkins. *We's Lives In Da Ghetto* is introduced into Ellison's narrative on a television talk show hosted by Kenya Dunston, whose resemblance to Oprah Winfrey is reflected in the meter and number of letters in both women's names. In case there was still any lingering doubt about the resemblance, Juanita Mae Jenkins's novel is selected for Dunston's television book club, where Jenkins explains what inspired it: "I got this job at a publishing house. I watched these manuscripts come by and these books come out and I thought, where are the books about our people? Where are our stories? And so I wrote *We's Lives In Da Ghetto*" (Everett 2001, 53). As a writer, Jenkins is exceptional in the way Monk Ellison is. However, in their writing both invent versions of familiar racial clichés for mass consumption. The fact that Ellison's fictional protagonist shares the surname of the author of the now-celebrated novel makes an obvious point about lineage but also, perhaps, causality. Van Go becomes Juanita Mae's son. She gives birth to him. More importantly, the misogynist Van Go, whose story opens with his dream about stabbing his mother to death and proceeds to follow the destructive swath he cuts through his world, is characterized as "so honest, so raw, so down-and-dirty-gritty, so real, that talk of objectivity is out of place" (ibid., 260), when the fictional novella is reviewed enthusiastically in the *New York Times.* Van Go's appalling behavior exhibits what honesty and rawness amount to when applied to the African American man. Objectivity is out of place in evaluating this character because the racial cliché is a subjective creation based not on fact but on opinion refracted through convention.

The *New York Times* review is a fascinating example of the use to which African Americans are often put in order to satisfy audience desires. Wayne Waxen, the reviewer, does indeed become a mannequin—as his surname suggests—who stands in for much that Everett targets here. Waxen describes Van Go's life as,

> one of sheer animal existence, one that we can all recognize. Our young protagonist has no father, is ghetto tough and resists education and reason like the plague. It is natural, right for him to do so. He is hard, cruel, lost and we are afraid of him; that much is clear. But he is so real that we must offer him pity. He is the hood whom Dirty Harry blows away and we say, "Good, you got him," then feel the loss, at least of our own innocence. (ibid., 260)

The Waxen review is especially significant in its account of the role "we" play in the relationship set up between "our" protagonist and the reader. Not only does Waxen not imagine his *New York Times* reader as black, he does not imagine someone like Van Go as a potentially real person with real problems but only as an animal to be feared, pitied, avoided, and finally destroyed. The final sense of loss is not for lost potential in a young man, but for "our" lost innocence. Waxen's review performs the ideological alchemy in which someone else's problems do not count unless they are turned into "ours," and also makes clear who "we" are in this instance. His review stresses the function to which Van Go is put by the dominant culture, here represented by the newspaper that decides what is "fit to print."

Wayne Waxen is confused about what is real and what is not, but he does not have to confront his confusion, in part because there is no one around him who views African Americans any differently than he does. This is a frequent confusion in *Erasure*. When one of the jurors for the Book Award, *Erasure*'s stand-in for the National Book Award, for which Stagg Leigh's novella (eventually published under the title *Fuck*) is nominated, says that the "energy and savagery of the common black is so refreshing in the story" (ibid., 254), he fails to realize that Van Go Jenkins is most interesting precisely because he is so *un*common. As Appiah has put it, "Thoroughgoing ignorance about the ways of others is largely a privilege of the powerful" (Appiah 2006, xviii). Within the literary world, instruments such as the *New York Times* and the Book Award represent the kind of power Appiah identifies. Monk Ellison—who is nominated to serve on the Book Award jury—makes this point clearly in response to a fellow juror telling him how happy he should be to see "your people so vividly portrayed." Monk answers: "These are no more my people than Abbot and Costello are your people" (Everett 2001, 261). The choice of two comedians whose signature routine is based in an inability to communicate to one another something as basic as the positions of players on a baseball diamond adds an incisive, self-referential comic undertone to Ellison's remark. Ellison's assertion makes a point that Appiah would consider a gesture toward cosmopolitanism, which, in his words, "shouldn't be seen as some exalted attainment: it begins with the simple idea that in the human community, as in national communities, we need to develop habits of coexistence: conversation in its older meaning, of living together, association" (Appiah 2006, xix). Waxen and the members of the Book Award jury do not engage in such a conversation because, simply put, they do not have to. Their positions of power and privilege free them from such self-conscious considerations, and, as a result, contribute further to their own unwitting and unnoticed confusion.

In his exhaustive study of the nature of stereotyping, David J. Schneider reminds us that

> in the days before television and when segregation along race, ethnic, gender, religious, and class lines was more pronounced than it is now, most of what most people knew about other groups came from hearsay and limited exposure to stereotyped portrayals on radio and in the movies. In the 1930s it would have been comparatively rare for a white person in the United States to know an individual black person at all

> well, so white stereotypes of blacks had to be based primarily on culturally transmitted information rather than detailed individual experience. (Schneider 2004, 22)

What Schneider is describing is exactly what is being enacted by the Book Award jurors in *Erasure*. One of them frankly admits as much: "I haven't had a lot of experience with color—black people—and so *Fuck* was a great thing for me" (Everett 2001, 261). The juror's reflexive use of the anachronistic "colored" before updating it to "black" situates his experience as, if not in the 1930s, certainly not at the beginning of the twenty-first century. When Ellison expresses his concern that the novel will leave people with the ill-founded impression that "there is truth to it" (ibid.), another juror delivers one of the punch lines of *Erasure*: "This is the truest novel I've ever read. It could only have been written by someone who has done hard time. It's the real thing" (ibid.). Since the novella was in fact written by a university professor whose grandfather, father, and two siblings are all doctors, and who has done no time at all, hard or otherwise, the point about truth as it pertains to *Fuck* is aggressively called into question. The "real thing" is not what the jurors think it is. Instead, because of a lack of exposure to the Other (any Other, it would appear) and never having their erroneous assumptions challenged, they are able to transform an exception into the representatively real thing. Moreover, they occupy positions that enable them to declare what is real and have others, similarly confused, believe them. The story of Van Go Jenkins only proves his exceptional nature. That is, he is an exception to pretty much every rule of conduct in African American, not to mention human, life. The fact that he is accepted as representative of "real" African Americans is one of the most disturbing points of Everett's satire.

The nature of this confusion of the exception with the much more mundane rule has been discussed by numerous commentators, who point up how profoundly it affects perceptions of African Americans within American culture. Ralph Ellison, for instance, in *Shadow and Act* gets to the heart of a desire persistently expressed within American society:

> In the beginning was not the shadow, but the act, and the province of Hollywood is not action, but illusion. Actually,

> the anti-Negro images of the films were (and are) acceptable because of the existence throughout the United States of an audience obsessed with an inner psychological need to view Negroes as less than men. . . . The anti-Negro image is thus a *ritual object* of which Hollywood is not the creator, but the manipulator. Its role has been that of justifying the widely held myth of Negro unhumanness and inferiority by offering entertaining rituals through which that myth could be reaffirmed. (Ellison 1995a, 276–77; emphasis added)

Ellison here uses the expression "ritual object" in the way I am using "racial cliché." When we remember that Ellison wrote these words in 1949, it becomes clear just how long the exceptional African American has enacted the role of desirable racial cliché, embodying the ad-man's old adage, "Give the people what they want." Of course, this expression really means: "Tell the people what they want, and then give it to them."

bell hooks also seizes upon the sense of desire that underlies the image of the African American subject, a desire that is central to *Erasure*:

> When the dominant culture demands that the Other be offered as sign that progressive political change is taking place, that the American Dream can indeed be inclusive of difference, it invites a resurgence of essentialist cultural nationalism. The acknowledged Other must assume *recognizable forms.* Hence, it is not African American culture formed in resistance to contemporary situations that surfaces, but nostalgic evocation of a "glorious" past. And even though the focus is often on the ways that this past was "superior" to the present, this cultural narrative relies on stereotypes of the "primitive," even as it eschews the term, to evoke a world where black people were in harmony with nature and with one another. This narrative is linked to white western conceptions of the dark Other, not to a radical questioning of those representations. (hooks 1992, 26; emphasis added)

The implicit rules that determine the "recognizable forms" that the Other must assume account for the persistence of the racial clichés I am speaking of. These clichés frustrate whatever radical questioning might otherwise be brought to bear on the use to which the Other is put by the dominant culture. Like Ralph Ellison, hooks points to a similar desire to objectify the African American subject.

More recently, Paul Gilroy has elaborated how recognizable forms of the Other continue to be determined by the dominant culture. In *After Empire*, Gilroy recounts different historical explanations for the political power imbalances that have tended to run along racial lines. While these imbalances formerly tended toward colonialist theories, Gilroy first sketches a historical trajectory of conceptions of race, and then introduces two "additional layers of raciological and geopolitical theory" (Gilroy 2004, 19) that explain late-twentieth and early-twenty-first century versions of the Other:

> The first had been originally invented to rationalize the era of Europe's great colonial empires, while the second was produced more recently to affirm the very different racial order that is becoming more visible now that U.S. specifications and assumptions about difference, culture, and phenotype are disseminated under the global reach of contemporary corporate powers. (ibid., 19–20)

As Gilroy explains, this latter theory "has sometimes been prepared to identify the same incredible subspecies as superhuman and even god-like in its physicality. Michael Jordan and Mike Tyson, Halle Berry and the tennis-playing Williams sisters are some of the *iconic presences* that embody the later possibility" (ibid., 20; emphasis added). In other words, this latter expression of what Gilroy calls "raciological and geopolitical theory" works in ways similar to the former, which had as its ideological underpinning the rationalization of Europe's great empires. In both cases the version of the Other serves the ideological desires of the dominant culture. What is notable in the interventions by Ellison, hooks, and Gilroy is that even as they mark a trajectory through different versions of the African American—from subhumanity to the noble savage to the superhuman—they are held together by a common and relentless ideological desire to objectify.

Everett himself has attempted to account for the pressure exerted by American culture on the African American writer who simply tries to represent an individual creative expression—as artists who are members of the dominant culture are allowed, in fact encouraged, to do. In his 1991 essay "Signing to the Blind" he writes:

> An army of liberal book-readers marches into stores and feeds on fad and trend and reads, but not too deeply, and so does to our work what the movies seek to do. I do not believe that the works we produce need to be any different; the failing is not in what we show but in how it is seen. And it is not just white readers, but African-American readers as well who seek to fit our stories to an *existent model.* It is not seeing with "white" eyes, it is seeing with "American" eyes, with brainwashed, automatic, comfortable, and "safe" perceptions of reality. (Everett 1991, 10; emphasis added)

The "existent model" of which Everett speaks carries the same resonance as the "ritual object," the "recognizable form," and the "iconic presence" identified by Ellison, hooks, and Gilroy respectively. This cultural brainwashing serves the hegemonic image of America as an exceptional nation when the need arises. Toni Morrison, for instance, as the latest American writer to have won the Nobel Prize for Literature, may be read as the sort of sign of progressive political change of which hooks speaks, even if such an honor to one exceptional figure does nothing for the lot of the many. The image of the successful black writer has yet to become the racial cliché that the famous black athlete has been over the course of the twentieth century and one would be ill advised to hold one's breath waiting for that day to come.

While male athletes have borne the brunt of much of the ideological use of the racial clichés of African Americans within American culture, with boxers such as Jack Johnson at the beginning of the twentieth century, and Joe Louis in the 1930s, followed by Jackie Robinson's entrance into major league baseball in 1947, it is crucial to note that much of the fame and fortune that accrues to Juanita Mae Jenkins for *We's Lives In Da Ghetto* also derives from a misapprehension of the cliché for the real. In her interview with Dunston, Jenkins acknowledges that she is not from the South but "from Ohio originally. Akron" (Everett 2001, 53). From here she reveals the origins of the novel: "When I was twelve I went to visit some relatives in Harlem for a couple of days and that's what the novel comes from" (ibid.). Furthermore, she attended Oberlin College "for a couple of years, then moved to New York" (ibid.). Her middle-class background and opportunities allow her to become a writer, as is the case with Monk Ellison. The unexamined "couple of days" that serve as the source for the "authentic" dialogue in her novel are elided by her ethnic identity as an African American woman. In other words, because they are given what they want, people believe her claim to authenticity.

Both Juanita Mae Jenkins and Monk Ellison are pressed into service by the same cultural machinery. This fact is made clear by their parallel celebrity, signified by appearances on Dunston's television program. While Ellison critiques his celebrity status, he nevertheless accepts the $600,000 advance for *Fuck*, the three million dollar movie deal, and the nomination to Dunston's book club, which promises to double his already hefty advance. He provides a telling revision of the problems of stereotyping when he sees himself as "sadly a stereotype of the radical, railing against something, calling it tradition perhaps, claiming to seek out new narrative territory, to knock at the boundaries of the very form that calls me and allows my artistic existence" (Everett 2001, 155–56). He has become what he once described in an undergraduate essay on *Finnegans Wake*: "What's different is that each sentence, each word calls attention to the devices. So, the work really reaffirms what it seems to expose. It is the thing it is, perhaps twice, and depends on the currency of conventional narrative for its experimental validity" (ibid., 185). This evaluation of Joyce's experimentation defines the relationship between the exception and the rule against which the exception inevitably must be defined. But the exception is also the thing it is, and seeing it as such should draw our attention to the devices by which it was deemed exceptional in the first place. This awareness is productive when analyzing how an exception becomes a cliché, since clichés emerge as a result of a lack of conscious engagement, an unwillingness to rethink a habitual usage.

The fact that Van Go Jenkins relentlessly mistreats women adds further complexity to understanding how the notion of the exception operates in *Erasure*. Perhaps the most disturbing aspect of *Erasure* is not Van Go's appalling behavior toward the women he encounters, as disturbing as that is, but the fact that this behavior is never subject to the opprobrium of the Book Award jury, the *New York Times* reviewer, or even Dunston herself. All of Van Go's actions are accepted unproblematically as "honest" and "real." The life of Van Go—"a nineteen-year-old urban, unemployed, unmarried, irresponsible, self-hating, violent black male rapist, killer, and father of four children by four different women" (Bell 2003, 476), as Bernard Bell summarizes him—can only be seen by a sensible person as the exception and not the rule as it is made out to be by pretty much everyone in *Erasure* who reads *Fuck*. Because Van Go's psychopathic and misogynist behavior is seen as "representative," then, his story is celebrated, as is the story of another "representative" character—the unwed young black mother at the center of *We's Lives In Da Ghetto*—who becomes a tap dancer (of all things) in order to feed her children. Monk eventually describes himself as "an overly ironic, cynical, self-conscious and yet faithful copy of Juanita Mae Jenkins, author of the runaway-bestseller-soon-to-be-a-major-motion-picture *We's Lives In Da Ghetto*" (Everett 2001, 221). The main difference between Jenkins and Ellison, though, is that Jenkins does not whine about the fragility of her ethical position while accepting great sums of money for her creation. She appears to understand much better than Monk does how American culture functions. While she is part of Everett's satire, then, she is not really one of its targets as Ellison is, although it is difficult to see her position as the more desirable one. He appears naïve while she's a cynic. But under the objectifying weight both endure, their best selves are unlikely to emerge.

The most complicated character in Everett's meditation on the exceptional African American man is Stagg R. Leigh, the pseudonym-come-to-life, who is the truly exceptional character in *Erasure*. He is exceptional in the "talented tenth" manner of Monk Ellison and Juanita Mae Jenkins by virtue of being a writer. He simultaneously embodies the racial cliché of the threatening, criminal African American man. Leigh, then, complicates the oppositional relationship between the Du Boisian ideal and the commercial product, standing at the exact midpoint of the continuum involving Everett's three principal characters. When Ellison decides to write his reactive novella, he refers to it as "a book on which I knew I could never put my name" (Everett 2001, 62). Stagg R. Leigh is a name that "puns on the pathological model that is too often used to interpret African American culture and character and on the name of the popular black vernacular character Stagger Lee" (Bell 2003, 476). Lee is an expression of the "bad man," the stock figure in many blues songs as well as in Langston Hughes's blues poems. In one of the many riffs that pay homage to *Invisible Man*, Monk Ellison wonders,

> how far I should take my Stagg Leigh performance. I might in fact become a Rhinehart [*sic*], walking down the street and finding myself in store windows, I yam what I yam.

> I could throw on a fake beard and a wig and do the talk shows, play the game, walk the walk, shoot the jive. No, I couldn't. (Everett 2001, 162)

And yet, in spite of his disclaimer, when he meets Wiley Morgenstein, the producer who buys the novella's movie rights, and when he appears (behind a screen) on Dunston's television program, Ellison's performance as Stagg Leigh demonstrates that the "have-your-cake-and-eat-it" position Ellison has adopted is very much playing the game.

This allusion to Rinehart is actually a double allusion to Ralph Ellison's *Invisible Man*, conflating two scenes that stress the significance of performance in both Ralph Ellison's novel and in Everett's. In the first scene, a street vendor comments that the narrator is "one of these old-fashioned yam eaters." The narrator replies, proudly: "They're my birthmark. . . . I yam what I am" (Ellison 1995, 266). As the scene continues, the narrator reflects upon his past attempts to conform to some model of behavior predetermined by others: "What and how much had I lost by trying to do only what was expected of me instead of what I myself had wished to do? What a waste, what a senseless waste!" (ibid.). The second scene occurs during the riot that ends *Invisible Man*, when the narrator discovers that he can move strategically among the rioters by adopting the guise of Rinehart, who is able to be all things to all people: "I was both depressed and fascinated. I wanted to know Rinehart and yet, I thought, I'm upset because I know I don't have to know him, that simply becoming aware of his existence, being mistaken for him, is enough to convince me that Rinehart is real. It couldn't be, but it is. And it can be, is, simply because it's unknown" (ibid., 498). What holds the two allusions together is a common existential anxiety, expressed most succinctly by the conclusion at which the narrator has arrived as he begins to recount his tale: "I am nobody but myself" (ibid., 15). But Monk Ellison, picking up where his namesake's creation leaves off, shows how difficult this self-knowledge can be to achieve and sustain when one is constantly being rendered as a cliché by the dominant culture or being told by others that he is, or is not, the real thing.

Stagg Leigh is an existential performance more than a person, as he crystallizes for Monk Ellison the anxieties realized with the commercial success but, in his view, the clear artistic failure of *Fuck*. Greil Marcus and Margaret Russett contend that Stagg Leigh threatens to consume Monk's personality, an understandable if somewhat overstated observation. Marcus asserts that as an "experimental novelist, Ellison has never made sense, but as *My Pafology* [the working title of *Fuck*] turns into a property, as it becomes clear that society will pay anything to hear the story it tells, Ellison ceases to exist." Russett says that the "last third of *Erasure* is concerned with how Monk reconciles his faith in art with his fame as a sell-out, and how his personality disintegrates under the pressure of *performing* the black stereotype he intended to satirize" (Russett, 359, emphasis in original). It is true that Monk wonders about Stagg:

> Had I by annihilating my own presence actually asserted the individuality of Stagg Leigh? Or was it the book itself that had given him life? There he was for public scrutiny and the public was loving him. What would happen if I tired of holding my breath, if I had to come up for air? Would I have to kill Stagg to silence him? And what did it mean that I was even thinking of Stagg as having agency? What did it mean that I could put those questions to myself? Of course, it meant nothing and so, it meant everything. (Everett 2001, 248)

Marcus and Russett overlook the fact that Monk thinks these thoughts as he prepares to appear as Stagg on Dunston's program, so these concerns are dictated by the immediate circumstances. Monk's reflections do indicate an existential crisis of a sort. But they come to the same kind of resolution as the narrator of *Invisible Man* regarding Rinehart. Both personae may be invoked to serve a strategic purpose. To the extent that he is real, Stagg is so in the minds of others, not Monk.

The real existential crisis is simpler and actually more compelling than the complete consumption of Monk's personality by Stagg Leigh. It is the public who loves Stagg, as Monk says, but there is never any doubt in Monk's consciousness about who he is when he talks to his mother, as she slips away from him into the dementia of Alzheimer's, and who knows him unfailingly as her "Monksie." His older brother, Bill, always speaks to Monk as Monk, reveals his intensely personal problems to Monk, and swears at Monk for not caring sufficiently (he thinks) about Bill's problems. In other words, the conflict between Stagg and Monk renders literal the problem of the African American subject dealing with the expectations of the society in which he lives. Of course

Stagg is preferred by the public. He is the racial cliché who stands for the representative black man and satisfies the persistent audience desire. Stagg is the "real thing" according to these cultural dictates. He gives the people what they want.

When Stagg finally appears in *Erasure* as an embodied character, it is an event. The private joke must finally take on a public form. Monk does have concerns about how to dress and conduct himself when performing Stagg, but these are minor questions because Monk knows that his performance will rely more upon his behavior than his appearance. He can play the role, in fact, as long as it is not really him. For Stagg's coming out, Monk decides on "brown weejuns, khakis and a white shirt with blue stripes and a button down collar. The clothes were available" (Everett 2001, 216). Here, clothes do not make the man. The contingency of availability conveys a sense of control that Monk has *within* himself. He can manage the performance regardless of what he wears.

At lunch with Morgenstein, the movie producer, and Morgenstein's assistant, Cynthia, Monk relies on two of the stereotypes of black maleness—hyper-violence and hyper-sexuality—to carry his performance. After ordering lunch in the confident manner of someone who has been in an upscale restaurant before, Stagg establishes his bad man *bona fides* in response to Morgenstein's question about why Stagg went to jail: " 'They say I killed a man with the leather awl of a Swiss army knife.' The qualifier *they say* was a stroke and Stagg smiled to himself, a move that served to underscore the quality of his crime" (Everett 2001, 218). Because the black criminal is an already recognizable racial cliché, Monk is able to rely on Morgenstein to fill in the blanks, as happens again when the producer registers his relief that Stagg is the real thing: " 'I'm the real thing,' Stagg repeated. 'Cynthia knows I'm the real thing. Don't you, Cindy' " (ibid.). In response to this comment, Cynthia squirms with delight and Morgenstein laughs nervously. Again, Monk is able to rely on both of his lunch companions to fill in the blanks about what "the real thing" might entail in this innuendo. What is of note, though, is that Monk is in complete control of the performance. Morgenstein, predictably, likes Stagg all the more after meeting him.

In a telephone call with Paula Baderman, a senior editor at Random House, who eventually publishes *Fuck*, Monk notices how excited she gets at the prospect of just talking to the real thing, an angry black man who has been in prison. When she says, "If you don't mind my mind asking, what were you in prison for?" (Everett 2001, 156), he replies, "I mind your asking," and notices to himself: "My abruptness was apparently pleasing to her, if not downright exciting. I detected a change in her breathing" (ibid.). He plays on her expectations throughout their exchange and finally thinks to himself: "if I had been in her office (looking the part), she would have been tearing off her blouse and crawling across her desk toward me, perhaps not literally, but at least literarily" (ibid., 156–57). Ellison is so aware that his bad man illusion, as opposed to the editor's "badder man" reality, is crucial to the success of his novella and his credibility as its creator that he can even make a private pun on the literal and literary nature of the editor's excitement. He must look the part, and looking the part will make him the real thing, as Baderman, like Cynthia and Morgenstein, completes the fantasy in her imagination.

To the extent that Monk has been insecure about his "realness" or for that matter his "blackness," this insecurity has always been a part of his life, irrespective of his Stagg Leigh performance. If his personality is in fact coming apart, then, it was doing so long before his performance as Stagg R. Leigh began. At the wedding of Lorraine, his family's long-time housekeeper, Monk has an awkward exchange with a black guest named Leon, who is dismissive and aggressive because of what he perceives as Monk's wealth. The encounter ends with Monk expressing his desire not to be exceptional: "Leon would have no trouble with my having money, no matter how much a figment of his imagination it was, if I were [a] ballplayer. The problem was the one I had always had, that I was not a *regular* guy and I so much wanted to be. Can you spell *bourgeois*?" (Everett 2001, 195; emphasis in original). Significantly, Monk expresses his desire not to be exceptional at all. He simply wants to be a "regular guy." In his attempt to make sense of Leon's hostility, Monk resorts to an expected form of the African American man, the athlete, whose money would be acceptable to Leon whereas money earned working as a novelist and an academic only shrouds him in suspicion. Leon's reaction and Monk's reflections illustrate how the cliché expectations that African Americans experience daily cannot help but affect how they see themselves and one another and how their self-images can easily come to resemble the images held of them by other Americans. Most important for my immediate purposes, though, is that all of Monk's internal turmoil in moments like this one occurs outside of the ambit of his Stagg R. Leigh performance.

The problem of competing versions of Ellison's personality is finally brought to its critical point in the most practical terms. Both existentially and physically, he cannot be in two places at once. This problem is put plainly when Monk travels to New York for a meeting with the jury deciding the Book Award:

> Thelonious and Monk and Stagg Leigh made the trip to New York together, on the same flight and, sadly, in the same seat. I considered that this charade might well turn out of hand and that I would slip into an actual condition of dual personalities. But as I nursed my juice through turbulent skies I managed to reduce the whole thing to mere drama. I was acting, simple and plain, and my pay was substantial and deserved. So, *we* were there dressed as myself, once Monksie in my mother's eyes, once artist in my own eyes. I checked into the Algonquin as was arranged by the staff of the National Book Association, put down my bags and took a nap. (Everett 2001, 237–38; original emphasis)

It is noticeable that whether as Thelonious (his professional name), Monk (his family nickname), or Stagg (his alter ego), Ellison knows that *they* are dressed like *him*. The dual personality anxiety is actually a red herring as he shows that he is divided into at least three, and these three components are determined not by a sketchy sanity but by his relationships with others. He knows who he is and is, in fact, like Eliot's Prufrock, preparing a face to meet the faces that he meets. And what he lacks is what Prufrock lacks, the privilege to take for granted this daily exigency. He can, however, reduce the prospect of a condition of dual personalities to "mere drama." He is acting and is aware he is acting.

Appiah describes the commonness of this sense of a divided self:

> Kumasi is where I grew up; but I haven't lived in Ghana for more than thirty years. Like many people today—like, for example, more than a hundred thousand Ghanaians in England—I live a long way away from the home of my earliest memories. Like many, I return there from time to time, to visit family and friends. And, again like many, when I am there I feel both that I do and that I don't belong. (Appiah 2006, 90–91)

What he is describing is the experience of being a cosmopolitan, a complex human being interacting with a complex world. The cosmopolitan knows that complexity is disallowed, by ideological and commercial necessity, for the cliché and works consciously against seeing himself or herself or seeing others as mere clichés. One device *Erasure* employs to destabilize the cliché is the allusiveness of the characters' names. With Stagg R. Leigh's reference to the blues bad man, and the double allusions in both Van Go's and Monk Ellison's names, the characters embody the sort of multifarious, layered identities that cosmopolitanism prefers. Moreover, the names remind us to see them in multivalent ways.

What gets out of hand is less Monk's performance of Stagg than the outrageous reception of the novella he has written. Once the novella wins the Book Award, the various personae collide because there is nothing left to hold them apart. As he prepares to receive the Book Award, Monk reflects:

> Stagg Leigh would in fact be awarded the Book Award. I considered my motivation in creating Stagg in the first place, felt again my anger and dissatisfaction with my world and my course of action became clear to me. I dressed and as I did I hummed. I had not hummed in a very long time; music had left me. I felt the spirit of Mother in my humming. I felt the spirit of my sister in my pithiness and that of my father in my playful arrogance. I even felt something of my brother and I knew that tonight I would be exposed. (Everett 2001, 262)

Monk's contentment in his psychic communion with his family members demonstrates a sense of relief, a fully integrated personality in touch with his various components, as he sees the prospect of his performance finally coming to an end.

The anxiety that attends Monk's walk to the podium to receive the Book Award looks something like a nervous breakdown. But, again, his anxiety is attributable not to the dissolution of his own personality but to the insanity of the reception of *Fuck* and his loss of control over a fictional persona so obviously intended as a rebuke to the same social, psychological, cultural, commercial, and ideological forces that end up contributing to the novella's popularity in the first place. Russett comments that the conclusions of Everett's novels are often "cryptic or abrupt, sometimes dissonant" (Russett, 364), and that they "spurn closure to the point of eliciting aesthetic dissatisfaction" (ibid.). In the case of *Erasure*, I have to disagree. The simple question with respect to this novel is: what could Monk Ellison possibly say that might resolve in a convincing manner the long-standing confusion engendered by the racial cliché and the use to which it is put in American culture? Moreover, how might an audience who pride themselves as serious and perceptive readers react to having been told that they had lacked the wit to have seen the novella for what it was? One need only remember the incident near the beginning of *Erasure*, when Monk delivers a parodic talk at an academic conference, which leads to someone hurling a set of keys at him, challenging him to a fistfight, and later threatening his life. The prank that is *Fuck* is much worse and has made fools of many more people. The conference paper Monk delivers ends with the statement: "A reiteration of the obvious is never wasted on the oblivious" (Everett 2001, 17). But, in fact, the events of *Erasure* prove that one can never be completely confident that what is obvious to one is obvious to another. Reiteration can sometimes be just a waste of time. It can also, ironically, contribute to continued obliviousness. Appiah provides what might serve as a corollary to the statement that ends Monk's conference paper: "What it's reasonable for you to think, faced with a particular experience, depends on what ideas you already have" (Appiah 2006, 39). This is the frustration of the cosmopolitan. It is also the frustration of the individual turned into a racial cliché.

The novel's conclusion leaves us to speculate on the riotous events that ensue after Monk Ellison takes the podium. Commenting on the ways *Erasure* deconstructs the novel form, Kimberly Eaton reminds us that "the book exists as both a novel and a journal" (Eaton 2006, 223). Because of the convoluted happenings over the course of the narrative, it is easy to forget or overlook the significance of the words with which *Erasure* opens:

> My journal is a private affair, but as I cannot know the time of my coming death, and since I am not disposed, however unfortunately, to the serious consideration of self-termination, I am afraid that others will see these pages. Since however I will be dead, it should not much matter to me who sees what or when. My name is Thelonious Ellison. And I am a writer of fiction. This admission pains me only at the thought

> of my story being found and read, as I have always been severely put off by any story which had as its main character a writer. (Everett 2001, 1)

This portentous and dire tone suggests that something went horribly wrong after the banquet at which the Book Award was presented, though we are not told what that event is. So, really, both the beginning and the ending resist closure. But since *Erasure* draws our attention to the seemingly endless cycle of ideological use to which the racial cliché is put, this formal decision on Everett's part is completely consistent with the novel's content and its comment. Like the novel itself, the figure of the racial cliché appears to have no beginning and no end. Monk assumes that he will be dead by the time his words are read. More than merely a journal, then, *Erasure* serves as the last testament of one individual's high-stakes attempt to resist being turned into a racial cliché.

Everett wants his reader to understand the satire even as most of his characters within *Erasure* do not. Satire relies on someone *getting* the joke, and Everett uses Monk skillfully to effect this getting. Monk Ellison's function within the layered narrative is crucial to understanding *Erasure*'s satire. On the one hand, the status of the text as a private journal implies a desire for truth and self-comprehension on the part of the writer, irrespective of reader reception. On the other hand, it is clear that Monk shares with Everett a desire that his reader, not the characters who praise *Fuck* but the reader who stumbles upon the text that becomes *Erasure*, get the joke. As he sits down to write the novella, he has what appears to be an out-of-body experience: "I sat and stared at Juanita Mae Jenkins' face on *Time* magazine. The pain started in my feet and coursed through my legs, up my spine and into my brain and I remembered passages of *Native Son* and *The Color Purple* and *Amos and Andy* and my hands began to shake." (Everett 2001, 61). Conspicuously, not a single character within *Erasure* recognizes Van Go Jenkins as the updated version of Bigger Thomas that he clearly is, even though the plot of *Fuck* bears obvious parallels to Richard Wright's novel, including Van Go working briefly as a chauffeur for a family (black in this case) named Dalton. However, *we* are supposed to notice these parallels and, as a result, get the joke. We are both Monk's and Everett's intended audience.

Monk wants to understand himself; Everett wants the reader of *Erasure* to understand the satire, and understanding Monk is a requirement of this end. Monk's reflections on why *We's Lives In Da Ghetto* offends him so profoundly aid in both projects of comprehension:

> Those books [by writers such as Tom Clancy or John Grisham] didn't bother me. Though I had never read one completely through, I had peeked at pages, and although I did not find any depth of artistic expression or any abundance of irony or play with language or ideas, I found them well enough written, the way a technical manual can be well enough written. *Oh, so that's tab A.* So, why did Juanita Mae Jenkins send me running for the toilet? I imagine it was because Tom Clancy was not trying to sell his book to me by suggesting that the crew of his high-tech submarine was a representation of his race (*however fitting a metaphor*). Nor was his publisher marketing it in that way. If you didn't like Clancy's white people, you could go out and read about some others. (Everett 2001, 214; emphasis in original)

As Monk struggles to understand why Jenkins's book offends him in ways other books do not, this struggle is presented for our information. We are to understand Monk better as a result of private moments like this one. We are also to understand how the racial cliché works to limit versions of African Americans, since clearly Monk is arguing that there are fewer alternatives to the black characters promoted by the publishing industry than need be the case. The satire also asks that we think more deeply than perhaps is habitual about why this state of affairs persists.

As Monk walks to the podium in the guise of Stagg Leigh to accept the Book Award for the story of Van Go Jenkins, the final scene deflates any prospect that the novel will resolve itself definitively: "I chose one of the tv cameras and stared into it. I said, 'Egads, I'm on television'" (Everett 2001, 265). These words echo Van Go's words as his story comes to an end in a standoff with the police: "The cameras be full of me. I on TV. I say, 'Hey, Mama.' I say, 'Hey, Baby Girl. Look at me. I on TV'" (ibid., 131). Both Monk as Stagg and as Van Go sum up their experiences using the same words. All three—Monk, Stagg, and Van Go—see their worlds in similar terms, confined by and presented for mass consumption through the primary instrument of American popular culture.

Everett presents another version of resistance to the uses to which the racial cliché of the African American is put in one of his short stories. In "The Appropriation of Cultures," published in 2004, a young black man by the name of Daniel Barkley skillfully reverses a scene initially intended to humiliate him. When urged to play "Dixie" by a group of white frat boys, the heartfelt rendition Barkley delivers is met with wild applause by the other patrons in the club. As he says to a friend later, "You should have seen those redneck boys when I took 'Dixie' from them. They didn't know what to do. So, the goddamn flag is flying over the State Capitol. Don't take it down, Just take it. That's what I say" (Everett 2004, 99). Barkley subsequently buys a used pickup truck with a Confederate flag emblazoned across the rear window in an attempt to take that symbol as well. The story ends with black South Carolinians all over the state taking the symbol of the Confederacy as their own, until finally, "after the emblem was used to dress the yards and mark picnic sites of black family reunions the following Fourth of July, the piece of cloth was quietly dismissed from its station with the U.S. and State flags atop the State Capitol. There was no ceremony, no notice. One day, it was not there" (ibid., 103). Barkley's taking of the symbol expresses the same frustration that leads Monk Ellison to write his novella. After all, Ellison, in writing *Fuck*, tries to take the racial cliché of the menacing black man as Barkley takes the rebel flag. As it turns out, both characters do not want more; they actually want less. Each wants not to be an exception but merely to be accepted as an individual, and not capitalized upon as a product whose emotional reactions (in Barkley's case) or artistic productions (in Ellison's) may be predicted or prescribed based on a coincidence of skin color. Whereas the reception of *Fuck* demonstrates that a reiteration of the obvious *can* be wasted on the oblivious, "The Appropriation of Cultures" provides a more sanguine outcome. Perhaps most importantly, both outcomes are similarly uncontrollable.

Even when the United States is criticized for its exceptionalist self-image, that image serves the ideological purposes of the dominant culture and is defined by American politicians and commentators, historians, artists, and publishers. When the same term is applied with respect to its African American citizens, however, it turns into something paradoxical that is imposed upon these citizens. Van Go is an exception pressed into service as the representative real thing, while Monk simply wants to be free to express himself as an individual, a desire that leads to his constant sense of alienation from the society in which he lives. Perhaps, as Daniel Barkley and, in a different way, Monk Ellison point out, this conclusion means that the African American is actually most exceptional when he or she attempts merely to lay claim to the mundane rights of life, liberty, and the pursuit of happiness that appear as the historical birthright of his or her white brothers and sisters. If that is the case, then the more exceptional the African American will become, the less exceptional he or she will appear.

Works Cited

Appiah, Kwame Anthony. 2006. *Cosmopolitanism: Ethics in a world of strangers.* New York: Norton.

Bell, Bernard. 2003. Review. *Erasure. African American Review* 37, no. 2–3: 474–77.

Eaton, Kimberly. 2006. Deconstructing the narrative: Language, genre, and experience in *Erasure. Nebula* 3, no. 2–3: 220–32.

Ellison, Ralph. 1995. *Invisible man.* New York: Vintage.

———. 1995a. *Shadow and act.* New York: Vintage.

Everett, Percival. 1991. Signing to the blind. *Callaloo* 14, no. 1: 9–11.

———. 1999. *Glyph.* Saint Paul: Graywolf.

———. 2001. *Erasure.* New York: Hyperion.

———. 2004. The Appropriation of Cultures. In *Damned if I do.* Saint Paul: Graywolf.

Gilroy, Paul. 2004. *After empire: Melancholia or convivial culture?* Abingdon, UK: Routledge.

hooks, bell. 1992. *Black looks: Race and representation.* Boston: South End.

Hughes, Langston. 2004. Theme for English B. In *Norton anthology of African American literature.* 2nd Ed., ed. Henry Louis Gates Jr. et al., 1309–10. New York: Norton.

Marcus, Greil. 2002. Invisible scam. Review. *Bookforum* (Winter). http://www.bookforum.net/archive/win_02/marcus.html. Accessed 29 April 2007.

Nwankwo, Ifeoma. 2005. *Black cosmopolitanism: Racial consciousness and transnational identity in the nineteenth-century Americas.* Philadelphia: University of Pennsylvania Press.

Russett, Margaret. 2005. Race under erasure. *Callaloo* 28, no. 2: 358–68.

Schneider, David J. 2004. *The psychology of stereotyping.* New York: Guilford.

9

"Just an American Boy"

American Exceptionalism and Steve Earle versus Capital Punishment

Roxanne Harde

During a 2003 interview with Steve Inskeep on National Public Radio, musician, author, and activist Steve Earle relied on the discourse of American exceptionalism to explain why he works against the death penalty. "In a democracy, if the government kills someone, then I'm killing someone," Earle said, "and I object to what that does to my spirit." Democracy is, for Earle, America's exceptional quality, the thing that makes his country unique and special for its citizens and on the world stage. However, for as often as Earle wields the rhetoric of American exceptionalism it is, for him, Seymour Martin Lipset's "double-edged sword," with egalitarianism on the one edge and the promotion of violence and intolerance on the other.

Earle entrenches his abolitionist writing in American exceptionalism even as he questions that ideology with speaking subjects who examine the various positions in which capital punishment places them. On the one hand, Earle seems to be saying, Americans should abolish capital punishment because America as a democracy holds a special place in the world and offers opportunity and hope for all of humanity; on the other hand, with vengeance and violence and racist and classist tendencies ingrained in every social structure, maybe America simply is not that special after all. Earle's need to draw on the ideologies and discourses of American exceptionalism seems symptomatic of the problems David W. Noble outlines in *Death of a Nation: American Culture and the Death of Exceptionalism*. In tracing the trends of postnationalism, Noble points out that those who reject the authority of American exceptionalism and bourgeois nationalism do so because of commitments to "the vision of a bounded nation" and "the dangers of incoherence that faced those who rejected a national narrative" (Noble 2002, 285). While grounding his activism in the authority of America as a bounded democratic nation and an exceptional one at that, Earle still seems willing to complicate his abolitionism with ongoing critiques of the national narrative. In the following I attend to American exceptionalism in Steve Earle's abolitionist writing, as I examine how Earle brings together competing ideologies to offer a potent voice and vision in this arena of American activism.

"Could you pull that switch yourself": Exceptional Responsibilities

Long before he became an activist for the abolition of capital punishment in America, Earle recorded his first anti–death penalty song. In "Billy Austin," from his 1990 album *The Hard Way*, Earle's eponymous part-Cherokee speaker offers a brooding narrative that challenges preconceived notions about the death penalty.[1] The ballad solemnly relates the details that comprise Billy Austin's disadvantaged life: native and poor, always in prison and always alone, committing a murder about which he seems completely dispassionate, and finally facing the death penalty at the age of twenty-nine. The ballad concludes:

> I ain't about to tell you
> That I don't deserve to die
> But there's twenty-seven men here
> Mostly black, brown and poor
> Most of 'em are guilty
> Who are you to say for sure?

So when the preacher comes to get me
And they shave off all my hair
Could you take that long walk with me
Knowing hell is waitin' there
Could you pull that switch yourself sir
With a sure and steady hand
Could you still tell yourself
That you're better than I am
My name is Billy Austin
I'm twenty-nine years old
I was born in Oklahoma
Quarter Cherokee I'm told

This last quarter of the song discusses who goes to prison and who dies for their crimes and calls into question the economic manifestations of power politics that see mostly the poor and nonwhite in prison. Earle challenges listeners to consider the demographic of death row inmates and the very real chance that some of them are innocent. However, as Billy Austin invites his audience to walk with him to the execution chamber, asks his listener to pull the switch, and questions the difference between them, Earle enters fully into the abolitionist debate. And, instead of asking his listeners to imagine themselves on death row, a move toward empathy and the humanization of inmates that Earle makes in his other abolitionist songs, Billy Austin asks them if they could actually execute a condemned prisoner. In so doing, he insists they face the issue of civic responsibility in a democracy that includes capital punishment in its penal code. Under the terms of the exceptional nature of American democracy, as Earle puts it so plainly, if your government is putting people to death, then so are you.

"Exceptionalism describes the perception of Massachusetts Bay colonists that as Puritans they were charged with a special spiritual and political destiny: to create in the New World a church and a society that would provide the model for all the nations," Deborah Madsen explains, and although "the arguments themselves change over time, the basic assumptions and terms of reference do not change, and it is the assumptions that are derived in important ways from the exceptionalist logic taken to the New World by the first Puritan migrants" (Madsen 1998, 1). I draw my understanding of exceptionalism—particularly as I apply it to Earle's consideration of what it means to be an American—as a root of American cultural identity from Madsen's work, and, like her, I rely on the earlier theorizing of Sacvan Bercovitch and Perry Miller to understand contemporary American thought through the prescriptive force of Puritan exceptionalism.

The understanding of the United States as a nation vested in its history of redemption, which thus interprets all events into the providential signs of nationalism, continues a line of thought that began in 1831 when Alexis de Tocqueville described America as a nation with a uniquely formed ideology and image of itself. Tocqueville coined the term to refer to America's perception of itself as qualitatively different from other developed nations, and while he seems most fascinated with laissez-faire as distinctively American, he notes that the country's citizens, like Earle almost two centuries later, consider democracy to be their most exceptional institution and quality. However, Lipset explains the chief quality that makes America exceptional, an open democratic society, as a double-edged sword, because its norms and behaviors are inherently linked to negative (and equally characterizing) traits, "such as income inequality, high crime rates, low levels of electoral participation, [and] a powerful tendency to moralize which at times verges on intolerance toward political and ethnic minorities" (Lipset 1997, 13).

In following Madsen and other theorists who argue that the United States views itself as an exceptional nation, a redeemer nation, I do not use the term in the manner of social scientists, who employ it to refer to some aspect of American uniqueness, such as anti-authoritarianism, individualism, the failure of socialism to take hold, or high levels of religious influence, particularly Protestantism. Social scientists thus use exceptionalism without attaching to it the qualities that Tocqueville considered part and parcel of this national ideology, and their discussions might be better termed exemptionalism than exceptionalism. Lipset points out that social scientists use the term to imply that America is different, an outlier, but he uses the term in the manner of Tocqueville. Lipset's understanding of the ways in which this ideology is rooted in the American democratic system and his consideration of exceptionalism as a double-edged sword—"we are the worst, as well as the best, depending on which quality is being addressed"—are key to my own readings of Earle's abolitionism (Lipset 1997, 18). Lipset rarely discusses the judicial system in his study of exceptionalism, but in asking, "Why does the United States have the highest crime rate, the most persons per capita in prison?" he adumbrates my reading of Earle's social critique (ibid., 17).

I started thinking about American exceptionalism, in the manner of Madsen, Lipset, and others, when I came across Harvard law professor Carol Steiker's theories about capital punishment as an exceptional American practice.[2] Steiker offers an exhaustive accounting of why America so vigorously employs the death penalty when it has "been abolished, either de jure or de facto in every single country in the Western industrialized world except for the United States" (Steiker 2002, 97).[3] The juxtaposition of cultural studies and social science theories thus seems a fruitful way to approach a social and political practice that is both supported and negated by exceptionalist ideology, even as it positions the nation as exceptional in the world's view of human rights issues.

I refer to capital punishment as both social and political practice, rather than as a strictly legal practice, for a number of reasons. In the first place, the legal system is itself a social practice meant for control, and law is a political concept; people use politics to form claims of law, claims that prohibit or permit or require certain actions, or that lead to certain entitlements or punishments. The law is thus a vast social practice centered in making, contesting, defending, and ruling on such claims. In the United States, the application of the law is sensitive—to a far greater degree than is equality or democracy—to the history and standing practices of the society that administers it. On the world stage, capital punishment has been adopted and abolished according to political and social changes. Juridical practice, particularly in tracing the history of capital punishment, reflects the shifting features of political practice and structures. A political community displays legality by keeping faith in certain ways with its past and by keeping pace with its present. The nature of the law might remain static, but its practice always reflects contemporary social values. To think of the death penalty as only a legal practice is to camouflage it and its deeper social and political implications. The pervasive presence of the federal government in the administration of capital punishment, particularly in election years, and the equally pervasive rhetoric of American exceptionalism surrounding that administration demonstrate just how deeply embedded is the death penalty in American political and social practice.

Using the term *exceptionalism* in the way of political scientists and historians, Steiker finds the United States exceptional in the case of capital punishment because, as she notes,

> the countries that most vigorously employ the death penalty are generally ones that the United States has the least in

> common with politically, economically, or socially, and ones that the United States is wont to define itself against, as they are among the least democratic and the worst human rights abusers in the world. (Steiker 2002, 97)

Like Earle, however, Steiker emphasizes individual responsibility for national practices in a democracy. After pointing out the soaring numbers that prove America is pursuing the death penalty with a vengeance, Steiker elaborates ten interconnected theories regarding why America is being exceptional about this practice, or rather, why it exempts itself from the standards held by the countries it sees as peers. Overall, her ten points tell what she terms "America's recent 'death penalty story'" and offer something of a how-to manual for the abolitionist movement, in that activists against capital punishment should be able to find in Steiker's theories the means to counter public and political endorsement of the practice. Steiker repeatedly emphasizes how complex are, as she calls them, the "powerful forces unique to the United States [that] have compelled . . . anomalous American retention of capital punishment" (Steiker 2001, 101). Her attention to this "most complex phenomena" as an exceptional American trait contrasts sharply with the relative simplicity of American exceptionalism as distinguished by Tocqueville, who noticed the beginnings of peaceful capitalism in a successful democratic state and identified the values crucial to this success as liberty, egalitarianism, individualism, populism, and laissez-faire.

Earle's approach to democracy is even starker than Tocqueville's. In concerts, he often introduces "Christmas in Washington," from the 1997 album *El Corazón*, a song that pleads, "come back Woody Guthrie, come back to us now," by describing it as a song about his heroes and by pointing out—as he does in Amos Poe's 2004 documentary *Just an American Boy: A Film about Steve Earle*—that "it is never ever unpatriotic or un-American to question any fucking thing in a democracy." Questioning something in America might not be unpatriotic, but "Christmas in Washington" lists Emma Goldman, Joe Hill, Malcolm X, Martin Luther King Jr., and Jesus as some of Earle's heroes, and if Woody Guthrie went relatively unscathed for his critiques of social practices, the others did not; they gave up everything from freedom to their lives as they protested various injustices. Notably gloomy, Earle's song, written on the occasion of the first election of George W. Bush to the presidency, may claim that "They cannot break our will," but it also notes that the country is "going straight to hell." Still, while American populism, particularly in the South, may persecute and murder the speaker's heroes and put another Bush in office, the song shoulders responsibility for the nation and its actions nonetheless. Yearning for the road traveled by these earlier radicals, the singer resolves to take his part in the democratic process (much as Earle later worked against popular opinion to try and get Bush out of office) and concludes with plans to go, possibly following the ghost of Martin Luther King Jr., "marching into Selma / As the bells of freedom ring."

"I can't ever pay enough": Individual Responsibilities

Among the complexities Steiker considers are the role of populism in the American criminal justice system and what she describes as Southern exceptionalism and American cultural exceptionalism, which are manifested in the much higher rate of executions in the American South and Southwest, and a subculture of violence. Earle directly addresses both of these phenomena in a series of songs narrated by Southern "good ol' boys" that connect military service and the high ratio of poor and working-class soldiers to domestic gun culture and the high ratio of the poor and nonwhite in prison. Earle's lyrics suggest that economics are a marker of techniques of domination that are rooted in a military culture. The connections Earle makes between overseas service and gun culture at home, in songs such as "Good Ol' Boy," "Copperhead Road," and "The Devil's Right Hand," imply that the schema of war might be the basis of the workings of power in American civil society. In his inextricable tracing of ties between military service, domestic gun culture, legalized execution of the disadvantaged, and the judiciary, Earle makes clear that, in American society, judicial and political power can be analyzed as a continuation of war. While Earle especially focuses on this subject as he protests against the war in Iraq in his songs and other media, his work has always made the connections between military service and violence at home. In short, Earle's critique of American power structures makes clear that when war is a matter of course in a nation's foreign policy, the distinctions between killings at home and abroad seem less and less important. The American boys he creates carry the threat of military violence turning into criminal action and capital punishment at home and explain how characters such as Billy Austin commit capital crimes and end up on death row. Military service has trained them for the penal system, either as guard or inmate, and little else.

In "Ellis Unit One," written for the film *Dead Man Walking* (1995), Earle constructs another veteran who returns home and, finding few choices about his future, becomes a prison guard working on death row. The song describes the immediacy of this guard's experiences with the dead men walking as he moves from irony, "And since they got the injection / They don't mind as much I guess," into an uneasy combination of responsibility and pity: "Well, I've seen 'em fight like lions, boys / I've seen 'em go like lambs / And I've helped to drag them when they could not stand." Foucault may declare that "the punishment-body relation is not what it once was in the torture during public executions," but Earle's abolitionist work is vested in the spectacle that is American capital punishment (Foucault 1995, 11). In Earle's view, there seem to be enough witnesses and enough pain to circumvent Foucault's view of the new era of punishment as lacking both torture and spectacle. In an interview, Earle comments on the term *abolitionist*: "It's pretentious, but that's what we call ourselves," but the chorus of "Ellis Unit One" borrows from "Swing Low Sweet Chariot," an African American slave spiritual ("Interview with Andrew Weber"). The song thus aligns the nineteenth-century Abolitionist cause with contemporary abolition activism, even as it implies that the men on Ellis Unit One are poor and often other than white. Capital punishment, then, is as much a social and political practice as was slavery, and in this, Earle follows at least two of Foucault's governing principles in *Discipline and Punish*: "Regard punishment as a social function. . . . Regard punishment as a political tactic" (Foucault 1995, 23). In this regard, the distinction between the condemned and the guard becomes a mutable boundary, and Earle ends the song with his guard-narrator dreaming himself into the experiences of the men on death row: "Last night I dreamed that I woke up with straps across my chest / And something cold and black pullin' through my lungs / 'N even Jesus couldn't save me though I know he did his best." This man's transition from soldier to executioner to condemned prisoner shows him to be just another pawn in a judicial system that is both political tactic and social function.

In her discussion of the salience of crime as a political issue, Steiker points out that the death penalty often serves as a focal point in electoral politics already organized around law and order. Particularly horrific murders grab the public imagination, while the drama of the death penalty provides an easily accessible symbol of righteousness and order to aspiring politicians. George W. Bush's involvement in the execution of Karla Faye Tucker, the first woman to be executed in Texas since the Civil War, provides one such case in point.[4] As governor, Bush rejected Tucker's pleas for clemency, although public figures interceding on her behalf included UN officials, Pope John Paul II, Pat Robertson, and the prime minister of Italy. Despite these pleas, and those of the parents of her victims, Bush, who set a gubernatorial record for presiding over executions (152 in his six years as governor), signed her death warrant, and she was executed in 1998.[5] In the 1999 presidential race, each of the initial eleven candidates supported the death penalty. Anyone working against the death penalty must take an active role in party politics, and aside from writing dour songs when Bush is reelected, Earle, like many other activist-musicians, Michelle Shocked among them, both campaigns and plans his tours in support of pro-abolition candidates. In an interview with Mark LePage, Earle notes his hope that change may come soon, and he quotes Sister Helen Prejean, author of *Dead Man Walking*, who contends that "support for the death penalty in this country is a mile wide, but it's only an inch deep" (Earle 2005).

Earle also counters public support for the death penalty and responds to the Tucker case in his play *Karla*. Staged in Nashville in 2002 and in New York City in 2005, *Karla* is a one-act, intensely emotional play that opens with her execution and continues with confrontations in purgatory between Tucker and her mother, co-murderer, and victims. The play, off-Broadway though it may be, engages with the worldwide attention on Tucker's case. Drawing from her biography and her death row interview with Larry King, Earle's fictional account forces Tucker to take responsibility for her crimes, something, he points out in a *New York Times* interview, she never did in life. The play turns on violently emotional intensity, but it ends up being about forgiveness and the recognition of suffering, as the characters recognize the suffering of the others and themselves and proceed to forgive themselves and each other. Ultimately, the play becomes about all human suffering and the capacity to forgive and to heal. *Karla* challenges those belief systems that continue to make capital punishment an electoral issue, as it argues Earle's view that "the death penalty diminishes all of us" (Earle 2005). The play refigures execution as a re-victimization of the victims, and no one leaves unscathed, not the victims, executed, executioners, friends, family, nor, given the play's level of intensity, the audience.[6]

Steiker credits homicide rates as the main reason for public support of capital punishment, and however much abolitionists are against politically endorsed murder, they tend to draw heavily on the statistics that prove capital punishment does not prevent homicide any more than prisons prevent any type of crime. And, of course, they complicate the issue with evidence of wrongful convictions and executions, a more common occurrence with the increasingly sophisticated development of DNA testing. The American Civil Liberties Union, for example, points out that 119 prisoners sentenced to death have been exonerated since 1976, most by DNA evidence (Earle 2005b). Combining the unique character of American egalitarianism and the propensity of the legal system to enact racialized codes of justice, Earle's discussion of guilt and innocence challenges support for the death penalty. The condemned characters he writes in "Billy Austin" and *Karla* are guilty, and their deaths are figured as a social and political wrong. In these and other works, Earle argues that the colored and poor are more likely to end up in jail, and after making the listener culpable for that, he also makes the listener decide on social responsibility for killing those who might not be guilty. As Billy Austin points out, "Who are you to say for sure?" However, Earle also engages with the idea of the wrongfully convicted inmate on death row. In "The Witness," a story in Earle's collection *Doghouse Roses* (2001), the title character is a wealthy white corporate lawyer who murdered his wife, then stood by while their uneducated and non-English-speaking gardener was tried and sentenced to death. The narrative takes place as the lawyer travels to witness the execution, and it follows his journey as witness while he remembers killing his wife for the insurance money, aiding the police in convicting his Hispanic gardener for the crime, and, most recently, murdering his mistress. Earle draws this character in subtle strokes, as he offers details about how the death penalty affects everyone involved. This witness acts and reacts in the manner expected of him by the penal system, while the man whose language skills prevented him from aiding in his own defense dies declaring his innocence in Spanish.

Earle embeds a good deal of irony in the title of "The Witness." In abolitionist rhetoric, a witness is someone who has seen an execution, either as a family member of the victim/s, family member or invited guest of the condemned, or officer of the court. In 1998, Earle witnessed the Texas execution of Jonathan Wayne Nobles, with whom he had corresponded for ten years, and he discusses this experience, which he describes as "horrific," in several interviews, an essay and a song. Like the story, these pieces invoke the one issue about American popular support for the death penalty that Steiker does not elaborate: the notion of execution as some sort of compensation or vengeance or closure for the family and friends of murder victims. In an Australian TV interview, Earle says that he agreed to contribute to Tim Robbins's *Dead Man Walking* project partly because the album would benefit an organization called Murder Victims' Families For Reconciliation. As sensitive to the families of the victims as Robbins and Prejean, Earle argues:

> If you say you're opposed to the death penalty, the first thing thrown at you is, "What about the victims?" Because the idea is that somehow they're benefitting the victims by executing people. . . . That's never seemed right to me and . . . I know it's not true anymore because I've actually stood [there with them]. (Earle 2004a)

Arguing that everyone involved, every witness and every correctional worker, and the wider population, is damaged by capital punishment, Earle points out that victims' family members are allowed to witness executions if they want to, and he calls the death penalty states "grossly irresponsible for allowing that to happen . . . I still have bad dreams" (Earle 2004a). Earle thus figures witnessing as another form of victimization.

In an interview with Rick Halperin immediately after Nobles's death, Earle again considers the issue of responsibility: "I still believe that what I just witnessed was murder, although nobody in this prison is any more responsible than anybody else in the state of Texas or the country for that matter" (Earle 1998). He details his friendship with Nobles, the time they spent together and the execution in an article for *Tikkun*, a bimonthly magazine that analyzes American and Israeli culture, politics, religion, and history. He focuses on the changes Nobles underwent in prison, going from being a universally hated addict to a sober Catholic who embodied the Hebrew principle of *hesed*, or lovingkindness. Describing Nobles's conversion as a means of *tikkun* (a Hebrew word meaning the repair of the world), Earle focuses on what society lost with Jonathan; "Given as many people as we lock up," he concludes, "we better learn to rehabilitate someone. I believe Jon might have been able to teach us how" (Earle 2000, 30). Along with the essay, Earle released "Over Yonder (Jonathan's Song)" in 2000, a quiet ballad about Nobles's final hours that draws from his letters and conversations with Earle:

> The warden said he'd mail my letter
> The chaplain's waitin' by the door
> Tonight we'll cross the yard together
> Then they can't hurt me anymore.
> I am going over yonder
> Where no ghost can follow me
> There's another place beyond here
> Where I'll be free I believe.
> Give my radio to Johnson
> Thibodeaux can have my fan
> Send my Bible home to Mama
> Call her every now and then.
> I suppose I got it comin'
> I can't ever pay enough.

After giving away his possessions, the speaker offers his regret and concludes by hoping that his death will bring peace to everyone who hates him. However, in attending to the suffering of victims' families and everyone involved in executions, Earle makes clear that witnessing an execution never brings anyone anything positive, which is borne out by the comments made by the mother of one of Nobles's victims after his death: "It's not a pleasant thing watching someone die, no matter the circumstances," she said. "There's no such thing as closure. The punishment was just. It doesn't mean we have to like it" (Earle 1998). There is grim heroism here as Nobles shoulders an unending responsibility for his crimes, and an even bleaker heroism as the mother takes on the responsibility of witnessing. Like Earle, she likely had bad dreams for a long time. Earle introduces "Jonathan's Song" in the terms of universal responsibility for Nobles's death: "My own opposition to the death penalty is pretty core. I object to the damage that it does to my spirit, for my government to kill people, because my government's supposed to be me, and I object to me killing people" (Poe 2004).

Individual responsibility is not the whole of it, though; even as Earle and Halperin relate the stories of this death in Texas, they insist on awareness that everyone in this democratic nation is responsible. Bad dreams about executions ought to be nationwide.

"The land of the infidel": Taking Exception

The privileging of individual voices is, of course, one of the chief underpinnings of American exceptionalism. Earle defines patriotism as "remembering as an American—that it's never, ever unpatriotic to question anything in a democracy, no matter what," and he clearly enjoys relating an anecdote about Senator Patrick Leahy's response to Attorney General Ashcroft's comment that anyone who questioned anything that the Department of Homeland Security did in the area of terrorism was aiding and abetting terrorism (Earle 2004b). When questioned about it, Leahy pointed out that the attorney general has the same First Amendment rights as every American. Earle concludes the story by affirming the First Amendment is "one of the most important things and one of the best things about being in America and living in a democracy" (ibid.).

Earle's patriotism, then, begins with his view of the American democratic system as exceptional, even as he takes exception to its flaws. In "John Walker's Blues," from his 2002 album *Jerusalem*, Earle gives a voice to John Walker Lindh, the so-called American Taliban, tried and imprisoned for fighting alongside al-Qaeda forces in the Middle East:

> I'm just an American boy raised on MTV
> And I've seen all those kids in the soda pop ads
> But none of 'em looked like me
> So I started lookin' around for a light out of the dim
> And the first thing I heard that made sense was the word
> Of Mohammed, peace be upon him
> A shadu la ilaha illa Allah
> There is no God but God.

Not ostensibly a song in support of abolition, Earle's anxiety about capital punishment comes into play when he performs "John Walker's Blues," as he ponders the similarities between Lindh and his own son, calling them "skinny kids you can't fill up" (Earle 2004a). Earle's tension rests in the fact that once returned to America, "the land of the infidel," Lindh faces the possibility of execution for his role in Taliban activities. What Earle sees as choices made out of youthful disillusionment could result in execution, something that thinking Americans should be protesting. In speaking about Lindh and against capital punishment, Earle became the target of nationwide anger. Regarding the recent backlash against politically active celebrities, Earle says this is "a relatively new idea in a democracy, as far as I know. Last I knew, we were citizens and had a right to comment about anything we wanted" (Earle 2004b). David Carithers finds in Earle's activism "an Emersonian brand of pragmatism in his provocative stories meant to rouse the mind to action, and a Whitmanesque poetics in his vision of a better democracy" (Carithers 2005, 2), and I agree but suggest that Earle acts under the prescriptive force of American exceptionalism. In short, for Earle, America's exceptionalism insists that he critique everything he finds problematic in all of its social structures. "Democracy is hard work. American democracy requires constant vigilance to survive and nothing short of total engagement to flourish," Earle argues in the liner notes to *The Revolution Starts Now* (2004), itself an exercise in exceptionalist discourse:

> The Constitution of The United States of America is a REVOLUTIONARY document in every sense of the word. It was designed to evolve, to live, and to breathe like the people that it governs. It is, ingeniously, and perhaps conversely, resilient enough to change with the times in order to meet the challenges of its third century and rigid enough to preserve the ideals that inspired its original articles and amendments. As long as we are willing to put in the work required to defend and nurture this remarkable invention of our forefathers, then I believe with all my heart that it will continue to thrive for generations to come. (Earle 2004)

Rather than turning to David Noble's postnationalism, Earle, with "John Walker's Blues" and the texts discussed above, turns to the narrative of American democracy as an exceptional national quality. As a patriot, Earle, also "just an American boy," must record the narratives of capital punishment, those of Jonathan Nobles, John Walker Lindh, and others, as he takes exception to this social and political practice.

Notes

1. In *Just an American Boy*, Amos Poe's 2004 documentary, Earle sings this song after John Terzano presents him with a Human Rights Award. It is an apt choice and a stark performance.

2. I started thinking about the death penalty—which was abolished in my country, Canada, in 1976—and American culture when I arrived in Waco, Texas, for a conference and turned on the television in my hotel room just in time to hear live play-by-play commentary on the death of Betty Lou Beets by lethal injection, Feb. 24, 2000, narrated as it happened by Warden Jim Willett. Beets was the second woman to be executed in Texas under Governor George W. Bush.

3. Steiker's essay also appears in Michael Ignatieff's collection *American Exceptionalism and Human Rights*. Ignatieff notes that he does not "revisit wider historical and sociological debates about why Americans have seen their society exceptional at least since the Pilgrim Fathers" (2), but he does refer to them as he considers America's "paradox of being simultaneously a leader and an outlier" (2).

4. On June 11, 1983, in Houston, Karla Faye Tucker and Danny Garrett hacked two people to death in the midst of a drug- and alcohol-fueled rage. Only twenty-four at the time of the murders, the petite and pretty Tucker already had a long history of substance abuse and prostitution. Tucker and Garrett were tried separately, found guilty, and sentenced to death. Between being charged and tried, Tucker became a born-again Christian and changed her plea to guilty. She showed genuine remorse for her crimes and repeatedly asked the families of her victims for forgiveness. She later married, by proxy, the prison chaplain. Her conversion was both genuine and compelling; in her fourteen years on death row, Tucker attracted the attention of religious leaders and political activists around the world, including Sister Helen Prejean. Under Bush, the Texas Board of Pardons and Parole denied her request, and Tucker was executed on February 2, 1998.

5. After Tucker's execution, Bush mocked her during an interview with Tucker Carlson for *Talk Magazine*. According to Carlson, Bush misquoted Tucker's interview with Larry King and mocked her by pursing his lips and using a falsetto to say "please don't kill me Mr. Bush" (Bush 1999, 106).

6. To date, the play is unpublished; a scene from the Nashville run is featured in Poe's documentary.

Works Cited

Bush, George W. 1999. Interview with Tucker Carlson. *Talk Magazine*, September: 106.

Carithers, David. 2005. Steve Earle and the possibilities of pragmatism. *Americana: The Journal of American Popular Culture, 1900 to Present* (ejournal) 4, no. 2.

Earle, Steve. 1986. *Guitar town* (Album). MCA.

———. 1988. *Copperhead road* (Album). UNI.

———. 1990. *The hard way* (Album). MCA.

———. 1997. *El corazón* (Album). Artemis.

———. 1998. Interview with Rick Halperin. Associated Press, October 7.

———. 2000. A death in Texas. *Tikkun* 15: 25–30.

———. 2000a. *Transcendental blues* (Album). Artemis.

———. 2001. The witness. In *Doghouse roses.* New York: Houghton Mifflin.

———. 2002. Interview with Jody Denberg, October 17.

———. 2002a. *Jerusalem* (Album). Artemis.

———. 2002b. *Side tracks* (Album). Artemis.

———. 2003. Interview with Steve Inskeep. National Public Radio, December 7.

———. 2004. *The revolution starts now* (Album). Artemis.

———. 2004a. In concert. Ottawa. November 9.

———. 2004b. Interview with Andrew Denton. *Enough Rope.* Australian Broadcasting Corporation Television, April 5.

———. 2005. Interview with Bruce Weber. *New York Times*, October 22.

———. 2005a. Interview with Boris Kachka. *New York Magazine*: October 24.

———. 2005b. Interview with Mark LePage. *Montreal Gazette*, October 30.

Foucault, Michel. 1995. *Discipline and punish: The birth of the prison.* Trans. Alan Sheridan. New York: Vintage.

Ignatieff, Michael. 2005. Introduction. In *American exceptionalism and human rights,* ed. Michael Ignatieff, 1–26. Princeton: Princeton University Press.

Lipset, Seymour Martin. 1997. *American exceptionalism: A double-edged sword.* New York: Norton.

Madsen, Deborah L. 1998. *American exceptionalism.* Jackson: University Press of Mississippi.

Noble, David W. 2002. *Death of a nation: American culture and the end of exceptionalism.* Minneapolis: University of Minnesota Press.

Poe, Amos, dir. 2004. *Just an American boy: A film about Steve Earle.* E-Squared/Sheridan Square Entertainment.

Steiker, Carol S. 2002. Capital punishment and American exceptionalism. *Oregon Law Review* 81: 97–130.

Tocqueville, Alexis de. 1851. *American institutions and their influence.* New York: A. S. Barnes.

10

Oprah's Vigilante Sentimentalism

Sara Humphreys

"The children of this nation—the United States of America—are being stolen, raped, tortured and killed by sexual predators who are walking right into your home," declares Oprah Winfrey in the short film that is activated upon entrance into Oprah's Child Predator Watch List, which was an online environment devoted to capturing wanted child molesters.[1] With the inauguration of Oprah's Child Predator Watch List, located on the Oprah.com network, in October 2005, Oprah promised to rid the nation of an "evil that's been going on for far too long." Not surprisingly, Oprah's hyperbolic claim to eradicate an evil that threatens to destroy the American home does more to promote American exceptionalism than alleviate the complicated problem of child molestation. That is, Oprah's Child Predator Watch List represents American, specifically white and female, children as the embodiment of threatened national purity in order to market a brand of righteous, moral American identity.

I will take up two sections of the website where multilayered narratives operate to create a righteous "us" who will protect the nation's children from an evil "them": Oprah's filmed evangelical speech and a memorial to six white, female victims of abduction, rape, and murder. In each section, the complex problem of child sexual abuse is misrepresented in favor of coercing viewers to collectively mourn and avenge the victimized child. As a secondary argument, analyzing the visual, oral, and written rhetoric that comprises Oprah's Child Predator Watch List sheds light on the power of new media environments to support national agendas.

Web Sites as National Narratives

Oprah's Child Predator Watch List[2] is only one narrative thread within the narrative universe of Oprah.com. Comprising complex story lines and narration, Oprah.com is a multilayered narrative; however, analyzing the components that produce this multimedia narrative is challenging, according to Lev Manovich, because the analytical tools to facilitate such study are not yet fully developed (Manovich 2001, 228). Undoubtedly, if Oprah.com was not published via the Internet, but instead was produced as a pulp fiction series, for example, the narrative formulas and traditions that the Watch List draws from would be much more apparent. However, Oprah.com is a new media object that assembles narrative formulas into interfaced layers that are published using Internet protocols.

The Internet, like Gutenberg's printing press, has revolutionized how we circulate the narratives that construct our reality. When Mark Poster asserts that no one "can doubt the role of print and television in . . . profoundly [altering] the way people think, fantasize and behave" (Poster 2002, 103), he makes a case for the power of the medium that carries the message. The Internet has certainly changed reading habits, but it does not stop the narratives, and the discourses they circulate, from reproducing the stereotypes and ideologies that create a stable, knowable reality. Therefore, media do not simply carry messages; they transmit cultural lessons and knowledge via, for example, narrative formulas. The Watch List uses formulaic characters, such as the female captive and the exploited child, to influence the mass public[3] to "think, fantasize and behave" in specific ways, but how do we read these narrative formulas and figures when they appear within Web environments?

In traditional creative forms, such as the novel or impressionist painting, "the interface and the work were the same; in other words," suggests Manovich, "the level of the interface did not exist" (Manovich 2001, 227). However, in websites, it is "possible to create different interfaces to the same material" (ibid.). For instance, in the Watch List, viewers[4] can click on an image, such as a photograph of murder victim Jessica Lunsford, and then interface with another narrative layer that contains the same image combined with a description of Jessica's rape and murder. While the Watch List is not a traditional narrative, the word *narrative* aptly describes the Watch List as a new media object that assembles and connects (or interfaces) visual and written material to create a coherent violent, sentimental, and national narrative.

Mieke Bal suggests that multimedia cultural objects, such as museum exhibits and websites, should be analyzed as narratives that express points of view through narrative voices that are aimed toward a reader/viewer. Further, these narratives must be viewed as conduits for cultural discourses, which are the "semiotic and epistemological habits that enables and prescribes [*sic*] ways of communicating and thinking" (Bal 1996, 3). While not all websites suit this analytical model, the Watch List displays and narrates cultural objects that are "anchored in a belief, almost tautologically referred to as positivist, [and communicate that] what you see must be real, true, present, or otherwise reliable" (ibid., 5). Oprah's exposition of child abduction and sexual abuse as an epidemic, combined with the display of murdered white girls as proof, is "anchored to a belief" in the threatened national home. The viewer's introduction to this belief system is through a film of Oprah narrating her site's purpose.

Oprah's Narrative Function

When the viewer enters the site, a somber Oprah, dressed in black, evangelically orates the purpose of the Watch List via a film powered by Flash technology. Usually, the viewer must use a mouse click to activate Flash or Shockwave before an object, such as a film, can be viewed, but in this case, developers bypassed this function in favor of having the film activate automatically each time the viewer enters the homepage, entitled "Oprah's Message" (Steffans 2007, 1). Thus, this short film aggressively positions Oprah as an authoritative, narrating presence.

As Oprah begins to speak, the camera zooms in from a wide shot, starting within Oprah's studio audience and ending mid-speech with a close-up on Oprah. The opening shot establishes a relationship between the viewing audience and Oprah, "whereby meaning emerges and a subject-position is constructed for the viewer" (Silverman 1999, 138).

This shot situates the viewer within Oprah's audience, while she stands on the stage of her talk show set. The viewer is, as a result, sutured into the audience while the camera controls the viewer's gaze, settling upon Oprah as the prime subject framed within the shot. However, while this shot controls the viewer's gaze, Oprah's words transform "the cinematic space into a dramatic space" (ibid., 146):

> Today I stand before you to say in no uncertain terms—as a matter of fact, in terms that I hope are very certain—that I have had enough. With every breath in my body, whatever it takes and, most importantly, with your support, we are going to move heaven and earth to stop a sickness, a darkness that I believe is the definition of evil that's been going on for far too long. The children of this nation—the United States of America—are being stolen, raped, tortured and killed by sexual predators, who are walking right into your home. How many times does this have to happen? And how many children have to be sacrificed? What price are we as a society willing to continue to pay before we rise up and take to the streets and say, "enough"—"enough"—"enough"? (Oprah's Message 2007)

The speech operates within an extremist evangelical tradition that unites a righteous "us" who must vilify an evil "them" that must be excised from the nation, thereby perfecting the national order. Oprah cleverly moves from one narrative voice to the next; she first establishes herself as a first-person narrator; she then addresses the audience directly in the second-person plural, implicating her viewers as essential members of her national project; finally, she encloses her viewers within the collective "we," who "can move heaven and earth to stop a sickness." Such a movement from the first-person singular to the first-person plural progressively repositions the viewer from passive observer to an interactive member, who stands beside Oprah, ready to join in her national fight against evil.

Oprah defines herself as the designated protector and/or divinely appointed leader, who can save the nation from a scourge. Eva Illouz persuasively argues that Oprah Winfrey "is best understood as a criss-crossing of expert knowledge, multiple media technologies, and orality intertwined with multiple forms of literacy, overlapping media industries, cyberspace, support groups and traditional charismatic authority"; within the framework of the Watch List, Oprah also performs a specific narrative function (Illouz 2003, 5). Clearly, she is not a traditional literary narrator, but her opening speech undoubtedly informs the viewer that she is an omniscient presence within the Watch List narrative.

Oprah's on-screen authoritative presence draws from her prodigious cultural capital, which includes ideals attendant to the American way of life, such as financial success, self-sufficiency, individualism, and self-improvement. While her cultural capital supplies ethos, Oprah's manipulation of pathos compels the viewer to join her vigilante project. Specifically, Oprah expertly wields sentimentality, an American structure of feeling that constitutes social perception (Williams 1977, 132). Sentimentality is not simply an aspect of a nineteenth-century literary genre but describes a national economy in passionate emotion, whereby apparently disparate social groups and individuals are invited to bond via sentimental tears. Sentimentality creates the fantasy of a unified, consensual national culture that glosses over and distracts from the real and highly complex difficulties of everyday life (Berlant 2000). Using specific literary constructions, such as repetition and word choice, Oprah emotionally invests the reader/viewer in her vigilante project that is not only anchored in the pain of traumatized children but also in Oprah's value as a consumable sentimental object.

The Oprah Winfrey Show operates as a confessional forum, from which Oprah shares her intimate pain as the survivor of child sexual abuse, among other traumas, with millions of viewers. Oprah's ability to command her audience to perform as bounty hunters in the name of protecting the nation's children does not simply draw from her wealth and influence; more accurately, the rhetorical force of her words rests in her status as a "political model of identity trauma [that] stands as truth" (Berlant 2000, 72). Oprah's appeal rests in her apparently contradictory positions as the all-powerful mogul and as the victimized figure of pain; the former status provides an illusion of fulfilling the American Dream, while the latter status enables Oprah to perform as an expert in pain, who can translate her guests' trauma for the audience. On her show and in articles published in popular magazines, Oprah brings her private pain into the mass public sphere to create the fantasy of intimate connections with a vast viewing audience (Illouz 2003, 16, 29). This performance of pain and suffering is "the true core of national collectivity," explains Lauren Berlant,

> when the pain of intimate others burns into the conscience of classically privileged national subjects, such that they feel the pain of flawed or denied citizenship as their pain. Theoretically, to eradicate pain those with power will do whatever is necessary to return the nation once more to its legitimately utopian odor. (Berlant 1999, 53)

Oprah simultaneously operates as the privileged national subject who can voice others' pain and as the intimate other who can claim the wounded image.

Consequently, vigilantism, which is fuelled by extreme anger and pain, provides an easily accessible outlet for the politics of pain within which Oprah operates. In technical terms, vigilantism occurs mainly when a constant set of value expectations appears to be in decline. In this case, the expectation that adults will not violate children is perceived as being transgressed on a national and increasing scale (Rosenbaum and Sederberg 1974, 544). On the Watch List, right beside the film of Oprah's speech, is a blurb that states: "You see it regularly on newscasts, innocent children abducted, raped and murdered." This inflammatory statement communicates the idea that the most extreme form of child sexual abuse—the abduction/murder scenario—is the norm, when, in reality, such cases are extremely rare (Finkelhor 2005, 6). Such inflation of the most horrific cases of sexual abuse into proof of a national crisis not only makes for good ratings but also creates a national collective that righteous and moral Americans can join.

The type of national vigilantism that Oprah proposes reproduces America as an exceptional, sacred space in need of protection. In her speech, Oprah claims the authority to vilify evil members of the population in the name of saving more important members. Those who join her crusade are, in turn, members of the elect who have the opportunity to not only enjoy the privilege of divine membership but also gain social status and monetary rewards. Oprah offers all those who turn in wanted child molesters one hundred thousand dollars in reward money, which she awards on her show. Oprah offers the opportunity for American citizens to become bounty hunters, who—if successful—can share the national stage with her.

While Oprah is an imposing narrative presence within the Watch List, she is not the only narrator. Just below Oprah's stern visage is a link to the reason the Watch List exists: the victims of child molestation.

"The Victims" link transports the viewer into a page narrated by Oprah and a cinematic narrator. The cinematic narrator "is not to be identified with the voice-over narrator" but should be viewed as a "composite of a large and complex variety of communicating devices," such as the treatment of image and visual structure (Chatman 2004, 482). Each of these components influence the "semiotic processing performed by the viewer," who can translate the assembled sequence of words and images presented into a narrative. That is, the viewer, who is trained to "know the rules of language and culture," will decode the images and visual structure of the Watch List narrative as an invitation to join a righteous "us" who fight against an evil "them" for the good of the nation (ibid., 484).

The American Economy in Female Captivity and Dead Children

The main sentimental characters within Oprah's violent national narrative are six white girls—Polly Klaas, Amber Hagerman, Carlie Brucia, Jessica Lunsford, Megan Kanka, and Samantha Runnion—who were each abducted, raped and murdered. These girls and their stories are distilled through the figures of the exploited child and the female captive, which converge on the Watch List to communicate the long-standing cultural formula of the threatened national family. The fusion of these iconic cultural constructs on the Watch List incites a vehement fear that "defines for us the very opposite of all that we choose or desire" (Fisher 2002, 15). These girls' images and stories are visually structured to create simplistic, clear-cut binaries between good and evil. While these children seem to be the focus of concern, they are nothing more than rhetorical tools to further a national project. As Mary Chapman and Glenn Hendler note, the sentimental tropes of the dead child and the destroyed family are repeatedly narrativized in a wide variety of media in American culture (Chapman and Hendler 1999, 9).

When the sentimental tropes of the afflicted family and the suffering white, female child are deployed through the captivity formula, the result is a powerful and intoxicating fusion of sentimental discourses. Indeed, the American captivity narrative has been credited with constituting the "first coherent myth-literature developed in America for American audiences," creating national collectivity through the tears shed for the female captive and defining white superiority by demarcating legitimate and illegitimate identities (Slotkin 1973, 95; Burnham 1997, 5; Barnett 1975, 49). Christopher Castiglia argues that the captivity narrative needs "to be a central part of current critical investigations into the constructions of gender, race and nation," because the captivity narrative still has remarkable influence in American culture (Castiglia 1996, 3).[5] The endurance of the captivity narrative can be attributed to its cultural purpose to construct and reinforce the "binary division between captive and captor," allowing for simplistic categories of good and evil (Burnham1997, 2). In addition, the white female captive, as the protagonist of the typical captivity narrative, operates as a marker for national status. Her role in the home as the "guarantor of American cultural superiority" means that if her body is threatened, then the national body is equally threatened (Sanchez-Eppler 1996, 413).

If the captive is a white female child, then multiple tropes of sentimentality proliferate: the dead child, white female captive, and the destroyed home operate together to produce an almost frenzied state of emotional distress in the reader/viewer, who, in turn, is willing to enact any means necessary to punish the perpetrators of such heinous actions. Indeed, the dead, white girls represented on the Watch List are not meant to depict the reality of child victimization but perform as powerful rhetorical tropes that support national values. Karen Sanchez-Eppler writes that America universally "trumpets its love of and concern for children, as it cynically deploys the 'poster child' to secure allegiance to any and all political agendas, and yet consistently fails to support the daily needs of children" (Sanchez-Eppler 1996, xv). According to Lauren Berlant, the American child represents the inspiring sign of the painless good life, but the child can equally become the figure of pain (Berlant 1999, 72). In the Watch List, these six girls fulfill both roles, at once representing a utopian past and a dystopian future. In the Watch List, the murdered female child supports the enduring ideal of "the properly pious and affectionate family as the guarantor of American cultural superiority" by reminding the viewer that destruction of the American way of life is always at hand and, therefore, "we" must be ever-vigilant (Sanchez-Eppler 1996, 414). These abducted and murdered girls reiterate long-standing national anxieties regarding the potential dissolution of American values (ibid., 66).

Displayed as the apex of desire, these girls are the objects of perverted desire and normative desire. Oprah is the "epistemic authority" who can point to these murdered girls and say: "Look! That is how it is" (Bal 1996, 2). Consequently, through the exhibition of these victims, she reinforces cultural myths of a racially pure national home and body. In Oprah's speech, she trumpets the abduction and sexual molestation of children as a national sickness, but she proves her point using memorials to white victims, who do not represent the social reality of child sexual abuse,[6] but instead are used to perform a sentimental function to connect with and, thereby, influence the viewer.

In combination with sentimental attachment, each page in the Watch List is designed to control and regulate the viewer's visual field. The Watch List is analogous to Jeremy Bentham's panopticon, situating the viewer as an official member of a national community that enforces the law through vigilant watching. In fact, a picture of Oprah's studio audience, in which each person appears to be gazing at the viewer, fills the background of each page. In the foreground, a graphic of a "police dossier" is placed; each file in the dossier contains information about the victims, child molesters, and Oprah's crusade. The background graphic of the studio audience positions us within the ranks of Oprah's viewing public. Much as in her opening speech, "we" are visually placed firmly within Oprah's "nation." In the upper righthand corner of each page a logo that resembles the crosshairs of a gun scope brands the Watch List as a space of corporate ownership and visual control; indeed, each page in the Watch List centers on acts of vigilant watching.

While each and every page regulates the viewer's gaze and, by extension, emotional reaction, the page that displays the victims uses a unique form of emotional control: the family and school photographs of each murdered girl. The Watch List uses family and school photographs of the victims in order to "[give] the illusion of being a simple transcription of the real, a trace touched directly by the event it records" (Hirsch 1997, 7). Through our ability to interface with the family and school photographs of the victims, we can create intimate connections with the six murdered girls. Yet, the logo, the color saturation and the graphics that package these photographs not only control our interpretation but also drastically change the original event to which each photograph refers. We are not privy to the moment in which the photograph was taken but are transported with a mouse click to the tragic, violent story of each girl's murder. The structuring of and the interface between the photograph and the written narrative transform these girls into mythic victims of capture and sexual torture.

Each photograph is placed in symmetrical relation to the next, which creates a homogenous visual field. These static, symmetrical photographs of smiling, dead children become dynamic when the Flash code is engaged. Once the cursor passes over a photograph, the color fades. The faded photograph is clearly designed to illustrate the child's passing or "fading" from the material world. The initial modality of these pictures is to communicate everyday reality, which is achieved, in part, through the realistic color saturation of each photo (Kress and van Leeuwen 2000, 159). Photographs of happy smiling children in family and/or school photographs are common to most American families, but if there is less color saturation than the norm "we judge [photographs as] 'less than real,' [and] 'ethereal" (ibid.). The faded photograph signifies each girl's passing from the living world while simultaneously highlighting the viewer's opportunity to voyeuristically engage with her traumatic story.

Once the viewer clicks the faded photograph, an enlarged photograph "returns" to the living world via normal color saturation and sits atop a faded background consisting of the other girls' photographs. The viewer's interest in each girl's traumatic story returns the girl's image to "reality," which supplies the viewer with a certain amount of power and agency. Beside the restored photograph is a mini-narrative of each child's abduction and rape, which is visually structured to resemble a newspaper story, enhancing the truth-value of the Watch List. For example, accompanying Amber Hagerman's photograph is the following story:

> In January 1996, 9 year old Amber Hagerman was riding her bicycle in a parking lot near her grandmother's home when a man grabbed her and forced her into his vehicle. Four days later, authorities found her naked body at the bottom of a creek bed. She had been raped and her throat was slit. Her killer is still at large. (Oprah's Watch List 2007)

Amber's story seems to be told with the disinterested rhetoric of reported speech, which suggests to the reader that this story correctly reflects the real event. However, this story carefully packages Amber's murder in a specific way. Rather than directly state that Amber had been raped and murdered, the viewer/reader is provided a graphic, verbal picture of a little girl, who lies "naked" with her "throat slit" in a "creek bed." As the reader reconstructs this violent scene, Amber stares dolefully at the viewer/reader from her family photograph, as if addressing the viewer directly and demanding that "we" respond appropriately.

Because each of these pictures "address[es] the viewer directly, realizing a visual 'you,'" they are called "demand" pictures (Kress and van Leeuwen 2000, 122). They require the viewer to "enter into some kind of imaginary relation with [an image that] wants something" (ibid., 118). These intimate photographs want the viewer to recognize these girls as once ideal children, who inhabited an idyllic world. Such "demand" creates tension and, therefore, heightened emotion in the viewer, who knows full well that this child and her world were destroyed. After the viewer clicks on the photograph and reads about each girl's gruesome end, this tension is released into sentimental tears, vehement fear, and righteous anger. The visual structuring of these pictures powerfully manipulates the viewer to believe that there is a "pseudo-social bond" between the viewer and the girl (ibid.). However, most viewers only know these six girls as murder victims; as such, these girls cease to be persons who once had complex lives and, instead, become mythic representations of violence and exploitation.

In addition to being faced with the demand of each girl's photograph to engage with her suffering, the viewer is forcefully directed by an imperative voice to "click for their stories." This omniscient narrator, who can logically be identified as Oprah, tells the viewer in bold type just above the photographs that "we will never forget these children"; the viewer is compelled by the visual and written rhetoric to identify with pain, hate the predator, and mourn the child. If the viewer can achieve each of these emotional stages, then the viewer can join with the narrating "we." This collective "we" is first introduced in Oprah's opening speech by way of a rhetorical question: "What price are we as a society willing to continue to pay before we rise up and take to the streets and say, "enough"—"enough"—"enough"? Like any good rhetorical question, its answer is already provided for the viewer, who is expected to realize that in the moral balance sheet of the nation vigilantism is an acceptable cost to save the nation's white, female children. Thus, the visual rhetoric and narrative devices within this page work together to produce a vigilant citizen, who fears and hates those who invade the imagined sanctity of the nation-home.

The white female captive, whose violated body is equated with a victimized nation, and the exploited child, whose defiled innocence becomes a rhetorical tool for social causes, supplant the real, complex lives of these six murdered girls. These children are reduced to cultural commodities to be consumed by a mass public hungry to indulge in the pain of others. Oprah's use of economic terms in her opening speech to describe these children as a "price" that the nation is paying for public apathy reflects the Web site's main goal, which is to make money. Oprah.com is filled with ads, and the Watch List is no exception. Located in the frame directly beside the girls' pictures are various ads that rotate on a continuous basis. As a result, these girls are doubly consumable as cultural objects around which a national collectivity can form and as profitable marketing tools that provide excellent product placement opportunities for advertisers. Consequently, "The Victims" page encourages viewers to indulge in righteous indignation, sentimental tears, and free market consumption.

False Premise versus Obvious Evidence

Oprah claims that child abduction and molestation are a type of national scourge, yet The Children's Bureau of the U.S. Department of Health and Human Services states that substantiated sex abuse cases declined in the 1990s by 57 percent (107). In fact, Dr. David Finkelhor, who is the director of the Crimes against Children Research Center (CCRC), and his team of researchers discovered, "based on available data, that at least part of the decline was a true decline in incidence" and not based on artificially inflated numbers (Jones et al., 2006, 107). The rigorous methodology employed by experts thus completely contradicts Oprah's evangelical rhetoric which would lead the viewer to believe that child abduction and murder is an epidemic.

The decline in child sexual abuse is generally attributed to improvements in child welfare and well-being, which is, in turn, due to greater public awareness, public prevention efforts and mobilization of law enforcement. In other words, the main agents involved in children's lives, such as families and teachers, are communicating; thus, abuse is prevented (Jones et al. 2006, 112). To be fair, the Watch List probably did contribute, albeit hysterically, to public awareness regarding a specific kind of sexual abuse; however, child abuse prevention programs in schools that teach children "to recognize and report abuse" are particularly successful in the prevention of all types of sexual abuse (ibid.). In fact, two separate studies found that "college undergraduates (Gibson and Leitenberg) and high school students (Ko and Cosden) exposed to sexual abuse prevention programs as children experienced fewer victimization experiences than those not exposed to such programs" (ibid.). Early prevention, not vigilantism, affects real social change.

Oprah creates a universalized fantasy that child predators "are walking right into your home," even though research shows that child sexual abuse differs in number and type from state to state, indicating a highly complex, regional problem (Jones et al., 109). By exaggerating and universalizing one, rather rare, form of child sexual abuse, the Watch List successfully incites fear but does not assist children in real need. The Watch List joins the ranks of other voyeuristic television shows that entrap alleged child molesters, such as the incredibly popular "To Catch a Predator" segment on NBC's *Dateline*, a prime time news program. These shows are based on a "false premise [that] not only survives against obvious evidence. It powers on the[se] show[s] . . . and encourages hysterical and abusive laws" (Tristam 2007). Besides participating in mass hysteria, Oprah's Watch List underestimates the social impact of other forms of child abuse.

A major problem associated with focusing on only one form of child abuse is that such a limited focus "underestimates the burden" of other forms of victimization, including emotional abuse and neglect (Finkelhor et al. 2007, 5). Oprah's hyperbolic representation of the abduction scenario places child abuse on a distorted scale of value because "unless the other forms of victimization are assessed . . . it is easy to overestimate the ostensible impact of one kind of victimization alone." Furthermore, such a fragmentary approach toward child sexual abuse ignores the interconnected nature of child victimization (ibid., 6). For instance, certain kinds of victimizations serve as "precursors or catalysts for new victimizations"; therefore, identifying and treating these "precursors and catalysts" before they develop into new forms of abuse represents yet another preventative measure (ibid.). Because the Watch List solely supports punitive rather than therapeutic measures, the concern is not really for abused children but for the furthering of national ideals.

Conclusion

While Oprah's intended effect is to end child molestation, her sentimental vigilantism actually works to continue American exceptionalism.

The Watch List does not enact social change but, instead, caters to the concept that the nation-home is under threat from a lurking evil; according to this logic, the national home and its occupants are special because they are threatened and threatened because they are special. Even though the threat is internal and comprises perverted citizens, this characterization of certain citizens as evil incarnate communicates that even America's flaws are exceptional. As such, Oprah's Child Predator Watch List uses the deaths of these six girls to further an insidious form of American exceptionalism to promote a righteous and divinely enfranchised national "we."

Notes

1. As of October 2008, the Child Predator Watch List has fundamentally changed in design; however, a less divisive form is still available for viewing at http://www.oprah.com/article/oprahshow/profiles_victims; http://www.oprah.com/slideshow/oprahshow/slideshow1_ss_captured_davis; http://www.oprah.com/article/world/globalissues/profiles_instructions/1. I have supplied a detailed description of the original design in this essay, and I possess the screenshots of the original site. I had intended to use the screenshots in this chapter, but upon reading the essay, Harpo Productions refused to give State University of New York Press permission to publish the screenshots.

2. For the sake of brevity, I will refer to Oprah's Child Predator Watch List as simply Watch List.

3. Oprah.com states that the site receives 3.6 million new visitors each month. In addition, per month, each opening page is viewed 65 million times (<http://www.oprah.com/adsales/audience.html>).

4. I use the term *viewer* to refer to the implied viewer/reader Wayne Booth discusses in *The Rhetoric of Fiction*: "The author creates, in short, an image of himself and another image of his reader; he makes his reader . . . and the most successful reading is one in which the created selves, author and reader, can find complete agreement" (Booth 1961, 138). The actual reader may well not agree with the textual intentions of the author; however, the endurance and popularity of a literary work speak to the successful synchronization of moral values among reader, text, and context.

5. While Castiglia focuses mainly on female-authored narratives as a type of emancipatory discourse for white women, his call for captivity narratives to take a more central role in discussion of current national identity politics is crucial to this argument.

6. Child sexual abuse does not significantly occur in only one racial or ethnic group (Finkelhor et al. 2005, 14).

Works Cited

Bal, Mieke. 1996. *Double exposures: The subject of cultural analysis.* New York: Routledge.

Barnett, Louise. 1975. *The ignoble savage: American literary racism 1790–1890.* Westport, CT: Greenwood Press.

Berlant, Lauren. 1999. The subject of true feeling: Pain, privacy, and politics. In *Cultural pluralism, identity politics, and the law,* ed. Austin Sarat and Thomas Kearns, 49–83. Ann Arbor: University of Michigan Press.

———. 2000. Reading of John M. Stahl's *Imitation of Life.* After great pain: From sentimentality to trauma. Graduate course offered at the University of Toronto, Winter.

Booth, Wayne. 1961. *The rhetoric of fiction.* Chicago: University of Chicago Press.

Burnham, Michelle. 1997. *Captivity and sentiment: Cultural exchange in American literature, 1682–1861.* Hanover, NH: University Press of New England.

Castiglia, Christopher. 1996. *Bound and determined: Captivity, culture-crossing, and white womanhood from Mary Rowlandson to Patty Hearst.* Chicago: University of Chicago Press.

Chapman, Mary, and Glenn Hendler. 1999. Introduction. In *Sentimental men: Masculinity and the politics of affect in American culture,* ed. Mary Chapman and Glenn Hendler, 112–24. Berkeley: University of California Press.

Chatman, Seymour. 2004. The cinematic narrator. In *Film theory and criticism,* ed. Leo Braudy and Marshall Cohen, 473–86. New York: Oxford University Press.

Finkelhor, David, Richard Ormrod, Heather Turner, and Sherry L. Harnby. 2005. Child victimization. *Child Maltreatment* 10, no. 1: 5–25. Accessed March 20, 2007, at <http://www.unh.edu/ccrc/>.

Fisher, Philip. 2002. *The vehement passions.* Princeton: Princeton University Press.

Hirsch, Marianne. 1997. *Family frames: Photography, narrative, and postmemory.* Cambridge: Harvard University Press.

Illouz, Eva. 2003. *Oprah Winfrey and the glamour of misery.* New York: Columbia University Press.

Jones, Lisa M., David Finkelhor, and Stephanie Halter. 2006. Child maltreatment trends in the 1990s: Why does neglect differ from sexual and physical abuse? *Child Maltreatment* 11, no. 2: 107–20.

Kress, Gunther, and Theo van Leeuwen. 2006. *Reading images: The grammar of visual design.* London: Routledge.

Levander, Caroline F., and Carol J. Singley, eds. 2003. Introduction. In *The American child: A cultural studies reader,* 3–12. New Brunswick: Rutgers University Press.

Manovich, Lev. 2001. *The language of new media.* Cambridge: MIT Press.

Oprah's Message. 2007. Oprah.com. April 12. <http://www2.oprah.com/presents/2005/predator/predator_main.jhtml>.

Poster, Mark. 2002. Digital networks and citizenship. *Proceedings of the Modern Language Association* 117, no. 1: 98–103.

Rosenbaum, H. Jon, and Peter C. Sederberg. 1974. Vigilantism: An analysis of establishment violence. *Comparative Politics* 6, no. 4: 541–70.

Sanchez-Eppler, Karen. 1996. Raising empires like children: Race, nation, and religious education. *American Literary History* 8, no. 3: 399–425.

———. 1999. Then when we clutch hardest: On the death of a child and the replication of an image. In *Sentimental men: Masculinity and the politics of affect in American culture,* ed. Mary Chapman and Glenn Hendler, 64–85. Berkeley: University of California Press.

Silverman, Kaja. 1999. [On suture]. In *Film theory and criticism: Introductory readings,* ed. Leo Braudy and Marshall Cohen, 137–47. New York: Oxford University Press.

Slotkin, Richard. 1973. *Regeneration through violence: The mythology of the American frontier 1660–1860.* Middletown, CT: Wesleyan University Press.

Steffans, Karina. 2006. ObjectSwap: Bypassing the ActiveX activation issue in IE. *Sitepoint.* Accessed April 5, 2007. <http://www.sitepoint.com/article/activex-activation-issue-ie>.

The victims. A link on the home page entitled Oprah's Message, Oprah.com. Accessed April 12, 2007. <http://www2.oprah.com/presents/2005/predator/predator_main.jhtml>.

Tristam, Pierre. 2006. "To catch a predator." *Daytona Beach News-Journal,* June 27.

———. 2007. To lose a war. *Candide's Notebooks*, April 12. <http://www.pierretristam.com/Bobst/Archives/C062706.htm>.

Williams, Raymond. 1977. *Marxism and literature.* New York: Oxford University Press.

11

The City under the Hill

Allegorical Tradition and H. P. Lovecraft's America

Matthew Strohack

Much criticism of H. P. Lovecraft's work is concerned with his fictive explorations of disorienting and unchartable regions of space and dream; yet, despite these excursions into the uncharted, the majority of even his weirdest tales return vividly and almost obsessively to New England with carefully incorporated descriptions of its geography, history, and cultural traditions. His short fictions "The Unnamable" and "The Festival" reveal that the function of this motif of return is to allow for an imaginative examination of New England, not just as another region of America, but as the place of origin from which America and its cultural patterns emerged—patterns that, for Lovecraft, were largely responsible for creating the America he knew in the early twentieth century, the America by which he was appalled. He was appalled by its industrialization, its Christianity, its democracy, and its people—all things that he could identify with allegories of progress originating from a specifically Puritan construction of New England. According to Deborah Madsen, these allegories were often typologically constructed to restrict interpretative freedom, silence dissenting voices, and claim for New England the status of an exceptional "city on the hill," a beacon of progress to other states and peoples. By inverting allegorical tropes deployed by the Puritans, "The Unnamable" and "The Festival" symbolically return to New England, the geohistorical origin of these allegories, to disrupt them at their roots and challenge the enduring vision of an exceptional America that they helped create. But rather than follow the impulse to use typology to *fix* a new image of America as other American writers have done, Lovecraft's allegorical strategies hold in suspension the signification of signs that the Puritans sought to contain; the result is at once horrifying and enabling, and points to broader political possibilities and dangers that are inherent in the allegorical mode itself.

One way Lovecraft challenges these allegories is in the form of semiautobiographical renderings of his various protagonists. His letters and much of his nonfiction prose create a portrait of a paranoid misanthrope who preferred uncreated dream or historically distant ties to Anglo-Saxon Europe to the social realities of America in the twenties and thirties. For example, in a short essay entitled "Americanism," in which he claims that "nearly all would-be definers of 'Americanism' fail through their prejudiced unwillingness to trace the quality to its European source" (Lovecraft 1995, 264), Lovecraft sets himself apart from what he perceives to be the dominant trend in national self-fashioning in the 1920s. He rejects America's exceptional New World status as he apprehended it in, for example, Woodrow Wilson's public speeches and the writings of Ralph Waldo Emerson, and instead seeks to identify anachronistically with various English antiquities such as Henry VIII. In this way, Lovecraft fashioned himself as an outsider, and according to Maurice Levy, he had come to be seen as such by his contemporaries (Levy 1988, 34). It is this position of cultural marginality, cultivated from within and projected from without, that Lovecraft assigns to his protagonists, who are often found skulking about the peripheries, the margins, the dark and decayed places outside New England's political center.

Although these characters exist outside the American mainstream, this is not to say they exist outside of American tradition entirely. Just where we might find types of nationalistic and religious conformism with certain aspects in the American ethos, we will also discover a spirit of individualism and dissent that appears, for example, in figures such as

Roger Williams, Nathaniel Hawthorne, and Edgar Allan Poe; it is to this spirit or tradition that the protagonist in "The Unnamable" and "The Festival" belong. Lovecraft appears in his fiction and in comments such as those made in "Americanism" regarding Roger Williams's rejection of "ecclesiastical machinery" (Lovecraft 1995, 266) to trace both national characteristics of enforced conformism and individualistic dissent to early settlers of New England who, for the purposes of this chapter, we will consider henceforth as belonging to two groups: the orthodox Congregationalists and the dissenting Antinomians. While the reasons for this division within the Massachusetts Bay Colony are complex and numerous, it is generally agreed that differences in religious practice, biblical interpretation, and attitudes toward the relationship between church and state underlie the conflict.

Deborah Madsen argues that such differences in religious perspective can be explained by examining the ways in which Congregationalists and Antinomians, in various documents regarding settlement, appropriated literary tropes, especially allegory, to construct their respective visions of America. At New England's political center were orthodox Congregationalists such as John Winthrop. Congregationalist discourse relied upon typological allegory, which, according to Madsen, places "a formal restriction of the interpretative possibilities opened up by allegorical exegesis" (Madsen 1996, 3). In this way they sought to transform the continent into what she calls a "redeemer nation" (ibid., 10) or, in the words of Winthrop, an exceptional "city upon a hill" that would serve as a beacon of progress to all peoples (Winthrop 2003, 216). Antinomians such as Anne Hutchinson, on the other hand, were banished from this city upon a hill that had become a religious and political center, because they exploited the indeterminacy inherent in allegory to undermine the interpretations of the New World that typology had fixed as if in stone. For example, Hutchinson rejected the Congregationalist doctrine that one's union with God could be secured in performing material acts of goodness in the community. She preached, to those who would listen, of a more esoteric relationship with God in which salvation could be granted only on the basis of individual faith—a relationship that, in its private nature, is inherently resistant to typological conformism. Because Antinomians such as Hutchinson were banished to Providence, Rhode Island, Providence itself becomes symbolic of the marginal space outside the central city on the hill. It is no coincidence, then, that Providence becomes Lovecraft's primary region of psychological identification and provides so much of the energy for his fictions. His own unique manipulations of the different forms and uses of allegory that Madsen describes reveal that he belongs to the tradition of dissent begun by the Antinomians which finds its geographical manifestation in Providence, Rhode Island, Lovecraft's birthplace.

Lovecraft's identification with Antinomian dissent is apparent in the narrator protagonists from "The Festival," and especially "The Unnamable," who both bear an uncanny resemblance to Lovecraft himself insofar as they occupy positions outside mainstream or insider American culture. "The Unnamable" takes place in a cemetery in Arkham, a fictional city somewhere in New England. Carter, the tale's narrator and protagonist, is an undervalued and underpaid Lovecraftian writer of terror tales. His friend, Joel Manton, a high school principal, against whom Carter stands in stark contrast, feels that Carter's "constant talk about 'unnamable' and 'unmentionable' things was a very puerile device, quite in keeping with [his] lowly standing as an author" (Lovecraft 2004, 82). Unlike the principal, who is interpellated as insider by an occupational title that clearly names and demarcates social position and function, Carter is interested in that which cannot be named, that which cannot be defined by the signs that determine mainstream American culture; he is interested in that which exists outside the center. The principal's somewhat bitter and mocking reaction to a line of work that participates in de-centering mainstream America reveals an anxiety toward modes of thought which allow for such a loss of center that are similar to those that were so unacceptable to the Congregationalists in the 1600s. For the principal, knowledge and meaning are obtainable only through "the correct doctrines of theology" (ibid.), which privilege God as transcendental signified and identifiable center of meaning. This doctrinal logic ultimately institutionalizes the illusion of a stable relationship of correspondence between signifier and signified, and between word and world, thus foreclosing alternative interpretations of the universe that depend upon a semantic environment where meaning is unfixed and the sign is precarious at best. This is the same precarious semantic environment that Carter inhabits as outsider in "The Unnamable" and that gives rise to the bizarre world of "The Festival."

In "The Festival" the unnamed narrator/protagonist is summoned by his ancestors to return to a small New England town for a Yuletide celebration. Lovecraft's choice to leave the narrator unnamed becomes significant when the reader is introduced to the history of the narrator's ancestors, and even more significant when we consider this history in relation to the philosophical idea of the unnameable that Carter and the principal debate in their own tale. In "The Festival" we are informed that four of the narrator's ancestors were hanged for witchcraft in 1692. By linking his characters so closely to historical events surrounding the Salem witch trials, Lovecraft invites us to consider the ways in which Puritans sought to define the ideological boundaries that would designate the political centrality of the dominant group. According to Ann Kibbey, "the Puritan deity steadily acquired [maleficent] powers, so much so that the power of the medieval *wicche* came to characterize divine power" (Kibbey 1998, 127). In this sense, Puritans could, sometimes by feats of extreme interpretative contortion, construe all inexplicable events that either harmed or benefited the individual or community as signs of divine providence and benevolent consideration for them as a chosen people, thus indulging readily in the processes of typology that Madsen describes. However, not all members of the community would hold interpretations of this kind. Kibbey argues: "The persistent resemblance between the Puritan deity and the witch was itself a displacement, mirroring a more fundamental tension in Puritan social thought: the resemblance between the Puritan concept of the father and husband and the concept of the witch as the author of *maleficia*" (ibid., 142). The responsibilities that came with such a power would often prove too great when it came to, for example, the deaths of family members. The witch, because he or she was believed to be capable of generating these tragic events, could provide a convenient scapegoat for fathers. But because accusations of witchcraft historically depended upon the same kinds of inexplicable events that in other instances Puritans would interpret as evidence of their deity, and, by extension, their specially ordained place in the world as a chosen people, this scapegoating of the witch proved to be more significant as a threat to the Puritans' sense of identity and political justification than it was a means for assuaging guilt and individual responsibility of fathers. Reconfigured as religious and political threat, the stereotype of the witch could then be used to contain and eradicate *by law* the semantic precariousness that could engender alternatives to the Puritans' conception of their place in the world.

This use of stereotype becomes even more apparent in the writings of Cotton Mather, a seventeenth-century New England writer, historian, and Puritan minister who wrote on and was involved with the Salem witch trials, and who often figures directly in Lovecraft's work. For example, in Lovecraft's "Dreams in the Witch House" Mather is invoked as an ironic authority on witchcraft and the supernatural to set off the absolute singularity of various diagrams that are discovered in the cell of the witch Keziah Mason, and in "The Unnamable" Mather's *Magnalia Christi Americana* is playfully referenced as the storehouse for what Carter refers to as Mather's "crazy country mutterings" (Lovecraft 2004, 84). Although Mather never actually sat on the jury during the witch trials, his influence on the witch craze and the trials was nevertheless significant. As a minister he was turned to as an authority to determine the authenticity of suspected cases of possession (Starkey 1949, 25). He conducted "laboratory observations on diabolism" and wrote a report on them entitled "Memorable Providences Relating to Witchcraft and Possession" (ibid., 24). New England court magistrates used Mather's "Memorable Providences" to construct a legal definition of witchcraft and to determine what qualified as evidence (ibid., 37). At the hanging of the notorious witch Reverend George Burroughs, Mather publicly refuted what would have been historically considered evidence of Burroughs's innocence—his recitation of the Lord's Prayer moments before his death on the scaffold (Mather 2003, 202). And finally, in 1692 at the request of Judge William Stoughton, Magistrate John Hathorne, Court clerk Stephen Sewall, and John Higginson, Mather wrote and in 1693 published *On Witchcraft, Being The Wonders of the Invisible World*, which is largely an account and defense of the witch trials (ibid., 245).

From the writings and actions that constituted Mather's involvement in the Salem witch craze emerged the fantastic, yet typical examples of Puritan typologizing that are pertinent to discussions of Lovecraft. In *Wonders of the Invisible World*, Mather is quick to label as devils and witches those whose behaviors did not conform to Puritan social norms and hence were thought to threaten the utopian Christian community that settlers had struggled so hard to create. He proclaims: "An army of devils is horribly broke in upon the place which is the centre, and after a sort, the first-born of our English settlements: and the houses of good people there are filled with doleful shrieks of their children and servants, tormented by invisible hands, with tortures altogether preternatural" (Mather 2003, 393). In this passage, which sounds remarkably like Lovecraft's own frenzied writing, Mather constructs a very clear and direct image of New England at the center, or more specifically, New England *as* the center. Those who represent an alternative to its particular configuration are violently cast outside of its boundaries, where they become typologized as devils and witches.

What happens, then, to those who are cast to the outside? The intended consequence is to diminish the possibility that exiles will present an ideological threat to the dominant community. This is our initial impression of the consequences of exile in "The Festival": "And now they were scattered, and shared only the rituals of mysteries that none living could understand" (Lovecraft 1967, 187). Scattered and forgotten, the witches in "The Festival" do not seem initially to pose a threat. However, as the story progresses, these witches appear to harness an ancient power. This transition from powerlessness to power is possible in the story, because the witches are never explicitly named as such. And as we can gather from records of actual witch trials, naming can be just as important to disempowering as it is to its opposite. By naming individuals "witch," the Puritans were able to comprehend happenings that were otherwise unnameable and therefore too terrible to imagine or understand. But what was beyond understanding before the witch was labeled as such remains so in "The Festival." What we see in the story, then, is not the typological containment of that which escaped Puritan understanding, but its proliferation, which resists semantic fixity and expands the realms of incomprehensibility that so horrified the Congregationalists. And by refusing to give the narrator or his diabolical ancestors a name, Lovecraft links the voice of the story, and by extension the story itself, to semantic processes that deny the possibility of a clearly nameable center.

Although both this condition of namelessness and this place that has been legally constituted outside of the center seem to imply a denial of power, in Lovecraft's stories we see that this is not necessarily the case; instead they suggest the possibility that something inherently subversive obtains in this position at the margins. He exploits this possibility of peripheral subversiveness by exploring the objects and feelings of horror that Puritans associated with the physical and spiritual wilderness. In "The Unnamable," Carter and the principal are sitting in the Charter Street cemetery in Salem discussing the nature of horror and the related possibility that things in the universe can be unnameable. For the principal "all things and feelings had fixed dimensions, properties, causes, and effects" (Lovecraft 2004, 83). For the writer, the world is full of "gibbous and infamous . . . nebulosities" (ibid.,

87), "phenomena beyond all normal notions" (ibid., 83), and therefore "shapes—or absences of shapes—which must for human spectators be utterly and appallingly 'unnamable' " (ibid., 84). Following this discussion, in typical Lovecraft fashion, an unnameable, horrifying essence descends from the attic window of a nearby house, defying comprehension, and drives the principal and his writer friend to madness. When recovering later at the hospital, the principal is awestruck and converted: "It was everywhere—a gelatine—a slime—yet it had shapes, a thousand shapes of horror beyond all memory. There were eyes—and a blemish. It was the pit—the maelstrom—the ultimate abomination. Carter, *it was the unnamable!*" (ibid., 89). This amorphous "it" is more distant than human memory; its thousand shapes suggest the infinite deferral of its meaning; its incapacity to be accurately named is an attempt to thematize and suspend the gap between signifier and signified, the very space of indeterminacy that the allegorical impulse requires to construct its narratives but then seeks to control through typological fixity. And although the terror that this indeterminacy inflicts would seem to suggest for Lovecraft's hospitalized narrator a desire to flee from it, to contain it or extinguish it, this is not the case; like Lovecraft, Carter makes his living by exploring indeterminacy—for better or for worse he cannot resist its allure. The desire to contain and to fix belongs more to the Puritans and their typologically constructed America, which Lovecraft often treats as a subject of disdain in his stories as well as his life.

A closer examination of allegory will help illustrate how the manifestation of this dynamic in Puritan narratives of community formation explains the Puritans' particular claim to power and its accompanying violence, and it will also help us better understand how Lovecraft interprets this claim to power as bearing the responsibility for the modern America in which he found himself an outsider. Madsen argues that typology, in a Christian context, originally refers to the "interpretation of Old Testament events and characters as foreshadowings of the events of the New Testament" (Madsen 1996, 7); she adds that this process of interpretation, which always refers back to a primary text, would eventually be applied to all signs in the material world (ibid.). It follows, then, that within this interpretative model, the entire phenomenological world is enslaved by biblical exegesis. By continually looking to a pretext, the Congregationalists could ensure that their project would move forward, that history, as they defined it, would progress. From this interpretative position it is possible to begin explaining how their political choices were made and then justified.

There is an episode in the section of John Winthrop's journal that chronicles his journey to America in which he describes events that surround a seemingly trivial confrontation that occurs between a mouse and a snake that happened to be on board the *Arbella* with him; the confrontation ends with the mouse as victor. Of this event he writes: "The pastor of Boston, Mr. Wilson, a very sincere, holy man, hearing of [the outcome] gave this interpretation: that the snake was the devil, the mouse was a poor contemptible people which God had brought hither, which should overcome Satan here and dispossess him of his kingdom" (Winthrop 2003, 217). In Wilson's interpretation, an allegory for the formation of a nation emerges: a seemingly insignificant and singular mouse is symbolically expanded, and almost as if by magic transformed into a Christian emblem for an entire people; an ordinary snake, the actual victim of this encounter, is transformed into a solitary figure of evil, which will, in contradistinction to the function of the mouse, reduce the complex and diverse environment and peoples that the Puritans are about to encounter to an unambiguous singular image of Satan. Winthrop also transcribes Wilson's dream in which "upon the same occasion he saw a church arise out of the earth, which grew up and became a marvellous goodly church" (ibid., 205). For Wilson and Winthrop, this image of the church, which has sprouted magically from the earth in the New World, served as a beacon and an example of a way of life that they believed to be more righteous than what was offered by the Old World in England, the seat of Lovecraft's nostalgia.

The collapsing of the images of the mouse and snake into related but opposed terms creates a kind of emblem that, when interpreted alongside this dream of a marvelous church, forms the allegorical basis for what we have come to call American exceptionalism, and can be applied usefully to more explicitly violent concepts such as Manifest Destiny; the virtuous mouse conquering the evils of the serpent will serve as an example to the world. However, by the twentieth century, history had revealed enough about America to convince writers like Lovecraft that this particular model of the American nation based in a good/evil binary was far too simplistic to account for the spiritual and material complexities of the modern world. The interpretation of the mouse and snake as biblical promise was a sham. And although Lovecraft would not likely have had many moral qualms about specific *aspects* of concepts such as Manifest Destiny (his letters reveal that he was racked with an almost debilitating xenophobia for most of his life), he would still occupy a position of dissent regarding American exceptionalism in significant ways. Timo Airaksinen argues that Lovecraft, in response to the modern world, "looks back and rejects everything which is ahead in time" (Airaksinen 1999, 40). Significantly, biblical promises and the image of America as an exceptional model for other non-American places and peoples are concepts that promote futurity and a kind of historical advancement, which would be unacceptable to Lovecraft's atavistic sensibilities.

In his long essay "Supernatural Horror in Literature," Lovecraft argues that this forward-looking impulse is ironically responsible for restricting the imagination:

> Against [the weird tale] are discharged all the shafts of a materialistic sophistication which clings to frequently felt emotions and external events, and of a naively insipid idealism which deprecates the aesthetic motive and calls for a didactic literature to "uplift" the reader toward a suitable degree of smirking optimism. (Lovecraft 1967a, 347)

In this sense, optimism and idealism, both connotative of futurity, can be seen as forms of interpretative violence that work against Lovecraft's brand of fiction, which, he maintains, is invested primarily in "wonder and fancy" (Lovecraft 1967a, 412) rather than the frequently felt emotions he attributed to the modern America he so despised. So, by rejecting the futurity inherent in American exceptionalism, Lovecraft returns to the past not so much to regain meaning but to rework and revitalize what has been imprisoned by Puritan typology.

In "The Unnamable," Lovecraft alludes to the typology of the past to frame Carter's critique of the principal's limiting claim that we "know things . . . only through our five senses or our religious intuition; wherefore it is quite impossible to refer to an object or spectacle which cannot be clearly depicted by the solid definitions of fact or the correct doctrines of theology—preferably those of the Congregationalists" (Lovecraft 2004, 82). By locating this frame in the Congregationalist past when the character of America was still being formed, Lovecraft develops a connection between what he believes to be the typological origins of the principal's restrictive thinking and the modern world in which the story is told, and which clearly positions the principal in the center and Carter at the margins.

This connection becomes even more explicit when Carter discusses the Puritans' involvement in the perceived witchcraft epidemic in New England:

> It had been an eldritch thing—no wonder sensitive students shudder at the Puritan age in Massachusetts. . . . The witchcraft terror is a horrible ray of light on what was stewing in men's crushed brains, but even that is trifle. There was no beauty; no freedom—we can see that from the architectural and household remains, and the poisonous sermons of the cramped divines. And inside that rusted iron strait-jacket lurked gibbering hideousness, perversion, and diabolism. Here, truly was the apotheosis of the unnamable. (Lovecraft 2004, 85)

In this passage, Lovecraft presents us with a useful metaphor that conveys the restrictiveness of Puritan typology. What Lovecraft calls an "iron strait-jacket" is the typological mode of interpretation that Congregationalists used to create and understand their world. For Carter, this understanding excludes interpretative freedom and beauty. The image of the strait-jacket—the emblem of the lunatic asylum—implies that, to the Congregationalists, interpretative freedom was akin to madness or "gibbering." Madness is the fate of Carter and the principal when they are confronted with "the ultimate abomination," the unnameable incarnate, which I have argued is itself an emblem of radical interpretative freedom. And thirdly, the strait-jacket functions here as an image of torture and sadism. If this image is used as an allegorical device, we can begin to glean the dangerous relationship that exists between allegory, violence, and power. In *The Origin of German Tragic Drama*, Walter Benjamin theorizes this relationship and argues that the allegorist functions as a sadist who "humiliates his object and then—or thereby—satisfies it" (Benjamin 1977, 185). Furthermore, he adds that the allegorist, in an act of cruelty, strips his object bare to prepare it to perform according to his intention (ibid., 184–85). The object can no longer signify independently. The hideousness that Carter sees lurking and gibbering in Puritan men's "crushed brains" is effectively silenced by the closed system of sadistic typology. This process then forecloses on alternative interpretations of the world that would perhaps depend on the perception of a world as gibbering, indeterminate, and its signified as endlessly deferred. This is the world of horror that Lovecraft's writing presents as the object of both fear and desire.

Although allegory in its typological manifestation seeks to contain and mask this fear, in its classical form, the indeterminacy of this world of fear is laid bare. For Benjamin, allegory, when used in the classical sense, is capable of revealing rather than masking these horrors:

> in allegory the observer is confronted with the *facies hippocratica* of history as a petrified, primordial landscape. Everything about history that, from the very beginning, has been untimely, sorrowful, unsuccessful, is expressed in a face—or rather in a death's head. (Benjamin 1977, 166)

In other words, allegory reveals the events and character of history that are usually suppressed by totalizing narratives, such as the narrative of progress, or the narrative of providentially ordained authority that we see in the early days of New England. A useful connection now becomes apparent between the age of baroque cruelty discussed by Benjamin and the age of the witch trials in Salem. Both correspond roughly to the same time period, and both are concerned with the display of power. According to Lutz Koepnick, Benjamin's interest in allegory derives from his observation that it seemed to prevent monarchs from mesmerizing their subjects through the symbolism of political spectacle: "[P]olitical spectacles divert critical judgments about the configurations of modern life" (Koepnick 1996, 60). The scaffold has often been discussed as an exhibition of the power of a divinely ordained monarch, which, through sheer awe and symbolic power, renders the spectator incapable of questioning the stability and totality of this power. The public executions that Puritan legal functionaries performed during the Salem witch trials exhibited and entrenched the power of Salem courts in a nearly identical way to those performed by monarchs back in Europe. Kibbey argues that the very process of the witch trials enabled judicial authority to free itself "from the accidents of remarkable providences" (Kibbey 1998, 146) that were attributed to either the Puritan deity or to the witch. The court becomes its own form of providence; however, the process of this becoming is hidden beneath the symbolic veil of spectacle. The witch trials become like baroque spectacles of power. Benjamin and Lovecraft thus seem to diagnose a similar problem.

Benjamin argues that in baroque allegory "the false appearance of totality is extinguished" (Benjamin 1977, 176). Lovecraft's peculiar use of allegory is also invested in extinguishing this appearance of totality, which, in "The Festival," reverberates with Madsen's claims regarding the sinister aspect of typology, "that of coercion and, for those who refuse to submit, historical obliteration" (Madsen 1996, 57). In this historical obliteration, in the typological strait-jacketing of the imagination, the nation, and the world outside the center, Lovecraft's protagonists see an attack against freedom and beauty. However, the always misanthropic Lovecraft is perhaps not so much concerned with the historical obliteration of real people as with the historical obliteration of alternative modes of interpretation. The witch, for Lovecraft, is not so much important for the person behind the name, as it is for the unnameable qualities that the name is used historically to imprison. To figure the witch into the Puritan emblem of the Christian mouse and the satanic snake, as did Mather, neutralizes its signifying capacity by subjecting it to the Puritan double law which delegitimizes the witch and refuses its entry into the center.

The historical obliteration that was the tragic fate of many women accused of witchcraft is the subject of Lovecraft's "The Festival." However, we must also consider that significant to typology is literal or material obliteration. Benjamin argues that the allegorist best performs his function by ordering "the destruction of the organic so that the true meaning, as it was written and ordained, might be picked up from its fragments" (Benjamin 1977, 216–17). Furthermore, he maintains that the death of the body, the becoming of a corpse, and its subsequent potential for martyrdom is what "prepares the body of the living person for emblematic purposes" (ibid., 217). By becoming pure body, or pure corpse, the corpse becomes tabula rasa and is made fully available to allegory. The dead body ceases to have the capacity to signify on its own, whereas a living body, invested as it is with consciousness and agency, still has the potential to interfere with the intentions of the allegorist. It is in this way, by erasing subjectivity, that settlers eliminated so-called witches; they were symbolized in a manner that denied them a subjectivity from which they could speak against the dominant group. The emblematist humiliates, murders, and silences objects, or in this case subjects, that do not cooperate with his intentions. When we consider the fate of the New England witch, this aspect of allegory appears in the service of power.

However, this very same process, which orders "the destruction of the organic," can be used alternatively to allow the emblematized corpse to speak again, as though from beyond the grave, and become complicit in allegories of dissent. It was this use of allegory that dissenting Puritans like Anne Hutchinson and Roger Williams were able to deploy in their attempts to subvert the power structure that sought to delegitimize their dissenting beliefs. Madsen argues that "It is the indeterminacy at the heart of allegorical interpretation . . . that enabled such writers to appropriate allegorical rhetoric and apply it to alternative constructions of America's national destiny" (Madsen 1996, 10). I argue that this tradition of dissent is based in the indeterminacy inherent in the corpse and the witch. Lovecraft, despite others' claims to his *total* outsiderness, claims affinity with this tradition not only in his writings but also in his ironic sense of place and home. At the end of his life he chose as his epitaph "I am Providence." This inscription disrupts the idea of providential explanations of the world that were at the heart of Puritan typologies; the inscription implies it is not the Christian God that dictated the events which divided New England into dissenting and non-dissenting states but the individual, the ironic "I" behind providence. Being born in Providence, Lovecraft chooses to associate himself geographically and genealogically with the tradition of dissent that is buried in Providence's soil. For Lovecraft to say "I am Providence" is almost to say "I am dissent." Lovecraft, like the corpses that populate his fiction, continues to speak from beyond the grave by means of a perverse self-allegorization and continues to exercise his agency in this defiant assertion of individual providence inscribed eternally on his tombstone.

Although the macabre twists on allegory present on his tombstone are of much interest to the Lovecraft fan, they are perhaps more active and fleshed out in his fiction, which combines the allegorical potentials of the tombstone, the witch, and the corpse to maintain allegiance to the tradition of dissent that has always sought to undermine the typologized America that he so despises. It is in "The Festival" that Lovecraft deploys this allegorical dissent most effectively, inverting the allegory that narrates what Madsen refers to as America's "typological destiny," its self-construction as the model city on the hill (40). In classic allegorical fashion the narrator's return to a New England town is meant to signify something deeper than a family reunion: "It was Yuletide, that men call Christmas though they know in their hearts it is older than Bethlehem and Babylon, older than Memphis and Mankind" (Lovecraft 1967, 187). Lovecraft is here playing on the way that the Winter Solstice celebration of Germanic Pagans has been appropriated by Christianity to consolidate Puritan Christian values in New England. What the narrator returns to, then, is something that existed long before the birth of Christ and the emergence of values that would form Puritan culture in New England. In this way, Lovecraft will use Christian tradition as an ironic pretext for an extrinsic narrative that involves returns and redefinitions; where Puritans see Christian ideology as an end for their project, Lovecraft sees it as a point from which to depart.

After greeting his ancestors, the narrator is required to don a cloak and join a procession of other cloaked figures on their way to an abandoned church: "Up, up, up, the eery columns slithered, and I saw that all the travellers were converging as they flowed near a sort of focus of crazy alleys at the top of a high hill in the centre of the town, where perched a great white church" (Lovecraft 1967, 191). This scene, which moves deliberately toward "the centre of town" as its focal point, echoes uncannily Cotton Mather's image of the beleaguered "place which is the centre" (Mather 2003, 393). At the top of the hill, at the center of this New England town, at the center of the world, it might seem, the church stands as an emblem of the city on the hill where these cloaked figures will go to sanctify their culture in a fashion not entirely dissimilar to that of Puritan settlers in the 1600s. Lovecraft's exiled witches return allegorically to an image that bears striking resemblance to the church that Winthrop describes as rising "out of the earth" to form a symbol of American exceptionalism and optimistic futurity (Winthrop 2003, 205). But here, in Lovecraft's story, this upward procession of determined cultural ambassadors signifies differently and inverts the ideological implications of the structurally similar journey made by the early Puritans. In this allegorical inversion, the witches whom the Church had cast from its center have now returned to possibly redefine it.

Lovecraft gives this particular church careful description. In the churchyard are tombstones, undefined spectral shafts, and archaic houses—ruins of some sort—all of which, when taken together, create the atmosphere of an absent culture or civilization that is made eerily present in each ruin, each fragment. Once inside the church that has been erected amidst, on top of, and in spite of these cultural fragments, the procession descends a staircase that is revealed by a trapdoor positioned directly before the pulpit:

> They streamed up the aisle between the high pews to the trap-door of the vaults which yawned loathsomely open just before the pulpit, and were now squirming noiselessly in. I followed dumbly down the footworn steps and into the dark suffocating crypt. (Lovecraft 1967, 191)

Lovecraft imagines the suffocating and loathsome space of the vault or crypt beneath the church, beneath this symbol of a pure and Christian America whose authority has been bolstered by Puritan readings of the New Testament. But in journeying beneath the church, the narrator's ancestors also travel beneath the ruins upon which the church was built, penetrating layer after layer of cultural bedrock. The ruin, an image Lovecraft deploys obsessively in his writing, becomes especially significant here in terms of his play with allegory. The ruin is also significant to Benjamin's conceptualization of classical allegory: "[I]n the ruin history has physically merged into the setting. And in this guise history does not assume the form of the process of an eternal life so much as that of irresistible decay" (ibid., 177–78). Rather than treat history typologically as a totality with an eternal life, as the Congregationalists did, Lovecraft, by expressing history through the tomb, reveals that it participates in the process that Benjamin attributes to it, of irresistible decay. By doing so, Lovecraft is able to offer glimpses of the suffering and death that the city on the hill wants to efface—the stuff typology seeks to eliminate and mere symbolism seeks to cloud with aesthetic illusion. Typology is shaken loose and brought back to the indeterminate sphere of classical allegory as the procession descends below the pulpit, the place from which allegorical sermons are usually delivered, and the spatial orientation of which is directed upward to heaven. So beneath the pulpit and the church, beneath this foundational symbol of a pure and Christian America, lies a crypt that evokes horror, decay, and ruins.

The procession continues down into the hill, beneath the church, beneath the town, into the very bowels of the earth, where opens up a cavern swarming with light, music, columns, and towers, the site of the Yuletide ritual. The city *on* the hill has become the city *under* the hill. The narrator states: "I knew we must have passed down through the mountain and beneath the earth of Kingsport itself, and I shivered that a town should be so aged and maggoty with subterraneous evil" (Lovecraft 1967, 192). This strange subterranean space is described with excessive language and words that denote ambiguity and indeterminacy: "unimaginable," "amorphous," "abyssal," "uncanny," "undiscoverable" (ibid., 192–93). Despite this representation of chaos, Lovecraft adheres to the allegorical mode and relates chaos to a kind of textual authority. This ritualistic space beyond understanding appears to have its own sacred text, as the Puritans had their Bible. Madsen argues that "allegory seeks to sustain the authority of some culturally important sacred text by establishing the ongoing relevance of this text both to individuals and to the community at large" (Madsen 1996, 9). However, the sacred text of the city beneath the hill is not the Puritan's Bible, but the dreaded "Necronomicon," the fictional book that appears throughout Lovecraft's work with the function of a sort of inverted Bible—a book of demons and witches that promotes indeterminacy, chaos, and horror and recalls the infamous "Devil's Book" that many accused witches had historically confessed to signing (Kibbey 1998, 125). The Necronomicon, then, serves as a kind of anti-text, which, at least in the imaginative space of his fiction, wreaks havoc upon the legitimacy of typological constructions of America that are based in the Bible. "The Festival" ends with a rare quotation from this dreaded book:

> Out of corruption horrid life springs, and the dull scavengers of earth wax crafty to vex, and swell monstrous to plague it. Great holes secretly are digged where earth's pores ought to suffice, and things have learnt to walk that ought to crawl. (Lovecraft 1967, 195)

In this city under the hill, where things have learnt to walk that ought to crawl, the origins of dissent are reborn, and chaos and indeterminacy are unleashed back into the world that the Puritans struggled to simplify and regulate in terms of the New Testament.

But what does this chaos mean in the twentieth century? "The Festival" was written roughly during the same time that Benjamin was writing his treatise on allegory, shortly after World War I, a period which, according to allegory theorists, should provide fertile ground for allegorical work. Benjamin argues that "[a]llegory established itself most permanently where transitoriness and eternity confronted each other most closely" (Benjamin 1977, 224). This confrontation between transitoriness and eternity could not have been more apparent than in this period of mass violence and cultural crisis. For many, it would seem that the war would all but destroy humanist culture and its narratives of human-driven progress. Contemporaneous advances in the sciences, particularly physics (one of Lovecraft's pet interests) would further undermine the centrality of the human, leaving behind a massive cultural void. But for Lovecraft, and other moderns like him, this void often represented a possibility for rebirth or a redefinition of culture, which many would artistically render with antihumanist form and tone. While Benjamin's corpus suggests that he too would approach this void with thoughts of cultural reconstruction, he does so with arguably more hesitation and caution than would be exhibited by some of modernism's more aggressively antihumanist practitioners. Koepnick argues that his valorization of an aesthetics of fragmentation in allegory is conceptualized as a method of resistance to the coming of a fascist aesthetic, which Benjamin prophesies through his critique of the nexus between allegory and power. In classical allegory, Koepnick argues, Benjamin seeks "modes of representation that may interrupt the aesthetic allure of modern domination" (Koepnick 1996, 61). This involves a step into indeterminacy, into the horror and decay that lie at the heart of allegory.

While postmodernism would more fully accept this precarious psychological step, it was still very frightening to moderns such as Lovecraft. And while I have shown up to this point Lovecraft approaching the indeterminacy that postmodernism would soon embrace, I would argue that he hesitates to embrace it with the same enthusiasm and sense of play. Although characters such as Carter embrace the indeterminate to a certain extent, there are moments throughout Lovecraft's corpus where its capacity for horror proves too great. Even Carter ends up in the hospital upon his confrontation with the unnameable. The narrator in "The Festival" initially desires to follow his strange ancestors' ancient rituals, but in the very last moments of the narrative, his guide removes his hood and reveals a waxen mask, which is so horrible to behold that the narrator flings himself into an underground river to escape the madness of indeterminacy that the ritual evokes. Although Benjamin suggests that freedom can be rediscovered once allegory reveals "the lack of freedom" behind typological narratives of progress (Benjamin 1977, 176), Lovecraft's allegories and critique of Puritan typology rarely move beyond the stage of revelation. When they do, it is not to imagine a society where all peoples are free, but one where there are either no people or only one—an impulse that oddly resembles the fascist one that would plague the first half of the twentieth century. For Lovecraft, whose mother sheltered him from the world as a child, and who almost collapsed from xenophobic terror on a trip to New York, true freedom may have proved to be too great a psychological burden. Perhaps this can explain his own eventual gravitation toward fascism, which he would only shake near his death when the reality of the Holocaust was becoming apparent. When the world's stability was shaken, as it was by World War I, forces wishing to reassert stability came back with a vengeance; as we now have the benefit of knowing, this would lead to atrocities of totalitarianism and fascism that arguably exceeded in historical horror anything that had ever been experienced before. It is this tendency to replace fear of disorder with absolute domination that, according to Benjamin, the power of allegory can dangerously facilitate. And although Lovecraft's horrific city under the hill opens the door to indeterminacy, interpretative freedom, and dissent, in his actual life he falls prey to the horrors of his own project. For a contemporary reader, the consequences of this may prove to be more frightening than his world of horror and monsters.

Works Cited

Airaksinen, Timo. 1999. *The philosophy of H. P. Lovecraft: The route to horror.* New York: Peter Lang.

Benjamin, Walter. 1977. *The origin of German tragic drama.* Trans. John Osborne. London: NLB.

Kibbey, Ann. 1998. Mutation of the supernatural: Witchcraft, remarkable providences, and the power of Puritan men. *American Quarterly* 34, no. 2: 125–48.

Koepnick, Lutz P. 1996. Allegory and power: Walter Benjamin and the politics of representation. *Soundings* 79, no. 1–2: 59–78.

Levy, Maurice. 1988. *Lovecraft: A study in the fantastic.* Trans. S. T. Johsi. Detroit: Wayne State University Press.

Lovecraft, H. P. 1967. The festival. In *Dagon and other macabre tales*, ed. August Derleth. London: Victor Gollancz.

———. 1967a. Supernatural horror in literature. In *Dagon and other macabre tales*, ed. August Derleth. London: Victor Gollancz.

———. 1995. Americanism. In *Miscellaneous writings*, ed. S. T. Joshi. Sauk City: Arkham House.

———. 2004. The unnamable. In *The dreams in the witch house and other weird stories*, ed. S. T. Joshi. Toronto: Penguin.

———. 2004a. Dreams in the witch house. In *The dreams in the witch house and other weird stories*, ed. S. T. Joshi. Toronto: Penguin.

Madsen, Deborah. 1996. *Allegory in America: From puritanism to postmodernism*. Houndmills, UK: MacMillan.

Mather, Cotton. 2003. The wonders of the invisible world. In *The Norton anthology of American literature*. 6th ed. Vol. A. New York: Norton.

Starkey, Marion L. 1949. *The devil in Massachusetts: A modern inquiry into the Salem witch trials*. New York: Alfred A. Knopf.

Winthrop, John. 2003. A model of Christian charity. In *The Norton anthology of American literature*. 6th ed. Vol. A. New York: Norton.

Afterword

American Exceptionalism in American Intellectual Conversation, or How I Finally Submitted to Literary Criticism

Terri Baker

After I agreed to write this essay and submit it for possible inclusion in this anthology I wondered if and how America is exceptional, and who "wrote the book of love"? I was driven to dictionaries, to Wikipedia (yes, I know the problems). I know that American Exceptionalism is generally understood as a term that refers to the status of the United States as somehow being superior to other nations, perhaps because of its governmental structure, perhaps because of a perception that the United States is on the "cutting edge" of the progress of democratic principles and so on. We are on this edge, in some ways, but I think of the edge as a "bleeding edge." The edge bleeds (metaphorically) because we are a nation of laws. Because the United States is a nation of laws (not always enforced or obeyed), American Indians survived, and are now active as intellectuals in the universities. The issue is simple, the survival complex.

A Pequot, William Apess, for example, noticed the nature of the U.S. Constitution and published an essay concerning that in 1835. The essay is titled "Indian Nullification of the Unconstitutional Laws of Massachusetts Relative to the Marshpee Tribe; or, The Pretended Riot Explained." Isn't that a lovely title? One of the resolutions noted by Apess reads: "*Resolved,* That we, as a tribe, will rule ourselves, and have the right to do so; for all men are born free and equal, says the Constitution of the country" (qtd. in O'Connell 1992, 175). Apess was an intellectual, an activist, and knew what the Constitution said and what the words meant—pesky document to some, but oh so useful to others. He pushed at the edge.

Human beings always push at the edge. That is why we have laws in the United States. Americans love laws, because often laws prevent us from falling to fisticuffs and mob violence when we approach conflict, maybe even when we are engaged in it.

Consider Martin Luther King Jr.'s nonviolence philosophy, which came from Gandhi's which came from Henry David Thoreau. We have learned to protest unjust laws nonviolently, and an intellectual wrote the founding philosophical U.S. document which made the United States in this case "a city upon a hill" so far as this nonviolent protest of unjust laws is concerned. Good old Thoreau!

We have neither learned easily—witness historical mob violence in America—nor does the lesson always stick. Still, we are a nation of laws. Because of these laws we are, then, exceptional. And how I loooove laws that make it illegal for anybody to ride in at dawn and attack towns full of people, houses, hospitals, libraries, schools, and so on and then loot the food stores and museums. Indeed, U.S. citizens are today in a most fortunate, most exceptional position. But I urge you not to get too complaisant. The reasons for our exceptional position are not always what they seem.

Consider that the U.S. reached this enviable (exceptional) position by evolving in many ways from people with control issues—the Puritans. Indeed the phrase "a city upon a hill" is a paraphrase of Matthew 5:14 which reads: "Ye are the light of the world. A city that is set on a hill cannot be hid." The phrase "a city upon a hill" appeared in "A Modell of Christian Charity" by John Winthrop written in 1630 and then in 1838 published in full by the Massachusetts Historical Society. Thus, the idea of "a city upon a hill" or an exemplary society enters what will become the national consciousness at a dramatically early and therefore significant point. During his lifetime Winthrop was what we would think of today as a civic-minded citizen—acting as deputy governor or governor of the colony. Still, modern Americans should remember that Winthrop certainly did not believe in democracy.

He was also a Puritan and held those ideas about his own specific exceptionalism or election as did others of his society. John Winthrop lived between 1588 and 1649. William Bradford of *Mayflower* fame lived from 1590 until 1657 and was, like Winthrop, a civic-minded fellow, signer of the Mayflower Compact, and governor of the Pilgrims. He was elected to the office many times between 1621 and 1656. Bradford is the author of the famous document *Of Plymouth Plantation*, written between 1630 and 1650 and published in 1856.

The entries in *Of Plymouth Plantation* make it clear that Bradford believed and supported the belief within his Pilgrim group that the Christian God had brought them safely to shore and caused them to survive. He says in Chapter IX, "Of Their voyage, and How They Passed the Sea; and of Their Safe Arrival at Cape Cod": "Being thus arrived in a good harbor, and brought safe to land, they fell upon their knees and blessed the God of Heaven who had brought them over the vast and furious ocean, and delivered them from all the perils and miseries thereof, again to set their feet on the firm and stable earth, their proper element." Then in Chapter X, "Showing How They Sought Out a Place of Habitation; and What Befell Them thereabout" Bradford describes the Pilgrims looking around for a place to live and needing food:

> [A]nd so at length [they] got to the seaside and marched to this supposed river, and by the way found a pond of clear, fresh water, and shortly after a good quantity of clear ground where the Indians had set corn, and some of their graves. And proceeding further they saw new stubble where corn had been set the same year; also they found where lately a house had been, where some planks and a great kettle was remaining, and heaps of sand newly paddled with their hands. Which, they digging up, found in them divers fair Indian baskets filled with corn, and some in ears, fair and good, of divers colours, which seemed to them a very goodly sight. . . . So, their time limited them being expired, they returned to the ship lest they should be in fear of their safety; and took with them part of the corn and buried up the rest. . . .

> And here is to be noted a special providence of God, and a great mercy to this poor people, that here they got seed to plant them corn the next year, or else they might have starved, for they had none nor any likelihood to get any till the season had been past, as the sequel did manifest. Neither it is likely they had had this, if the first voyage had not been made, for the ground was now all covered with snow and hard frozen; but the Lord is never wanting unto His in their greatest needs; let His holy name have all the praise. (Bradford 1908, 126–27)

In this passage the reader will notice that while the Pilgrim explorers reburied some of the food stores, they stole the rest, and the Pilgrims know that they are stealing someone's food stores, because they are in fear of their safety. The reader will also notice that some of their stolen stuff is seed corn which, of course, means that they are stealing seed which the American Indians need for planting the next season's crop. Bradford calls getting the seed corn "a special providence of God," which means that Bradford believes God directly intervened and caused them to find it because "Providence" was a term used to refer to God's direct intervention in the world. Bradford clearly sees the Pilgrims as God's elect and says that the Lord or the Christian God is always willing to take care of their needs even to leading them to the food stores of the indigenous people, which the Pilgrims steal. Need I point out that there is no handy grocery store from which to replenish the food stores? The indigenous people may starve.

This "greatest needs" passage and the belief that the Christian God recognizes the needs of the elect but not those of other people is the founding statement of what will evolve into Manifest Destiny. And the beat goes on.

Modern Reader, time travel forward to William Apess. In "The Experience of Five Christian Indians" (1833), Apess (remember him from a few paragraphs back?) offers his understanding of the words of the Christian Bible:

> But, reader, I acknowledge that this is a confused world, and I am not seeking for office, but merely placing before you the black inconsistency that you place before me—which is ten times blacker than any skin that you will find in the universe. And now let me exhort you to do away that principle, as it

> appears ten times worse in the sight of God and candid men than skins of color—more disgraceful than all the skins that Jehovah ever made. If black or red skins or any other skin of color is disgraceful to God, it appears that he has disgraced himself a great deal—for he has made fifteen colored people to one white and placed them here upon this earth.
>
> Now let me ask you, white man, if it is a disgrace for to eat, drink, and sleep with the image of God, or sit, or walk and talk with them. Or have you the folly to think that the white men, being one in fifteen or sixteen, are the only beloved images of God. (O'Connell 1992)

The point seems pretty clear in this passage.

So the United States has founding documents stating concepts of exemplary behavior (a city on a hill) and stating that a particular group of Europeans is deserving of bounty and natural resources (Manifest Destiny) that will take the United States through American Indian Removal to Indian Territory, Slavery, Allotment, Oklahoma Statehood (important because that is the where many of tribes were removed to) as well as Apess, who is the intellectual and educated voice putting up his hand and saying EXCUSE ME! The voice of Apess was joined by Elias Boudinot, Sarah Winnemucca Hopkins, Charles Eastman, and some others until a small chorus was singing, not always in harmony, but singing in full voice. The chorus currently includes many modern voices of indigenous people, and American Indian writers have been included in courses in universities and in textbooks.

The United States has, then, the American Indians, the Puritans, the laws of the land, treaties (broken), education as a fundamental force for the country, and the Supreme Court. Never forget the Supreme Court!

And how? Some will ask, How did the Supreme Court get into this mix? Well that is a good story. And the story links in today's world at least, with the universal love affair with gambling. In 1831 in *Cherokee Nation v. Georgia* which was argued before the Supreme Court, the Court recognized the American Indian tribes as "domestic dependent nations with an unquestionable right to the lands which they occupy, until that right shall be extinguished by a voluntary cession to our government" (Supreme Court 1831).

Thus, the tribes were recognized as dependent sovereign nations within the United States. Because of this dependent sovereign status, today in 2010, gaming in American Indian tribes operates under the jurisdiction of the federal government rather than the government of the state in which the tribe resides. Profits from gaming in most of the tribes are used for the collective good of the tribal members. Gaming, for example, may pay for the tribe's share for (1) road construction and maintenance in state-tribal compact; (2) health care for tribal citizens; (3) elder care; (4) assisted living for those who qualify; (5) housing; (6) scholarships. These are just a few examples of how gaming benefits tribal citizens. This is part of the attempt to sustain tribal identity and maintain the welfare of the tribal citizens.

Now consider how higher education works in the United States—at least in theory. There was a time, Gentle Reader, when education was considered the mark of the successful person. There was a time when education was valued, and while the general perception of that value is diminished somewhat today, still in many areas of the United States, education is understood to be desirable and a shaper of values. For those reasons, education is political and it is always an area of tension. Those who want power need education for many reasons.

One of those reasons has to do with what is believed to be valuable to know. University professors and scholars are the authoritative voices in this matter (although the computer and Google have compromised that authority, and many university administrations are uncomfortable with that authority.). It works this way.

Students pay to attend university. The university offers classes taught by professors who are paid to teach students about specific subjects determined by professors as the professional authorities on what is valuable to know. One example is literature. How do we decide what literature is worth the time and money of a university to teach students? Well, first there is the canon, the holy list of titles thought worthy. This list developed in the nineteenth century and was devised by financially powerful white men who possessed the world view of European American Christians. These white men put together a list of the works of other men who had been significant in the education of the list makers. The list included classic titles, no women, nobody who today would be considered minority.

That list changed a bit for about eighty or ninety years but did not include the writings of minority people. What was considered to be valuable to know about literature as late as 1968 is exemplified by a book used by many students struggling to pass exams. That book is from the Barnes & Noble Outline Series, its subject *American Literature.* This study guide's third edition was copyrighted in 1953 and was reprinted in 1968. Examining the guide today in 2010 is a blast from the past, no American Indian writers that I could find, although I might have overlooked something. Indigenous people are absent from this 1968 book, except as dead or disappearing people and romanticized people (demon or noble). The book's subtitle is "A Complete History, with Biographical Data, Literary Trends, and Criticism." The reading list I received as a graduate student in a PhD program in 1974 contained not a single American Indian name.

But now, by 2010, the list has changed significantly and includes all kinds of readings by a mix of people who are writing about issues and subjects that are no longer limited to what was considered from the nineteenth until the mid-twentieth century and a bit beyond to be worthy. Now the writings of people with interests and worldviews outside the mainstream are considered to be worth university consideration.

The evolving list has created a propulsive tension in the intellectual life of the United States. "Propulsive tension" is a phrase I use with a bow to Joseph Faulds, a colleague. It means that sometime intellectuals fight, at least with words. This is not always a comfortable life. Long-held views on acceptable behavior are changing. Traditional ways of knowing are challenged. Majority viewpoints about what it means to be an American are questioned.

Understanding of what it means to be an American is changing.

Consider that the images of indigenous people in the United States during the latter half of the nineteenth century presented them as disappearing or just absent. One memorable and to me regrettable grouping is to be viewed in the National Portrait Gallery of the Smithsonian in Washington, D.C., a place of authority. The grouping is composed of two marble sculptures on either side of a painting. One sculpture presents "The Last of the Tribes," a bare-breasted Indian maiden created by Hiram Powers. The second sculpture, carved by Ferdinand Pettrick, is "The Dying Tecumseh," who breathes his last in tragic, marble pose. The painting that hangs upon the wall between the two large marble sculptures is "Westward the Course of Empire Takes Its Way, Mural Study U.S. Capital 1861." The artist is Emanuel Gottlieb Leutze (born in Schwabisch-Gmund).

"Westward the Course of Empire Takes Its Way" shows no American Indians in the Manifest Destiny image. Leutze does present European Americans on mountain tops, clearly alluding to Moses looking at the

Promised Land. I did not find a Bible in the picture, but there is a muted image of a cross at a grave with mourners which suggests the sacrifice of Jesus and also represents the sacrifices that lie before the European Americans. In the upper lefthand corner of the margin one sees three kings and the star announcing the presence of the Christ child. In this painting appear allusions to the messiah, Moses (as mountain men), the Promised Land, sacrifice, death, and promise of resurrection. I may have missed some detail, but clearly the painting and framing artistic marginalia are allegorical.

This grouping is what visitors to the National Portrait Gallery see when touring the nation's premier museums. A bit down the hallway in the Presidents' Gallery the visitor may find an iconic and heroic portrait of Andrew Jackson.

For the visitor's information about the real presence and attitudes of American Indians, there are no scholarly words alongside the art.

Alas!

Fortunately, there are words and an increasing number of words being produced by American Indians, or indigenous people. Some of these words appear in the National Museum of the American Indian in the Smithsonian. Some of the words are literary and are to be found in publications. The literature has become the focus of literary criticism, which is how the university consideration of literature develops muscle.

What this means is that the intellectual discourse of what it means to be an American is changing, evolving as more and more people enter into the discourse. I personally do not wish to control that discourse, but I do wish to participate in the discourse, and I can. Whoa! This is a real change, and it could happen only in a society that supports a university system—or as we sometimes grandly call it, the "Academy"—and Academic Freedom within the university system.

One recent and very interesting book to appear on the scholarly scene is *American Indian Literary Nationalism,* by Jace Weaver, Craig S. Womack, and Robert Warrior. These fellows clearly understand that literature is political, and, I add at no charge, Craig is a hoot.

I reviewed this book, and one of the things that action means is that I can participate in the discourse as a Choctaw woman because I hold a PhD in English, publish, present lectures to the public and at conferences, and teach university classes. One hundred years ago I could not have done any of that. Now I can.

Craig Womack authored, perhaps between howls of laughter, chapter 2 of *American Indian Literary Nationalism*. Like Womack. I too am concerned about gatekeepers and pressures to conform. His essay addresses concerns that must occur to intellectuals: Is relationship to community important to a critic, to a writer? Like Womack, I wonder if I must confess my hybridity, and when did I become a piece of corn? What is authentic? Must we all conform? After reading Womack, surely thinking people must wonder along with Womack, "Who made up these rules anyway?" Womack asks questions, and I liked that. He makes it quite clear that he is not an essentialist. That is, a scholar of American Indian Literature need not be an American Indian necessarily, but that scholar does need to be respectful and sensitive to the cultures that produce a work to the extent of learning something significant about the cultures. I point out that I wrote a PhD dissertation about the poetry of John Milton, and I learned about seventeenth-century England. What's so difficult about this idea?

Educational moments happen in many ways, and one takes the opportunities where they occur. Last week I conversed briefly in the Atlanta Airport with a total stranger who requested a list of authors whose writings he could explore concerning American Indians—you know how it is with the delays in air travel these days. I quickly wrote a list of four or five authors for him to look for—the educational moment. One learning moment at a time.

Publishing opportunities also are available if one works hard enough. With a colleague I edited and published in 2007 through the University of Oklahoma Press a book titled *Women Who Pioneered Oklahoma*. My colleague Connie Henshaw and I concluded from our research in the Oklahoma Indian-Pioneer Papers that American Indian women and African American women pioneered right along with their Anglo sisters.

In November I am scheduled to lecture about Native American literature as a guest presenter at another university. Who knows who will learn what from that?

In addition to the publishing and presenting, I chair a department that includes the only degree-granting major in an indigenous language (Cherokee) in the continental United States as far as I know. Oh yes indeedy, I participate in the discourse.

So, are we a good example, a city on a hill? Well, I think that we are for any number of reasons. I invite you to consider some of them.

We vote and can throw the scoundrels out in all levels of elections, including tribal elections. Such participation nurtures patriotism.

As an American Indian (Oklahoma Choctaw) I live, as in "not dead, not absent" and wear clothes that look much like the clothes of other, ok older women. Of course, I believe that my appearance is fashionable and I maintain the illusion that I am tall too.

Is it my manifest destiny to wear modern clothes and pretend I am tall? Well, if you read (please read) you find the roux of Manifest Destiny in the literature from early Puritan New England. The roux made the sauce thicker and thicker until it became a goo. Sorry. Thinking about Manifest Destiny makes me giddy. Manifest Destiny requires that a person believe that the Christian God created the destiny and it manifested in actions that are still occurring, that is, that the Christian God gave North America to Europeans. That's a bit too Greek for me. Europeans took North America; that is, as the theorists might say, they exercised agency.

I suggest that we think about behavior. Is conquest destiny? Can human beings think about their behavior and consequences? Is environmental disaster destiny? Are human beings smart enough to control their behavior?

I do not pretend to know. We do not seem to be too good at controlling behavior historically. I do know that laws are good. It is possible for laws to keep people from killing each other. Learning to use the laws is an option. Because the United States has laws, a constitution, the possibility of education and the possibility of an informed public, then, yes, American Exceptionalism exists. During a recent trip to Washington, D.C., I thought that the cab drivers seemed more informed than the politicians. Oklahoma, home to some thirty-nine federally recognized tribes, for all of its flaws (and they are many) is proof that American Indians can live at peace in an integrated society and participate in the discourse. Such participation is an ongoing struggle but *ongoing*.

However, I must say that I do not really wish to live with the Puritans (modern or ghost) in that City on a Hill—sounds too much like "a praying town" to me. I want to live in a society where I can freely participate in the discussion about and formation of the laws; participate in the discourse about definitions, customs, values; live in a society where I can vote, publish, worship as I wish or not, and as far as it is possible help to shape my own destiny.

That to me is American Exceptionalism. The possibilities within a free society are exceptional. Living on a hill can be good. Although it makes you a good target, it also allows you to see what is coming and urges you to do what you can.

Works Cited

Bradford, William. 1908. *History of Plymouth Plantation, 1606–1646.* Ed. William T. Davis. New York: Charles Scribner's Sons.

O'Connell, Barry, ed. and intro. 1992. *On our own ground: The complete writings of William Apess, a Pequot.* Amherst: The University of Massachusetts Press.

Supreme Court of the United States. 1831. *Cherokee Nation v. Georgia*, 30 U.S. 1, 5 Pet. 1, January Term.

Weaver, Jace, Craig S. Womack, and Robert Warrior. 2005. *American Indian literary nationalism.* Albuquerque: University of New Mexico Press.

Winthrop, John. 1838. A modell of Christian charity (1630). *Collections of the Massachusetts Historical Society*, 31–48. Boston.

Notes on Contributors

James J. Allegro is an assistant professor at the Norfolk State University, Norfolk, Va., where he teaches African American history, Early American history, and courses on Race, Gender, and Class. He is the author of "'Increasing and Strengthening the Country': Law, Politics, and the Anti-Slavery Movement in Early-Eighteenth-Century Massachusetts Bay," *New England Quarterly* 75, no. 1 (2002): 5–23.

Terri McKinney Baker is Emeritus Professor of English, Northeastern State University, Tahlequah, Oklahoma, where she retired as Chair of the Languages and Literature Department, which houses English, English Education. Spanish, Spanish Education, Cherokee Language Education, and Cherokee Cultural Studies. As an academic, Professor Baker taught courses in the English Department and courses for the American Indian Studies Degree Program at Northeastern. A native Oklahoman, Professor Baker is a citizen of the Choctaw Nation of Oklahoma. She holds her PhD from Louisiana State University. Professor Baker along with Connie Henshaw co-edited *Women Who Pioneered Oklahoma, Stories from the WPA Narratives* (Norman: University of Oklahoma Press, 2007). She lives cheerfully in Tahlequah, Oklahoma, with her husband, two dogs, several cats, and a few cows, and enjoys a view of the Illinois River Valley.

Christine Bold is a professor in the School of English and Theatre Studies at the University of Guelph, Guelph, Ontario, and teaches on nineteenth-century U.S. popular print culture and on the politics of cultural production. She is the author of *Writers, Plumbers, and Anarchists: The WPA Writers' Project in Massachusetts* (Amherst: University of Massachusetts Press, 2006) and *Selling the Wild West: Popular Western Fiction, 1860 to 1960* (Bloomington: Indiana University Press, 1987).

Carl J. Bon Tempo is assistant professor in the Department of History, University at Albany, State University of New York, Albany, New York. His research and teaching interests include human rights and public policy, and he is the author of *Americans at the Gate: The Politics of Refugee Affairs in the Cold War United States* (Princeton: Princeton University Press, 2008).

Matthew L. Brophy is assistant professor of Communications, Arts, and Humanities at Delaware County Community College, Downington, Pennsylvania. In addition to his ongoing work on Melville and Irving, Brophy has published "Shadowing Afrikaner Nationalism: Jungian Archetypes, Incest, and the Uncanny in Marlene van Nierkirk's *Triomf*," *Journal of Literary Studies/Tydskrif vir Literatuurwetenskap* 22 (2006): 96–112.

Nathaniel Cadle is assistant professor of English at Florida International University in Miami, Florida, and is revising for publication his dissertation, "The Mediating Nation: American Literature and Globalization from Henry James to Woodrow Wilson."

James Taylor Carson is professor of History and chair of the Department of History at Queen's University, Kingston, Ontario, Canada. His scholarship focuses on the ethnohistory of native peoples in the American South, and he has published two books on the subject, *Searching for the Bright Path: The Mississippi Choctaws from Prehistory to Removal* (Lincoln: University of Nebraska Press, 1999) and *Making an Atlantic World: Circles, Paths, and Stories from the Colonial South* (Knoxville: University of Tennessee Press, 2007).

Emily García is assistant professor of English at Northeastern Illinois University, Chicago, Illinois. Her research focuses on Early American literature, Latino/a studies, and literary theory—particularly literature that crosses the colonial and revolutionary periods from the 1760s to 1820s.

Roxanne Harde is associate professor of English and McCalla university professor at the University of Alberta, Augustana Faculty. She studies American literature and culture, and teaches feminist literary theory and American literature. She has recently published *Reading the Boss: Interdisciplinary Approaches to the Works of Bruce Springsteen* and her essays have appeared in several journals, including *Christianity and Literature*, *Legacy*, *Studies in Puritan American Spirituality*, *Critique*, *Feminist Theology*, and *Mosaic*, and several edited collections.

Sara Humphreys is assistant professor of English at Trent University in Peterborough and Oshawa, where she teaches American literature, modern fiction, literary theory, and new media. Her current book-length project explores the role of literary material culture in shaping and defining the varied publics that vie for recognition in the U.S. national imagination.

Deborah L. Madsen is professor of American Literature and Culture at the University of Geneva, Geneva, Switzerland, where her teaching and research concentrate on American ethnic literary and cultural studies, comparative multiculturalisms, literature and diaspora, and gender studies. She is the author of *American Exceptionalism* (Jackson: University Press of Mississippi, 1998), *Allegory in America: From Puritanism to Pstmodernism* (Basingstoke, UK: Palgrave Macmillan, 1996), and editor of *Beyond the Borders: American Literature and Post-Colonial Theory* (Ann Arbor: University of Michigan Press, 2003).

Sylvia Söderlind is professor of English Language and Literature at Queen's University, Kingston, Ontario, Canada, where she teaches North American literature and literary theory. She is the author of *Margin/Alias: Language and Colonization in Canadian and Québécois Fiction* (Toronto: University of Toronto Press, 1991) and articles on fiction in English, French, and Swedish. Her recent scholarship focuses on translation theory, and she is also a practicing translator of drama.

Anthony Stewart is associate professor of English at Dalhousie University, Halifax, Nova Scotia. His scholarly interests include Twentieth-Century African American Literature and Culture, Ralph Ellison, and Percival Everett. He is the author of *George Orwell, Doubleness, and the Value of Decency* (New York: Routledge, 2003) and *You Must Be a Basketball Player: Rethinking Integration in the University* (Black Point, NS: Fernwood, 2009).

Matthew Strohack is a PhD candidate in English Language and Literature at Queen's University, Kingston, Ontario. His dissertation is entitled "Popular Modernisms and the Business of Horror." His research and teaching interests include modernism, horror, the Frankfurt School, and commodity theory.

Index

Adams, Brooks, 133
Africa, 32, 135, 141, 142, 143, 144; counterpoint to Europe, 32, 46; immigration from, 150; north, 41, 47, 6; "scramble for," 139–40; west, 32, 34
African Americans as subjects, 174–75, 180
African peoples, 118, 143, 144; biblical origins of, 82; enslavement of, 119, 142
"Age of Exploration," 9, 10, 32–33, 38–40, 44–45
al-Qaeda, 203
Alden, Diane, 27
Alden, Henry Mills, 115
allegory, 3, 223–41; and exceptionalism, 12; and Puritans, 225
American Civil Liberties Union, 200
American Defense Society, 108
American dream, 3, 28, 66, 174, 211
American history, 33, 38, 73, 81, 134–35, 194
American Home Missionary Society, 125, 126, 129
American Indians. *See* Native American peoples
American literature, 51, 72, 211
American Revolution, 51–66
American Studies, 2, 5, 8
Americanists, 2, 3, 5, 8, 72, 89
anti-federalists, 59
antinomians, 225–26
Anglicus, Bartolomaeus, 37, 38
Anglo-Saxonism, 108, 138, 145 n.5
Apess, William, 244, 246, 247
Appiah, Kwame Anthony, 168, 172, 183, 185
Arab, 35, 36, 133, 140
Aravamudan, Srinivas, 67 n.2
Arbella, 2, 4, 18, 53, 54, 67 n.1, 231
Articles of Confederation, 59, 60
Ashcroft, Richard, 203
Asia, 10; in European thought, 32, 35–38; immigration from, 104, 119, 150, 155; imperialism in, 35, 39, 42, 140; weakness of, 133
assimilation, 11, 111, 130, 131, 143, 159
Atlantic Ocean, 31, 33, 34, 35, 39, 40–41, 43, 61, 63, 130; crossing, 31, 33, 43, 97, 104, 105, 107, 109

Atlantic history, 34
Averell, Jim, 98, 99

Babylon, 31–32, 44, 237
Baring-Gould, Sabine, 144 n.2
Barnes, Elizabeth, 54
Barnett, Thomas 26–27
Beets, Betty Lou, 205
Bell, Bernard, 177
Bell, Daniel, 6, 8, 33
Benjamin, Walter, 233–35, 239–40
Bentham, Jeremy, 215
Bercovitch, Sacvan, 6, 52, 67 nl, 72, 75, 79, 81
Berlant, Lauren, 211, 212, 214
Berry, Halle, 175
Bethlehem, 47, 237
Bible, 202, 239, 246, 250
Bill of Rights, 158
blackness, 167, 182
Blair Witch Project, 16, 20–21, 25
Boone and Crockett Club, 94, 96, 97, 98, 102, 107, 108, 115
Booth, Edwin, 144 n.2
Booth, Wayne, 220 n4
Boston, 97, 111, 112, 113
Bothwell, Albert, 98
Boudinot, Elias, 247
Bracciolini, Poggio, 38
Bradford, William, 245–46
Brett, George, 116, 117
British Empire, 40, 94, 98
British North America, 40, 43
Brown, Charles Brockden, 62
Buchanan, Pat, 161–62
Burlesque, 10, 12, 71–74, 76, 82, 86, 88. *See also* satire
Burroughs, George, 228
Bush, George W. 2, 6, 7, 16, 20, 25, 66, 156; and capital punishment, 196, 199, 205 n.2, 205 n.4
Butler, Judith, 67

Cabot, John, 39
Cabot, Sebastian, 39
Cabral, Pedro Alvarez, 39
Canada, 8–9, 21, 28, 33, 57, 114, 205 n.2
capital punishment, 12, 191–204
capitalism, 5, 6, 94, 98, 112, 138–39, 150, 155, 196
captivity, 17–18, 21, 213–14, 220 n5
Carter, John, 157
Castiglia, Christopher, 214, 220 n5
cattle barons, 96, 100, 103, 110, 111, 119
Caxton, William, 37
census, 103, 104, 118–19, 125
Central America, 155
Cervantes, Miguel de, 89
Chace Act, 114
Chanler, Winthrop, 96, 102
Chapman, Mary, 213
Cheney, Dick, 26
Cherokee, 192, 193, 251, 237
Cheyenne Club, 94, 95, 96, 98, 100–3, 104, 105, 109, 113
Chicago, 119
children, 141–42, 211–19
China, 36, 39, 40, 42, 45, 142, 155
Chinese people, 110; and Exclusion Act, 117; railroad workers, 111
Choctaw, 250, 252
Christianity, 25, 42–44, 126, 129, 132–33, 237; in American history, 81; conversion to, 36; history of, 37, 77, 85; missionization, 36, 83–84, 132, 143; and Native Americans, 83; and Puritans, 237; rhetoric, 39, 77, 83
cinema, 21, 21, 172, 176, 177, 181, 196, 198, 207, 210–13
"city on a hill," 1, 7, 15, 52, 53, 61, 78, 224, 225, 236, 237, 238, 244, 247, 251
civil rights movement, 148–49, 151

Clooney, George 24
Cody, Buffalo Bill, 94
Cold War, 3, 6, 148–49, 151, 153–54, 157
colonization, 35, 43, 44, 82, 83, 135; of the Americas, 19, 33, 45, 47; European, 39, 40–42, 45, 47, 83, 88; and race, 139
Columbus, Christopher, 33, 38, 39, 44, 45
Congregationalists, 125, 128, 225–26, 229–30, 233, 238
Conti, Niccoló dé, 37–38
Cooper, James Fennimore, 95
copyright, 114
cosmography, 32, 37–40, 44
cosmopolitanism, 44, 167–68, 172, 183–85
cowboys, 100, 102, 103, 111
Crèvecoeur, Michel Guillaume Jean de, 8, 52, 61–68
crusade, 16, 36, 73, 84, 210, 212
cultural studies, 5, 62, 195
culture, 33, 40, 79, 240; African American, 174; Anglo-American, 4, 9, 86, 89, 94, 125, 130, 149, 159, 160–62, 168, 178, 185, 187, 211, 213–14, 226; dominant, 87, 171, 174, 188, 211; exceptionalism and, 197; gentlemanly, 98; gun, 197; homogeneity, 126, 131; industries, 112; mass, 94, 103, 108, 116; Native American, 251; pluralism, 163; popular, 9, 11, 12, 16, 112, 187; Puritan, 237; southern, 197

Darwin, Erasmus, 78–79
death penalty. *See* capital punishment
Declaration of Independence, 58, 59, 158
DeCourcey Ward, Robert, 103, 105, 108, 119
democracy: American, 6, 11, 58, 60, 71, 88, 139, 193, 204; Christian, 71; and exceptionalism, 148, 150–51, 153, 156–58, 191–96, 203, 223; failure of, 139; and immigration, 156–58
Demos, John 17
Department of Homeland Security, 9, 203
devil, 19–20, 21, 25
DiMaggio, Paul, 112
dime novel, 95, 99, 113–15
Dobbs, Lou, 158–59
Drayton, Michael, 45
Drinnon, Richard, 85, 88
Du Bois, W.E.B. 11, 125, 128, 134, 138–44, 178. *See also* "talented tenth"

Earle, Steve, 12, 191–205
Eastman, Charles, 247
Eden, Richard, 39, 40, 43
Egypt, 35, 142
Eliot, T.S., 183
Elliott, J.H., 32, 33
Ellison, Ralph, 173–76, 179
Emerson, Ralph Waldo, 73, 75, 79–80, 88, 204, 224
England, 53, 64, 107, 108, 153, 183, 231, 251; colonization by, 41–44
Enlightenment, 54, 56, 61
Ervin, Sam, 153, 154
Eurocentrism, 10, 34, 153
Europe, 10, 32, 47, 61, 64, 65, 94, 130, 131, 142, 234; Christian, 42; culture, 62, 149, 161–62; eastern, 41, 47; immigration from, 65, 104, 107, 109, 111, 118, 129, 150–51, 155, 161; remapping of, 141; western, 31, 32, 33, 36, 37, 38, 47
eugenics, 104, 108

evangelicalism, 207, 209, 210, 218
Everett, Percival, 11, 167–89
exceptionalism: American, 15–16, 26–28, 31–33, 35, 51–61, 65–67, 71–75, 127–28, 131, 147–50, 219, 231–32, 154, 157, 167–68, 191–94, 204, 243, 252; African American, 11, 144, 168, 189; and Asia, 31–47; and capital punishment, 191–95; European origins of, 8, 31, 62, 224; 45; immigration, 149, 163–64; Mather, Cotton on 20, 22; in New England, 19, 52; Puritan origins of, 12, 75, 194, 245; and racism, 149, 151, 188; southern U.S., 197; Winthrop, John on, 20, 52–54, 61, 67 n. 1, 71, 149

Farbstein, Leonard, 154
fascism, 240–41
federalists, 58, 59, 60
Ferguson, Robert, 58, 61, 81, 84
film. *See* cinema
Fitch, Ralph, 41
Foster, Elizabeth, 75, 79, 85
Foucault, Michel, 72–73, 74, 89, 198
"Founding Fathers," 59–60, 84, 158
France, 38, 114, 140, 153
frontier, 17, 72, 126; club, 10, 11, 94, 95 (fig), 102, 108, 109, 111, 115, 119, 120 n.16; conflicts, 18; myth of 10, 94; symbolism, 81, 85; *See also* Turner, Frederick Jackson
Frye, William P., 126

Gama, Vasco da, 39, 41
Games, Allison, 34
gaming, 247–48
Gandhi, Leela, 35
Gandhi, Mohandas, 244
genocide, 17, 81, 82, 84
Gerstle, Gary, 163
Gilbert, Humphrey, 31, 39
Gilman, Charlotte Perkins, 100
Gilroy, Paul, 175, 176
globalization, 2, 4, 6, 11, 26, 27, 129, 138, 140
Goa, 41, 44, 47
Goldman, Emma, 196
Goughe, Hugh, 42
Great Britain, 34, 56, 57, 96, 114, 140
Greece, 31, 45, 153
Greene, Jack P., 33
Grinnell, George Bird, 94, 95 (fig.), 96, 116, 120 n.16
Guantánamo Bay, 23
Guthrie, Woody, 196

Hakluyt the Elder, Richard, 45–46
Hakluyt the Younger, Richard, 39, 40, 43, 44
Hall, Durwood, 152, 54
Hall, James, 74, 85, 87
Hall, Prescott Farnsworth, 103, 105, 108, 120 n.12
Halperin, Rick, 201, 203
Hariot, Thomas, 45
Harper & Brothers Publishing Co., 112, 113, 114, 116
Harper, Fletcher, 115–16, 120 n.16
Harper, J. Henry, 114, 115, 116
Harper, Joseph W., 114
Hartz, Louis, 149
Harvard University, 94, 96, 97, 101, 103, 106, 107, 137, 138, 168, 195
Harvey, George S., 116, 120 n.15
Hathorne, John, 23, 24, 228
Hathorne, William, 23, 24
Hawthorne, Nathaniel, 16, 22, 23, 225

Hayworth, J.D., 162
Hebrew, 201
Hedges, William, 81, 88, 89
Henry VIII, 224
Hendler, Glenn, 213
Henty, G.A., 129
Herodotus, 35, 76
Higden, Ranulf, 37
Higgins, Iain Macleod, 35
Higginson, Henry Lee, 97, 107, 112
Higginson, John, 228
Highman, John, 54
Hill, Joe, 196
Hodgson, Godfrey, 8
Hoffman, David C., 55
Hofstadter, Richard, 5
Holocaust, 241
Hollywood, 23, 173, 174
Holt, Henry, 95 (fig.), 113, 114
hooks, bell, 174–76
Hopkins, Sarah Winnemucca, 247
horror, 12, 13, 229, 230, 232, 234, 238–41
Howells, William Dean, 115
Hughes, Langston, 169, 178
human rights, 7, 195, 196, 205 n.1, n.3
humanities, 4
Hunt, Michael, 133, 138, 144 n.4, 145, n.5
Huntington, Samuel P., 3, 5
Hutchinson, Anne, 225, 236

identity; 28, 73, 163, 211, 214; African American, 177; Anglo-American, 4, 62, 73, 79, 93, 127, 129, 131, 152, 157, 194, 207, 227; cultural and racial, 162, 169, 177, 184; personal and political, 62; politics, 163, 220 n. 5; postcolonial, 145 n.6 "subnational," 5; tribal, 248
Ignatieff, Michael, 7, 8, 205 n.3
Illouz, Eva, 210–11
immigrants, 33, 40, 62, 65, 103–5, 107, 108, 110, 118, 129–31, 149–64
immigration; 11, 93, 111, 113, 114, 117, 126, 130, 131, 147; debates, 147–64; federal policy, 104, 112; illegal, 155– ; law, 151–55; opposition to, 104, 105, 107, 108, 111, 119; pamphlets, 105; patterns, 103, 110; quotas, 118, 119, 125, 129; racism, 104, 151–55, 160; 162, 163
Immigration Restriction League, 95 (fig.), 103, 105, 107, 108, 110, 119
imperialism, 5, 33, 34, 35, 40, 43, 44, 46, 47, 47 n.1, 57, 73, 88, 89, 127, 129, 138, 140
India, 35, 36, 38, 39, 40, 41, 45, 47, 142, 155
Indian Ocean, 32, 40, 41
Indians. *See* Native American peoples
indigenous people, 33, 34, 72, 246, 247, 249, 250, 251
Indonesia, 40, 47
International Criminal Court, 7
internet, 208
Iraq War 6, 20, 197
Ireland, 33, 42, 47 n.1
Iroquoia, 47
Irving, Washington, 10, 12, 71–90
Islam, 34, 39, 41, 47
isolationism, 7, 18, 66, 130, 133, 134, 137, 143, 164
Italy, 43, 45, 110, 159, 199

Jackson, Andrew, 71, 250
Jamestown colony, 42, 47
Japan, 45, 136, 142
Jenks, Jeremiah W., 108

Jensen, Merrill, 59
jeremiad, 6, 52, 72, 75, 79, 88
Jerusalem, 36, 37, 47, 203
Jesus, 19, 44, 196, 198, 250
Jewish people, 107, 109, 111
Jim Crow, 161–62
Johnson, Jack, 176
Johnson, Lyndon, 150, 151
Johnson-Reed Act, 118
Jordan, Michael, 175

Kadir, Djelal, 44
Kammen, Michael, 7
Keil, James C., 89
Kennedy, Edward "Ted," 153, 156
Kibbey, Ann, 227, 234
King, Larry, 199, 205 n.5
King Jr., Martin Luther, 1, 196, 197, 244
King, Steven, 157
Klaas, Polly, 213
Koepnick, Lutz, 234, 240
Kupperman, Karen, 42–43
Kyoto Protocol, 66

labor: agitation, 93; anti-immigration, 107, 110; contract, 102; immigrant, 157, 158; and management, 155; organized, 106; and race, 139; -saving machinery, 130; slavery, 33
Lach, Donald F., 41
LaFeber, Walter, 126, 127, 134, 138, 144 n.1, 145 n.5
Larkin, Edward, 55, 60, 62
Lazarus, Emma, 148
League of Nations, 134
Leahy, Patrick, 203
Leutze, Emanuel Gottlieb, 249
Levant, 35, 41–43, 47; Company, 41
Levine, Lawrence, 112
Levy, Maurice, 224
Lippincott, J.B., 113
Lindh, John Walker, 203–4
Lipset, Seymour Martin, 3, 5, 7, 191, 194, 195
Lipsitz, George 3, 5
Lodge, Henry Cabot, 95 (fig.), 96, 104, 105, 107, 110, 114, 116, 117, 133, 134, 137
London, 41, 47, 94, 117
Louis IX, 38
Louis, Joe, 176
Lovecraft, H.P., 9, 12, 223–41; and allegory, 226, 235, 238; and New England, 223–28, 233–37
Lunsford, Jessica, 209, 213
lynching, 98, 100, 109–11

Macmillan publishing, 95 (fig.), 114, 116, 117, 120 n.16, 17, 20
Madsen, Deborah, 7, 67 nl; 193–95, 223–27, 230, 235, 236, 238
Mahan, Alfred Thayer, 126, 133–38, 142–43
Malcolm X, 196
Mancall, Peter, 42
Mandeville, John, 37, 38
manhood, 170–71, 178, 182
Manifest Destiny, 4, 10, 71, 73, 81, 84, 231, 232, 246, 247, 249, 252
Manovich, Lev, 208
Mapp, Paul, 34
Marcus, Greil, 179–80
Martyr, Peter, 39, 40, 43
mass media, 132
Massachusetts Bay; Colony, 52, 193, 225; Company, 71
Massachusetts Historical Society, 244
Matar, Nabil, 34
Mather, Cotton, 17, 19, 24; and witchcraft, 17, 19, 20, 22, 227, 235; as character in Lovecraft, 227–28, 235, 237

Mayflower Compact, 245
McCain, John, 1, 13 n.1, 156
McCarthy, Joseph, 16, 23
McClellan, John, 152
McClure, S.S., 116
Mediterranean Sea, 32, 34, 41, 43, 45, 61
Melville, Herman, 10, 12, 71–90
mental illness, 17
Mexico, 155, 156
Middle Ages, 32, 36, 40
Middle East, 6, 35, 41
militarism, 12, 26, 128–29, 136, 144 n.2, 197–98
Miller, Arthur, 16, 24
Miller, Perry, 6, 71, 1942
Mitchell, John, 95 (fig.), 102
Mitchell, Langdon, 95 (fig.), 102
Mitchell, Silas Weir, 96, 100, 101, 102, 120 n. 11
modernity, 136, 141, 150, 152; and Lovecraft, H.P, 230–34, 240; and Native American peoples, 247, 245
modernization, 141–42
Mongols, 36, 38
Morgan, J.P., 97, 112, 116, 120 n.5
Mormons, 126
Morrison, Toni, 176
Moses, 78, 249
movies. *See* cinema
multiculturalism, 11, 148, 155, 160, 163–64, 257
Munro, George, 113
Munsey, Frank, 113, 115
Murrow, Edward R., 23
Münster, Sebastian, 45

NAACP, 138
Nantucket, 65
National Museum of the American Indian, 250
National Origins Act, 117
National Portrait Gallery, 249, 250
nationalism, 8, 152, 194; "critical," 72, 89; cultural, 174; language and, 127; and universalism, 52–54, 66
Native American peoples, 21, 82, 111, 243, 246–52; and genocide, 81–82, 84; imagined, 46; literature, 251, society, 43; as "non-people," 117; antipathy towards, 84–87; survival of, 243, 246
Navarrette, Ruben, 157
"New Americanists," 3, 5, 8, 89
New England, 20, 21; "Brahmins," 103; Hawthorne on, 22; Irving's parody of historians on, 73, 74, 79
New Testament, 230, 238, 239
"New World," 10, 15, 16, 31, 32, 34, 38, 42, 44, 193, 224, 225, 231
New York City, 130, 112, 113, 199, 241
New York Times, 171, 172, 199
9/11, 2, 6, 7, 8, 25
Noble, David, W., 2, 4, 5, 7, 8, 192, 204
Nobles, Jonathan Wayne, 201–2, 204
North America, 33 34, 39, 40 42, 43, 47 n.1, 57, 64, 73, 82, 252
Nwankwo, Ifeoma, 167

Obama, Barack, 1, 2, 13 n.1
O'Connell, Barry, 244, 247
O'Gorman, Edmundo, 33
Ohmann, Richard, 103, 115, 116
Old Testament, 230
"Old World," 6, 33, 130, 231
Oliver, Egbert, 75, 79, 80
Orient, 34, 35, 142
Orientalism, 10, 32–35
O'Sullivan, John L., 71

Ottoman empire, 34, 36, 41, 42, 47, 140

Paine, Thomas, 10, 54–61; 64–66
Pan-Africanism, 11, 138, 143
Parker, Hershel, 85
Parmenius, Stephen, 31, 32, 44, 46, 47
Pastore, John, 153, 154
patriotism, 8, 13 n.1, 55, 56, 89, 140, 203, 252
Pearce, Roy Harvey, 85–86
Penrose, Charles, 102
Persia, 32, 35, 36, 45
Pettrick, Ferdinand, 249
Phelps, Austin, 128, 129, 136, 140 143
Philadelphia, 94, 95 (fig.), 100, 101, 102, 115, 159
Pilgrims, 73, 205 n.3, 245, 246
Pliny, 141
Plymouth Company, 42
Poe, Amos, 196, 202, 205 n.1, 205 n.6
Poe, Edgar Allan, 225
Polo, Marco, 37
Poster, Mark, 208
postmodernism, 9, 240
postnationalism, 4, 192, 204
poststructuralism, 89
Potter, David, 149, 157
Powers, Hiram, 249
Powhatans, 42
Prejean, Helen, 199, 201, 205 n.4
Prester John, 39
Prince, Thomas, 74, 75
promotional literature, 45
prophets, 75, 79
Protestantism, 11, 87, 129–30, 144, 194, 161
providence, 2, 52, 53, 54, 58, 71, 75, 126, 227, 234, 236, 246
Providence, R. I., 225, 226, 236
public sphere, 105, 211
Pucinski, Roman, 154–55
Puritans, 1, 2, 4, 9, 18–19, 71, 75, 81, 88, 193, 233, 244, 247, 252; "federal covenant," 28; ministers, 44, 227
Puritanism, 1, 8, 9, 12, 16, 19, 193, 223–41; Irving's critique of, 79; sermon, 4, 9 ("A Model of Christian Charity" 18; theology, 54; typology, 2, 12; and witchcraft, 9; and H.P. Lovecraft, 9, 224, 227–41
Quakers, 24
race, 5, 89, 126, 167, 172; cliché, 11, 168, 171, 174–77, 182, 185, 187; hatred, 87, 89; hierarchies, 138
racism: as foundation of democracy, 11; global institutionalization of, 139; and Christian symbolism, 83; Asiatics, 82, 103; and slavery, 32
railroads, 104, 110, 111, 114, 116
Raleigh, Walter, 39
Ray, Nick, 100, 110
Raynal, Guillaume-Thomas François, 63, 64, 65, 67 n.2
Reagan, Ronald, 1, 7, 11, 127
Remington, Frederic, 95 (fig.), 96, 102, 108, 109 (fig.), 116, 120 n.16
Renaissance, 32, 35, 39–47
Revolutionary War. *See* American Revolution
Ringe, Donald, 81
Roanoke colony, 39, 42, 44
Robbins, Tim, 201
Robertson, Pat, 199
Robinson, Jackie, 176
Rogin, Michael, 119, 22
Roosevelt, Franklin D., 7

Roosevelt, Theodore; 94, 95 (fig.), 96, 97, 102, 107, 108, 110, 111, 115, 120, 134, 159
Roth, Martin, 72, 74, 75, 76, 87, 88
Rothenberg, Nancy, 55
Rowlandson, Mary, 21–22. *See also* captivity
Russett, Margaret, 180, 184
Rut, John, 42

Said, Edward, 32–36, 43
Salem, 23–24; witchcraft trials, 17, 19, 21–23, 227, 228, 234
Sanchez-Eppler, Karen, 214
Satan. *See* devil
satire, 10, 72, 173, 186, 187
Saturday Evening Post, 105, 110, 117
Schneider, David J., 172–73
Schroeder, John W., 85
Schweitzer, Ivy, 67 n1
self-improvement, 211
sentimentalism, 207–20
Sewall, Samuel, 45
sexual assault, 207
Sheehan, Bernard, 42, 45
Shocked, Michelle, 199
Short, Mercy, 17, 18, 21, 22, 24
sin, 18
slavery, 12, 24, 32, 33, 65, 66, 119, 142, 198, 247
Slotkin, Richard, 94, 108, 214
Social Darwinism, 104, 108
social sciences, 195
socialism, 126, 194
Solomon, Barbara, 106
South America, 39, 84, 135
Spanish-American War, 134, 136
Spanos, William, 5, 6, 67 n1, 87, 89
Spivak, Gayatri Chakravorty, 145 n.6
Springer, Balthasar, 39
Starkey, Marion L., 228
Steiker, Carol, 195–98, 200–1, 205 n.3
Stereotyping, 172. *See also* cliché, race, racism
Strong, Josiah, 11, 125–44
Sturgis, Thomas, 97
Stuyvesant, Peter, 74, 89
sub-prime mortgages, 3

Taft, Howard, 134
"talented tenth," 11, 142, 144, 178
Taliban, 203
Tancredo, Tom, 160, 161, 162
Tawil, Ezra, 62
Tea Party Movement, 3
technology, 132–33
terrorism, 9, 15, 20, 25, 26, 203
Texas, 199, 201–3, 205 n. 2, 205 n. 4
Thoreau, Henry David, 79, 244
Tichi, Cecilia, 74, 85
Tocqueville, Alexis de, 3, 8, 125, 149, 194, 196
totalitarianism, 151, 241
Transcendentalism, 73, 80
travel literature, 32, 34, 37–38, 40–41
Treaty of Versailles, 134
Tucker, Karla Faye, 199, 205 n. 4, 205 n. 5
Turner, Frederick Jackson, 33, 35, 119, 128, 133–38, 143, 144 n. 3, 149
Twain, Mark, 115
Tyler, Royall, 61
Tyson, Mike, 175

U.S. Civil War, 199
U.S. Congress, 61, 114, 117
U.S. Constitution, 58, 59, 60, 61, 62, 66, 110, 117, 158
U.S. Constitutional Convention, 59, 61

U.S. Continental Congress, 55
U.S. Supreme Court, 247

Vespucci, Amerigo, 39
Vietnam War, 5, 6
vigilantism, 12, 100, 102, 211–12, 217, 219
Virginia, 42, 45, 156, 160

Walker, Francis Amasa, 104
Wallerstein, Immanuel, 67, 68 n. 3
Walsingham, Francis, 44
War of Independence. *See* American Revolution
War on Terror, 4, 23, 148, 157
Warner, Michael, 59–60
Warren, Charles, 103
Warrior, Robert, 250
Washington Post, 147
Weaver, Jace, 250
West Indies, 33
Western genre, 10; 93–119
Westernization, 142
Westrem, Scott, 38
White, Ed, 58–59
White, G. Edward, 94
whiteness, 11, 119, 139, 140, 152, 167, 169; and captivity, 217; and femininity, 208–9; and nationalism, 140
wilderness, 2, 6, 15, 20, 21, 71, 81, 84, 229
Williams, Roger, 225, 236
Wilson, James Q., 8
Wilson, Woodrow, 128, 129, 134, 137–41, 143–44, 144 n. 3, 144 n.4, 149, 224
Winfrey, Oprah, 12, 170, 207–20
Winthrop, John, 2, 10, 11, 15, 18, 52–53, 62
Wister, Owen, 10, 94–120
witchcraft, 16, 23–26, 227–29, 233–39
Wolcott, Frank, 100, 101, 102, 109, 110
Womack, Craig, 250, 251
Wood, Gordon, 149, 163
Woods, Lawrence M., 98, 102, 104
World War I, 136, 139, 239, 241
World War II, 2, 33, 136
Wright, Richard, 186
Wyoming, 94, 96, 100–11

Yankee, 73, 75, 79, 80, 88, 103

Zakaria, Fareed 147–48